CASSELL'S GUIDE TO
written english

CASSELL'S GUIDE TO
writtenenglish

james aitchison

CASSELL&CO

First published in the UK 1994 by
Cassell & Co.
Wellington House
125 Strand
London WC2R 0BB
First paperback edition 1996
Reprinted 1997, 1999
This edition 2001

British Library Cataloguing-in-Publication Data
A catalogue record for this book is available from the British Library

ISBN 0-304-37587-1

Typeset by Colset Pty Ltd, Singapore

Printed and bound in Great Britain by
Bookmarque Ltd, Croydon, Surrey

Contents

Acknowledgements

I am grateful to students of publishing and journalism at Napier University for testing much of this material. I am indebted once again to my former colleague, Mr Gordon Lang, Senior Lecturer in the Department of Print Media, Publishing and Communication at Napier University, for his generous support while this book was being written.

Introduction

'Does it matter?' students sometimes ask about written standard English. It matters little to people whose lives and work do not require them to write, just as navigation matters little to people who never go to sea, but standard English is essential for people who are required to express themselves in writing.

Written standard English is an agreed international code that is used throughout the English-speaking world. A person who can read *The Times* of London can also read the *Irish Times*, the *New York Times* or the *Times of India*. Journalists writing for one of those newspapers could, with a slight change in their prose style, write for the others. The code was developed by printers and publishers in order to impose general rules, or standards, on their authors' use of the English language. No other form of written English has this kind of recognition; if you break the code you will be misunderstood by some of your readers.

Students and other writers who have an uncertain command of written English are unable to express their thoughts clearly and find it particularly difficult, perhaps impossible, to express subtleties and complexities of thought. People who are capable of forming and analysing profound or intricate ideas may be considered less intelligent or less mature than they are because the quality of their writing cannot convey the quality of their thinking.

Writers, including writers of essays, reports and dissertations as well as writers of newspapers, magazines and books, are responsible for making their meaning clear; it is not the responsibility of the reader to deduce the meaning that may underlie the badly written prose. The penalty for the writer could be severe: if the reader cannot trust the writer's use of the medium, the English language, how can the reader trust the writer's message?

A text that is written with fluency and precision not only wins the reader's trust but gains an added authority from the quality of the writing. Fluency and precision, however, can be acquired only through practice and an understanding of the principles and techniques of written English. With this understanding you will not only be able to write more effectively but also begin to see how other writers achieve their effects. Failure to see this could leave you, as a reader, open to manipulation by politicians, advertising copy-writers or journalists.

Written English differs from spoken English to such an extent that the two are different versions of the English language. We speak before we write, and because speech is a natural activity that we develop within the family circle in the first few years of our lives, the acquisition of speech is normally an informal process.

Writing, on the other hand, is not a natural activity. Alphabets and writing systems are human inventions that have to be learned by each succeeding generation. Writing is normally an individual, planned and deliberate activity, whereas speech is a social or group activity and is often unplanned and spontaneous.

The written word, unlike the spoken word, is not limited by space or time but can be transmitted over vast distances and long periods. This permanence has given writing a greater authority than speech, an authority that was reinforced when writing began to be used as a record of human activity: wars, religions and laws, births, marriages and deaths.

The authority of the written word is sometimes inseparable from the authority of the writer. The priestly scribes, for example, were once the controllers of religion because only the scribes knew what was written in the manuscripts. Even today the historian is the con-troller of history and the news editor the controller of news; if events are not recorded in history books or in news media, these events remain unknown to most people.

Written English began to be standardized in Anglo-Saxon times when scribes copied manuscripts by hand. The process begun by the scribes was resumed by the early printers and publishers – the first book from William Caxton's press at Westminster appeared in 1477 – until most aspects of English were standardized. By 1755, the year of Samuel Johnson's *Dictionary*, there was agreement on the spelling, meaning and grammar of words, and some agreement on syntax, that is, the structuring of sentences and paragraphs, and on punctuation.

The agreement is flexible, and later chapters will show that the English language is in a state of continuous evolution. As civiliza-tions change, so new words, or new meanings added to existing words, are needed to identify the changes. The spellings of some words change; new words are sometimes formed by hyphenating two existing words and then, when the compound word is accepted as standard, the hyphen tends to be dropped and the two words become one. Grammar and syntax also change, but at a slower pace than vocabulary. English grammar is now simpler and less formal than it was fifty years ago. Syntax, the structure and length of sentences and paragraphs, is the basis of prose style and can vary from one writer to another, but the current preference is for supple, economic syntax. Despite this flexibility, written standard English remains constant and offers little scope for variation in the spellings and meanings of words, or in the grammar of words and sentences.

Today, some of the properties that were once exclusive to writing are shared by the spoken word. The electronic revolution, from the telephone to the computer and the communications satellite, has allowed the spoken word to overcome the limitations of space and time. As the electronic revolution advanced, enthusiastic revolutionaries predicted the end of letter-writing, the decline of newspapers, magazines and books, the paperless office – in effect, the death of the written word. But the prediction has proved false. Written standard English remains an immensely powerful medium of communication, and an essential medium for all educated persons in the English-speaking world.

PART ONE

1 Word Classes and Grammar

English has a greater number of words than any other language, but the standard English lexicon of over 500,000 words and the millions of words in scientific English can be grouped into ten classes. The four main word classes are nouns, verbs, adjectives and adverbs; six smaller word classes are pronouns, prepositions, conjunctions, determiners, numerals and interjections.

By grouping words into appropriate classes we can see more clearly the forms and functions of individual words and how words combine and interact to convey patterns of meaning. Without these patterns and the standards or rules that underlie the patterns there could be chaos. We need the rules to give meaning to language, just as we need rules to give meaning to most group or social activities: games and sports, driving a car, arranging a holiday, renting a flat or buying a house. This chapter will identify the classes of words – they used to be called parts of speech – along with the main characteristics and rules of each class. Some of these characteristics are worth noting here.

Inflections

An inflection is a change in the form of a word that indicates a change in the word's function and thus a change in its precise meaning. Inflections are usually suffixes – that is, short verbal elements, normally consisting of only a few letters, that are added to the ends of words.

The simplest inflection is the letter *s* added to the end of a noun in order to change the grammatical number of the noun from singular to plural: *computer*, singular; *computers*, plural. A few nouns have internal inflections to show the difference between singular and plural: *man* and *men*; *woman* and *women*. Pronouns too have grammatical number: *I*, *you*, *he/she/it* are singular; *we*, *you*, *they* are plural.

A similar inflection, an apostrophe and the letter *s*, or the letter *s* and an apostrophe, can be added to a noun to indicate the possessive case. The word case means the grammatical category of a noun or pronoun and the function of the noun or pronoun in a sentence. Cases have been drastically simplified over the centuries and English nouns now have only two cases: the standard or uninflected form and the possessive form. Pronouns have three cases: the subjective, objective and possessive.

Pronouns have another grammatical property known as person. There are three persons, known simply as first, second and third, and each indicates the narrative standpoint or viewpoint being adopted in a piece of writing. The first person, *I* and *we*, is the person speaking or observing; the second person, *you*, is the person being directly spoken to; the third person, *he/she* and *they*, is the person being spoken about.

Modern English uses the same form, *you*, for the second person singular and plural. In the colloquial grammar of Scotland and Northern Ireland the form *youse* indicates the plural, and in some of the southern States of the USA the colloquial form *you-all* is used as the plural.

The number expressed by the noun or the pronoun is also expressed by the verb. Here again English grammar has been simplified; verbs have one form for the singular – for example, *he/she/it walks* – and another form that is used for both singular and plural: *I* (singular) *walk*, *they* (plural) *walk*. Verbs also change their form to express the grammatical properties of voice, mood and tense (see pages 52–67).

Adjectives and adverbs are inflected to show degrees of size or intensity. The standard or uninflected form of adjectives and adverbs is known as the positive form; the other two forms are known as the comparative and the superlative: *tall* (positive), *taller* (comparative), *tallest* (superlative).

Content Words and Function Words

Another useful grammatical distinction is the one between content words and function words. Content words contribute most to the content or meaning of a piece of writing. The largest of the word classes, nouns, verbs, adjectives and adverbs, are content words.

Function words are as important for their grammatical effect or function as they are for their meaning. Although they play a vital role in indicating the relationships between words in a sentence, function words themselves sometimes add little to the actual meaning. Conjunctions and prepositions are function words. Verbs are an exception: all main verbs are both content words and also function words; they are essential for the meanings of sentences, and they play a vital grammatical role.

The terms content words and function words should not be treated as absolutes. Every word in a sentence should add something to the meaning and should have some grammatical function.

NOUNS

Nouns form a large class of content words, for they are the words that name people, towns, cities and countries, animals and plants, natural phenomena such as weather, manufactured commodities, and human values and emotions. They are essential not only for our understanding of language but for our understanding of the world, because it is through nouns that we identify our world and orientate ourselves within it.

This vast class of words is divided into sub-classes according to their type and function.

Proper Nouns

Proper nouns are the names of specific persons, places, organizations or things, and to mark this individuality proper nouns are always spelled with an initial capital, or upper case letter:

> Anna Desai, Miriam Levy, Matthew Ray; India, Taj Mahal, River Ganges; United Nations Organization, International Monetary Fund, European Court of Justice; Boeing 757, Spitfire Mark IV, Jaguar XJ40.

Some proper nouns – the titles of poems, short stories, films, musical compositions and recordings, of newspapers, magazines and books – take additional punctuation in the form of inverted commas or italic type (see page 108).

Common Nouns

Common nouns are the names of groups or categories that normally have some feature or features in common:

> dentist, guitar, poem, student, tree, whale.

They are also the names of commodities, phenomena or physical properties:

> aluminium, money, fire, snow, heat, noise, speed.

Concrete Nouns

Concrete nouns have a physical, usually visible and tangible, existence, like concrete itself. Nouns can be both concrete and common:

> axe, computer, guitar, paper, student, tree, telescope

or both concrete and proper:

> Mount Everest, Lake Tanganyika, River Nile, the House of Commons, the Kremlin.

Abstract Nouns

Abstract nouns have no obvious physical existence. They include human values and emotions:

> anger, courage, fear, greed, hatred, humour, love, zeal

and also concepts, philosophies and theories:

> capitalism, justice, liberty, relativity, tyranny.

Other words used above – *values*, *emotions*, *concepts*, *philosophies* and *theories* – are themselves abstract nouns.

Origin and Formation of Nouns

Many nouns in modern English have evolved from Old English and can be identified by their distinctively English suffixes: *-dom*, *-er*, *-hood* and *-ness*. In Old English the word *dom* meant judgement or jurisdiction. *Dom* survives as the word *doom* and as a suffix indicating a condition, a position or a quality of life and an abstract state:

> boredom, chiefdom, Christendom, freedom, kingdom, martyrdom, officialdom, serfdom, wisdom.

The suffix *-er* has kept its original meaning as an indication of someone's employment:

> archer, baker, barber, brewer, butler, carter, cutler

or someone who engages in an activity:

lounger, scrounger, dancer, romancer, loner, moaner.

Nouns that identify people with their occupations or with their actions are known grammatically as agent nouns (see page 23), since they identify persons as the performers or agents of the activities implied in the nouns. Men were once so closely identified with the work they did that the words for their occupations came to be used as personal family surnames:

Cooper, Hooper, Fletcher, Porter, Salter, Thatcher, Turner.

Similarly, the -ier suffix from Middle English and from French gives the agent nouns:

cashier, collier, courier, farrier, furrier, glazier

and the military occupations:

bombardier, brigadier, cavalier, chevalier, fusilier, grenadier, soldier.

The suffix -hood, from the Old English word had, originally meant rank or order and gives nouns denoting stages and conditions of life:

childhood, boyhood, girlhood, brotherhood, sisterhood, father-hood, motherhood, manhood, womanhood, parenthood.

In addition to -dom and -hood there is yet another suffix, -ness, that denotes a state or condition of life, or a quality or property of a substance, and gives us hundreds of nouns in modern English:

madness, sadness, goodness, rudeness, quickness, homesickness, spotlessness, thoughtlessness.

The noun suffixes -er and -ier denote workers, while the suffix -ery, from Middle English and French, denotes the trade or the place of work:

bakery, bindery, chancellery, colliery, creamery, drudgery, iron-mongery, midwifery, piggery, scullery, surgery.

Nouns from Verbs and Adjectives

The flexibility of English grammar allows us to form nouns from verbs and adjectives. The past participle forms of some verbs – that is, verbs preceded by the word has or had or by the words have been or had been – can function as nouns referring to classes of persons or things. For example, the noun the forbidden, means those things that have been forbidden. Similarly, we can write:

the beaten, the bereaved, the dispossessed, the educated, the fallen, the lost, the repatriated, the wounded.

The present participles of some verbs – that is, the form of the verb that ends in *-ing* – can also function as nouns, most obviously nouns that denote an activity:

Fat Sam tried various forms of exercise: *swimming, cycling* and *running*. He even tried *dieting* for two days, but Sam finally gave up all hope of *slimming* because he could not put his favourite pastimes – *eating* and *drinking*, and *dreaming* and *thinking* about *eating* and *drinking* – out of his mind.

All the '-ing' words in the paragraph above are nouns. *Swimming, cycling* and *running* are specific examples of the noun *exercise*; *dieting* and *slimming* extend the same idea; *eating, drinking, dreaming* and *thinking* are specific examples of the noun *pastimes*.

Nouns that are formed from the present participles of verbs are sometimes known as verbal nouns or gerunds. The expression, *a gerund-grinder*, was a derisive name for a nit-picking, hair-splitting grammarian, and the term serves as another reminder that our aim is to use grammar appropriately and effectively in our writing and not as an abstract exercise.

Nouns can be formed from adjectives, and the commonest group of nouns formed in this way refer to people who have the quality denoted by the adjective, for example, *the good* and *the bad, the weak* and *the strong, the rich* and *the poor*. Similarly:

the beautiful, the dutiful, the meek, the sick, the blameless, the homeless, the grotesque, the picturesque, the lecherous, the treacherous, the uneatable, the unspeakable, an academic, a schizophrenic, a mystic, a romantic.

Singular and Plural Nouns

Nouns can be singular – that is, one only – or plural – that is, two or more. These properties of singularity and plurality are known as number.

The plural form of most English nouns is formed simply by adding the letter *s* to the singular form:

car/cars, house/houses, submarine/submarines.

Some plurals are formed by adding *es* to the singular form, especially when the singular ends in *ch, sh* or *s*:

> arches, churches, thrushes, wishes, gases, kisses.

When the singular form ends in a consonant followed by *y*, the plural normally ends in *ies*:

> armies, delicacies, remedies, tragedies.

Some nouns have a singular form ending in *f*, and a plural form ending in *ves*:

> calves, halves, hooves, knives, lives, selves, wolves.

Variations on this pattern are the plural forms of the nouns *roof* (*roofs*), *chief* (*chiefs*), *belief* (*beliefs*) and *proof* (*proofs*).

A few irregular plurals are formed by changing the vowel in the singular:

> man/men, foot/feet, mouse/mice, woman/women

and some nouns keep the same form in the plural:

> aircraft, arms [weapons], cattle, deer, measles, milk, salmon, sheep, trout, trousers, wheat.

Words that English has adopted or borrowed from other languages form their plurals in a variety of ways, and these are discussed in Chapter 4.

Collective Nouns

Collective nouns are the names given to collections or groups of people or things:

> a board of directors, a cast of actors, a platoon of infantrymen, an armada/flotilla of ships, a squadron of aircraft, a school of porpoises.

Although a collective noun refers to two or more persons or things, the collective noun itself is grammatically singular:

> an archipelago (singular) of islands (plural)
>
> a constellation (singular) of stars (plural)
>
> a miscellany (singular) of essays (plural).

Countable and Non-countable Nouns

Standard English makes a distinction between countable nouns; that is, nouns that can be counted separately and individually:

> lorries, computers, shoppers, shoplifters

and non-countable nouns; that is, nouns that denote an undifferentiated quantity. The quantity may be measurable but the items that make up the quantity are not normally countable as individual units:

> freight, information, business, crime.

The difference between countable and non-countable nouns appears in statements such as:

> *Fewer lorries* were needed because *less freight* arrived at the depot.
>
> *A few computers* can process *much information.*
>
> *Many shoppers* create *much business*; with *fewer shoplifters* there is *less crime.*

Standard English does not allow the expressions:

> less lorries, fewer freight, less computers, many information, much shoppers, many business, less shoplifters, fewer crime.

The distinction between countable and non-countable nouns determines the collective noun that is used to indicate quantity. The collective noun for a group of countable nouns must indicate their separate, countable nature; the collective noun for non-countables must indicate their indeterminate quality. Thus:

COUNTABLE	NON-COUNTABLE
the number of vehicles	the volume of traffic
a series of accidents	a great deal of distress
a number of ten-pound notes	a sum of money
a succession of visitors	the amount of interest

Because the word *people* is a countable noun, standard English does not tolerate the expression, *the amount of people.*

Distinctions such as these are important because they make it possible to express more precisely the exact nature of reality and to differentiate one form of reality from another by adding detail and definition. Without these distinctions writing is less subtle, less precise and less effective.

Gender

The gender of modern English nouns is always biological – masculine, feminine or neuter – in contrast to Old English or modern languages such as German and French, which have grammatical as well as biological gender. In Old English, for example, the noun *ham* (home) was masculine, but the noun *stow* (place) was feminine. In French the noun *arbre* (tree) is masculine, but the noun *fleur* (flower) is feminine. English has masculine and feminine nouns for the males and females of various animal species:

> bitch/dog, cow/bull, dam/sire, doe/buck, duck/drake, ewe/ram, colt/filly, mare/stallion, goose/gander, hen/cock, pen/cob, sow/ boar

and where no separate word exists for the female animal, the feminine suffix *-ess* is used, as in *lion/lioness* and *tiger/tigress*. These words will remain in the language, and so too will the gender nouns for members of the aristocracy:

> duchess/duke, countess/earl, marchioness/marquis.

But attitudes to gender have changed, and with the change in attitudes has come a change in the language of gender. Apart from the worlds of animals and aristocrats, the feminine forms of some nouns have been replaced by the masculine forms or what were once the masculine forms, which now function as epicene, that is, unisex, nouns. The linguistic change reflects a social change, for the combined effects of legislation and changing public attitudes mean that few occupations are now carried out exclusively by men. Feminine nouns such as

> authoress, instructress, manageress, poetess

are seldom used. Agent nouns – that is, nouns that indicate a person's actions, or occupation or characteristic behaviour – that end with the feminine suffix *-trix*, for the masculine *-tor*, now seem archaic:

> administratrix, curatrix, directrix, executrix, inheritrix, mediatrix, proprietrix, prosecutrix.

The unisex process has not been complete or consistent; feminine nouns continue to be used, but some of them seem isolated or specialist or self-conscious:

> barmaid, heroine, housewife, lady, midwife, mistress, suffragette, usherette, waitress.

The suffix *-woman* can replace *-man* in some of the dozens of masculine agent nouns:

> countrywoman, forewoman, horsewoman, policewoman, saleswoman, spokeswoman, sportswoman, townswoman.

The verb *to man*, as in *to man the exhibition*, can be changed to *staff* – *to staff the exhibition*. But a masculine bias is inherent in the English language, and there is no obvious unisex alternative to the words:

> craftsmanship, human, husbandry, man-eating tiger, man-hole, man in the moon, manslaughter, masterpiece, mastery.

Case of Nouns

Old English nouns and pronouns had different cases or inflections according to their positions and functions in sentences. For example, the Old English noun *scip*, meaning *ship*, had three singular forms: *scip*, *scipes*, *scipe* and three plural forms: *scipu*, *scipa*, *scipum* – in other words, there were six different forms for one noun.

Modern English grammar is much simpler. Nouns now have only two forms for cases: the standard form and the possessive form, which is normally indicated by an apostrophe before or after the letter *s* (see pages 111–17). Modern English has, however, evolved in ways that are sometimes inconsistent or even illogical: nouns have lost their case endings but pronouns still have them (see page 26).

PRONOUNS

Pronouns are words that stand *pro*, that is, for or instead of, nouns. Although they are a fairly small class of words, pronouns divide into several sub-classes, most of which are frequently used in written standard English.

Personal Pronouns

The main sub-class, personal pronouns, has four grammatical properties: number, gender, person and case, and because of these factors the personal pronouns have a greater variety of grammatical forms than any other word class except verbs.

Number

Personal pronouns, like nouns, can be singular in number (one only) or plural (two or more):

SINGULAR	PLURAL
I	we
you	you
he/she/it	they

Gender

The gender of personal pronouns, like that of nouns, is biological:

MASCULINE	FEMININE	NEUTER
he/him/his	she/her/hers	it/its

The personal pronouns *I*, *you* (*you*, singular and plural), and the plurals *we* and *they* can be either masculine or feminine; the pronoun *they* can also be neuter. Neuter pronouns are not, strictly speaking, personal pronouns since they do not refer to persons.

Person

Personal pronouns refer to persons as people; they also indicate person in the grammatical sense of first, second and third person:

	SINGULAR	PLURAL
first person	I	we
second person	you	you
third person	he, she, it	they

The first person pronouns *I* and *we* refer to the speaker or speakers and express the narrative viewpoint of the speaker. The second person pronoun *you* refers to the person or persons being spoken to or directly addressed by the speaker. The third person pronouns *he*, *she*, *it* and *they* refer to the person, persons or things being spoken about, that is, persons or things other than the speaker or the person being spoken to.

When a pronoun is the subject of a verb, the number and person of the pronoun determine the form of the verb. In modern grammar the verb has only two forms to indicate number, the form ending in -s and the base form. Thus:

PRONOUN	VERB
he, she, it	walks
I, you, we, they	walk

This correspondence in number and person between pronoun and verb is known as concord or agreement.

Case

Personal pronouns change their forms for different cases. The word case means the grammatical category and form of the pronoun, depending on the pronoun's role in a sentence; the three cases of personal pronouns are subjective, objective and possessive.

Personal pronouns in the subjective case are:

> I, you, he, she, it, we, they

and, as the term subjective clearly indicates, these pronouns form the subjects of the verbs with which they operate:

SUBJECT	VERB
he, she, it	walks
I, you, we, they	walk

The subjective case is sometimes called the nominative case, but the word subjective is more often used because it clearly indicates that the pronoun is the subject of the verb.

Personal pronouns in the objective case are:

> me, you, him, her, it, us, them.

As the term objective suggests, these pronouns are the objects of verbs:

SUBJECT	VERB	OBJECT
The reporter	interviewed	me, you, him, her, us, them

Personal pronouns also take the objective case when they are governed by prepositions:

SUBJECT	VERB	PREPOSITION	PRONOUN
The reporter	wrote	about	me, you, him, her, it, us, them

Because pronouns take the objective case after prepositions, *between you and me* should be used, not *between you and I*, and *from him and me* instead of *from him and I*. The objective case is sometimes called the accusative case. The term objective is preferred because it clearly indicates that the pronoun is the object of the verb or the preposition.

There are two main exceptions to these rules for the objective case. First, when a pronoun is the object of the verb *to be* in any of its forms, the pronoun takes the subjective case. Formal standard English still requires:

> They are the winners; it is *we* who are the losers.

The best candidate was *she* who spoke first.

The usage is sometimes regarded as archaic, but rather than write

They are the winners; it is *us* who are the losers.

The best candidate was *her* who spoke first.

which are grammatically wrong, the tendency now is to avoid both the archaic, formal quality of the subjective case and the faulty grammar of the objective case by rephrasing such statements in forms like these:

They are the winners and we are the losers.

The best candidate was the woman who spoke first.

The second exception occurs when the pronoun follows a comparative statement such as:

more than, more fearful than, less than, less able than, worse than, better than, no better than, as good as.

In these contexts the pronoun takes the subjective form:

You need this even more than *I*.

I am probably more timid than *she*.

We are just as important as *they*.

A simple mnemonic for this use is to imagine that the verb in the first part of the sentence is repeated immediately after the pronoun:

You need this even more than I need this.

or

You need this even more than I do.

I am probably more timid than she is.

We are just as important as they are.

Personal pronouns in the possessive case are:

mine, yours, his, hers, its, ours, theirs.

Personal pronouns and nouns in the possessive case indicate possession or ownership. Other possessive forms:

my, your, her, our, their

are classified as possessive adjectives or, more simply, as possessive determiners. The distinction between these two similar classes of words – possessive pronouns and possessive determiners/adjectives

– is that possessive pronouns normally appear as the subjects or objects of sentences, or the objects of prepositions, while possessive determiners appear immediately before the nouns or noun phrases that they describe. In each of the pairs of sentences that follow, the first example contains the possessive pronoun, and the second example contains the possessive determiner:

> *Mine* is the smallest car in the car park.
> **or**
> The smallest car in the car park is *mine*.
> *My* car is the smallest in the car park.
>
> Even so, I would not exchange this car for *yours*.
> Even so, I would not exchange this car for *your* car.
>
> I cannot remember which suitcase is *hers*.
> I cannot remember which is *her* suitcase.
>
> *Theirs* is an early morning flight; *ours* is at noon.
> *Their* flight is early in the morning; *our* flight is at noon.

The possessive case is sometimes known as the genitive case. The preferred term is possessive because it clearly indicates possession.

These factors – number (singular or plural), gender (masculine, feminine or neuter), person (first, second or third) and case (subjective, objective or possessive) – are listed in this table:

person	*singular*			*plural*		
	SUBJECTIVE	OBJECTIVE	POSSESSIVE	SUBJECTIVE	OBJECTIVE	POSSESSIVE
first	I	me	mine	we	us	ours
second	you	you	yours	you	you	yours
third	he/she/it	him/her/it	his/hers/its	they	them	theirs

The Spelling of Personal Pronouns

One of the few absolute rules in English language is that the possessive case of personal pronouns never takes an apostrophe. The spellings are:

> yours, his, hers, its, ours, theirs.

Similarly, the word *whose*, the possessive case of the relative pronoun *who*, is never spelled with an apostrophe.

Confusion sometimes arises from the spellings of the words *its* and *it's*, and *whose* and *who's*. The confusion is easily avoided. The word *it's* is a contraction of *it is* and always means *it is*, as shown in square brackets in the example below:

> When it's [it is] winter in Sweden it's [it is] summer in Australia.

Compare that with the correct use of the possessive pronoun *its*, with no apostrophe:

> Three features of the city of Edinburgh are its historic Castle, its varied architecture and its annual Festival of the arts.

In each of the three phrases – *its historic Castle, its varied architecture* and *its annual Festival of the arts* – the pronoun *its* means of or belonging to it, that is, to Edinburgh.

The word *who's* is a contraction of *who is*, and it always means *who is*:

> Everyone who's [who is] elected to Parliament has an entry in *Who's Who* [Who is Who].

An example of the correct use of the possessive form of the pronoun *whose* is:

> Mark Mason, whose favourite putter was stolen the night before the tournament, took six strokes at the fourteenth hole.

The words, *whose favourite putter*, mean the putter of or belonging to him, that is, to Mark Mason.

The simple test is to decide whether you mean *it is* or *of or belonging to it*, and whether you mean *who is* or *of or belonging to whom*. If you want to avoid all possibility of mis-spelling *it's* and *its*, *who's* and *whose*, you should adopt this simple procedure. When you mean *it is* you should write *it is* and not *it's*; when you mean *who is* you should write *who is* and not *who's*. The full forms of these contracted words – *it is* for *it's* and *who is* for *who's* – are also the preferred forms in standard English. Other uses of the apostrophe are explained on pages 109–17.

Reflexive Pronouns

Reflexive pronouns form a small sub-group consisting of:

> myself, yourself, himself, herself, ourselves, yourselves, themselves.

They are called reflexive because they reflect, or refer back to, the personal pronoun or the noun in the same sentence:

> *They* cooled *themselves* with chilled drinks.

The bowler was disgusted with *himself* when he was hit for six.

In the examples above, the reflexive pronoun *themselves*, which refers back to the personal pronoun *they*, is the object of the verb *cooled*. The reflexive pronoun *himself*, which refers back to the noun *bowler*, is the object of the preposition *with*.

Emphatic Pronouns

Emphatic pronouns are identical in form to reflexive pronouns, but they are placed immediately after the personal pronouns or the nouns to which they refer and thus add emphasis to the first pronoun or noun:

He himself admitted he bowled badly.

The *pitch itself* was not to blame.

Interrogative Pronouns

Interrogative pronouns, so called because they interrogate or ask questions, are a small sub-class:

who, whom, whose, what, which.

An interrogative pronoun is often the first word in the sentence in which it appears:

Who chose the team?

Whom did you consult in the selection?

Whose idea was it to include that bowler?

Which batsman will open the innings, and *what* is his average this season?

Other 'wh-' words, *why* and *where*, are classified as adverbs or adverbial prepositions (see pages 76–7).

Relative Pronouns

Some relative pronouns are identical to interrogative pronouns:

who, whom, whose, which, that, what.

The grammatical difference is that the relative pronoun relates to a noun or pronoun in a preceding clause, and the relative pronoun is normally the first word in a sub-clause. Relative pronouns are discussed in detail on pages 204–11.

Demonstrative Pronouns

The function of a demonstrative pronoun:

> this, that, these, those

is to demonstrate the noun that the pronoun replaces. For example, in the sentence:

> *This* is the *handbook* for the IBM computer.

the demonstrative pronoun *This* refers to the noun *handbook*. Similarly, in the sentence:

> Whose compact *disc* is *that*?

the demonstrative pronoun *that* refers to the noun *disc*, and in the sentence:

> I tried other *print ribbons* but I prefer *these*.

the demonstrative pronoun *these* refers to the noun *print ribbons*.

If the demonstrative word appears immediately before a noun the word can be classified as a demonstrative adjective or a demonstrative determiner, but it is much simpler to call the word a determiner.

Indefinite Pronouns

Indefinite pronouns refer to people or to things without specifying who or what they are. Indefinite pronouns referring to people are:

> one, anyone, someone, anybody, somebody, everyone, everybody, no one, nobody.

> *Everyone* assumed that *someone* would order new ribbons. *Anyone* could have done it but *no one* did.

Other indefinite pronouns, all of which can refer to people or to things, are:

> all, few, enough, several, many, more, most, others.

If the indefinite pronoun appears immediately before a noun, or occasionally before another pronoun or an adjective, the indefinite pronoun changes word class and becomes an indefinite determiner, which can also be called an indefinite adjective. In the pairs of sentences that follow, the first example contains the indefinite pronoun, and the second example the indefinite determiner:

> *Most* had entered the industry straight from university.

All the best software designers were promoted.

Some joined the research department and *others* joined the marketing department.

Several designers were transferred to the training unit so that *enough* new designers would be available.

A common fault is the overuse or ambiguous use of the pronouns *this* and *it*, especially as the opening words of sentences. These two pronouns should be used only when they clearly refer to nouns or noun phrases in the preceding sentence.

ADJECTIVES

Adjectives form a large and varied class of words. They are normally placed immediately before nouns, and their function is to describe the nouns by adding detail and definition. The detail can be physical:

loud music, black coffee, new shoes, toxic waste.

In the examples above, the word *loud* is an adjective describing the noun *music*; *black* is an adjective describing the noun *coffee*; *new* is an adjective describing *shoes*; *toxic* is an adjective describing *waste*.

The detail expressed by the adjective can be abstract:

an insoluble problem, a fair decision, a melancholy mood, a controversial topic.

In these examples the words *insoluble*, *fair*, *melancholy* and *controversial* are adjectives; the words *problem*, *decision*, *mood* and *topic* are the nouns these adjectives describe.

Adjectives can also express the kind of metaphorical information that adds tone or metaphorical colour to nouns:

a bright future, a soft option, galloping ambition, a flimsy idea.

The words *bright*, *soft*, *galloping* and *flimsy* are adjectives describing the nouns *future*, *option*, *ambition* and *idea*. Each adjective in isolation expresses a physical quality, but because the nouns are abstract the result is a metaphorical expression.

Although adjectives are normally placed immediately in front of nouns, there are a few exceptions. English idiom does not allow:

an afraid child, an aware student, a glad mother.

Instead, we must rephrase these ideas as:

the child was afraid, the student was aware, the mother was glad.

Idiom, or idiomatic expression, is a form of words that has become acceptable through usage and convention, and convention is a powerful force in language as in other areas of society.

In a few idiomatic expressions the adjective is placed after the noun:

the body politic, chairman designate, crown imperial, heir apparent, inspector general, letters patent, malice aforethought, president elect, princess royal.

These expressions are similar to a few specialist phrases borrowed from French, and in French the adjective normally follows the noun:

court martial, band sinister, lion rampant.

Adjectives are sometimes separated from the nouns or pronouns they describe by intervening verbs or adverbs:

Miriam Levy was confident in rehearsal but she felt extremely nervous in performance. Her friend, Anna Desai, always seemed calm in front of an audience.

The adjective *confident* describes the proper noun, *Miriam Levy*, but the verb *was* comes between the noun and the adjective. The adjective *nervous* describes the pronoun *she*, but the verb *felt* and the adverb *extremely* come between the pronoun and the adjective. The adjective *calm* describes another proper noun, *Anna Desai*, but the adverb *always* and the verb *seemed* intervene between noun and adjective.

Origin and Formation of Adjectives

Many adjectives in modern English have evolved from Old English and Middle English:

alive, dead, good, bad, weak, strong, ghastly, wonderful, heavenly, hellish, hard, soft

and the colours:

black, blue, brown, green, grey, red, white, yellow.

Old Norse, which evolved and diverged from the same Germanic language as Old English, is the source of the adjectives:

flat, gusty, odd, ugly, ragged, rugged.

Adjectives from Suffixes

Sometimes the adjective is the root word, which is also known, illogically, as the stem: *good, bad, low, flat*. Many other adjectives are formed by adding a suffix to the root word. For example, when the suffix *-ful* is added to the noun *pain*, the word changes its class from noun to adjective, *painful*. The suffix *-ful* and its near-opposite *-less*, both of which entered modern English from Old English, give us the adjectives:

> skilful, wilful, blameless, shameless.

The adjective *full* is spelled with two *l*s but the adjectival suffix *-ful* is spelled with only one *l*. The nouns *skill* and *will* are spelled with two *l*s, but they drop one of the *l*s to form the adjectives *skilful* and *wilful*.

Other large groups of adjectives are formed from the Old English suffixes *-ish*, *-ly*, *-y* and *-some*:

> devilish, outlandish, English, Scottish; beastly, ghastly, godly, manly; filthy, healthy, stealthy, wealthy; handsome, wholesome, loathsome, lonesome.

The Old English suffix *-ward* or *-wards* gives us adjectives that indicate direction:

> backward/backwards, forward/forwards, eastward, westward.

Smaller groups of adjectives are formed from the English suffixes *-en* and *-like*:

> wooden, woollen, ladylike, lifelike.

The spelling and to some extent the pronunciation of the adjectival suffixes *-esque* and *-ique* are reminders of the French origin of most of these words:

> grotesque, picturesque, antique, unique.

Latin suffixes *-osus* and *-utus* became the English *-ous* and *-ute*:

> hilarious, precarious, absolute, resolute,

and Greek gave us *-oid* and *-oidal*, which are widely used in the language of science and medicine:

> cuboid, rheumatoid, gyroidal, typhoidal.

Other adjectival suffixes entered English by less obvious routes: some were adopted from Latin or Greek into French, and then from French into English; some were modelled on French forms, some on Latin and a few on Greek. One result of this multiple borrowing is that we have pairs of suffixes that are almost identical. The pairs include:

-*ant* and -*ent*:
arrogant, elegant, affluent, effluent

-*able* and -*ible*:
deplorable, ignorable, audible, legible

-*ary* and -*ory*:
necessary, voluntary, accusatory, introductory

-*atic* and -*ic*:
aristocratic, ecstatic, classic, heroic

-*al* and -*ial*:
clerical, spherical, cordial, primordial

-*an* and -*ian*:
Anglican, Lutheran, Churchillian, Gilbertian

-*ane* and -*ine*:
humane, mundane, equine, feminine

-*ate* and -*ete*:
considerate, desolate, effete, obsolete

-*ac* and -*ic*:
ammoniac, cardiac, drastic, enthusiastic.

Adjectives from Prefixes

Adjectives are also formed by adding prefixes, that is, verbal elements that are placed before the root word. In the word *prefix* itself, for example, the element *pre-* is a prefix. Prefixes, like suffixes, change the meanings of words, but a notable difference between adjectival prefixes and suffixes is that the prefix is often added to a word that is already an adjective, so that the prefix changes the meaning but not the class of the word. Many adjectival prefixes change the existing adjective into its antonym, that is, a word with the opposite or negative meaning:

abnormal, amoral, anticlockwise, counteractive, contradictory, disgraceful, distasteful, illiterate, illegitimate, immortal, immoral, indefensible, indispensable, irrelevant, irreverent, undrinkable, unthinkable.

Adjectives from Verbs and Nouns

The past participles of verbs – that is, the forms that verbs take after the auxiliary verb *has* or *had* – often function as adjectives:

> the beaten team, a dispossessed tenant, a lost child.

This process continues into the present with expressions such as:

> computerized production line, pressurized water reactor, recycled paper, televised debate.

Adjectives are also formed from the present participle of a verb, that is, from the form of the verb ending in *-ing*. As well as examples like:

> humming bird, stinging nettles, washing machine

there are more recent examples:

> alternating current, central processing unit, cooling cycle, expanding universe, leading/trailing edge, oscillating forms of energy, scanning electron microscope, sweetening/emulsifying agents.

Adjectives can be formed from nouns simply by placing one noun in front of another:

> brain waves, wave power, power boat, boat people
> communications satellite, satellite transmission
> cell culture, culture shock, shock wave, wave motion.

Comparison of Adjectives

In phrases such as *extremely nervous* the adverb *extremely* is used to show the degree, extent or intensity of the adjective *nervous*. Similar combinations of adverb and adjective are:

> acutely anxious, desperately sad, naturally fat, peculiarly pink, very small, wholly innocent.

Varying degrees of intensity can be achieved by using different forms of the adjective alone. The forms are known grammatically as positive, comparative and superlative. Many adjectives follow this pattern:

POSITIVE	COMPARATIVE	SUPERLATIVE
sad	sadder	saddest
fat	fatter	fattest
pink	pinker	pinkest

These adjectives are grammatically regular. Adjectives that break the pattern are grammatically irregular, and irregular adjectives include:

POSITIVE	COMPARATIVE	SUPERLATIVE
bad	worse	worst
good	better	best
little	less/lesser	least
many/much	more	most

Other adjectives can be compared or intensified only by placing in front of them the words *more* or *most*, which are themselves adjectives:

POSITIVE	COMPARATIVE	SUPERLATIVE
anxious	more anxious	most anxious
careful	more careful	most careful
helpless	more helpless	most helpless

A few adjectives are regarded as absolute and thus incomparable; that is, they cannot be compared to show different degrees of intensity but must be used in one form only:

> complete, dead, eternal, faultless, final, finished, incomparable, infinite, perfect, ultimate, unique.

Similarly, the ordinal numerals – that is, numbers that indicate rank order – cannot be compared:

> first, second, third

although the expression *the very first* is acceptable. Numerals can be treated as adjectives, but it is much simpler to classify them as numerals (see also pages 39–41).

DETERMINERS

The grammatical function of a determiner is to determine or fix the limits of a noun or a noun phrase; and because the determiner describes the noun in this way, it has an adjectival function. Determiners form a small, mixed class of function words that represent a simplification in English grammar. The word class is mixed in the sense that it brings together words that were once, and sometimes still are, assigned to several different word classes, and it is for this reason – the reduction of several word classes to a single class – that determiners mark a simplification in grammar.

Determiners, like adjectives, are normally placed before the nouns and noun phrases they describe. The most frequently used determiners are the words *a/an*, which are also known as indefinite articles, and *the*, which is also known as the definite article:

> a party, an opposition party, the political party.

Other common determiners:

> this, that, these, those

are sometimes known as demonstratives because they demonstrate or point out exactly which noun or noun phrase is meant:

> this cinema, that supermarket, these new town-centre offices, those building society branches.

A similar group of determiners:

> which, whichever, what, whatever, whose

can be used in normal indicative statements:

> Jack can afford to buy *whichever* computer he chooses.
>
> He knew *what* discount the dealer gave to students.

The same determiners can also be used interrogatively, that is, to ask questions:

> Which computer did you finally choose, Jack?
>
> Whatever reason led you to buy a Millenium X12?
>
> Whose recommendation was that?

The possessive determiners:

> my, your, his, her, its, our, their

clearly indicate possession, ownership or attribution:

> my computer, your pocket calculator, her expensive video recorder, their antique gramophone.

When the possessive words appear in their other forms:

> mine, yours, hers, ours, theirs

and are used instead of nouns rather than to describe nouns, the possessive words are pronouns (see pages 27–8). Determiners, unlike pronouns, seldom appear alone but are normally followed immediately by a noun or noun phrase. Some determiners indicate the scale or quantity of the noun or noun phrase:

> most vehicles, some family cars, all motor cycles, many furniture vans, every horse-box, much traffic congestion, each motorway filling-station, enough petrol, no car parks, less bad temper, few accidents, several slow-moving farm tractors, whole families.

Nouns and noun phrases can be preceded by two or more determiners:

> *a few* vintage cars, *this whole* stretch of motorway, *each and every* driver, *all the many* miles.

The grammatical terminology – definite and indefinite articles, demonstrative and possessive, and even the word determiner itself – is important only to grammarians. Most writers need only know that determiners offer a range of options that can bring greater clarity and precision to their writing.

NUMERALS

Numerals are the class of words that refer to numbers. The term numeral is preferred here because in any discussion of grammar the word number may be thought of as grammatical number – that is, singular or plural – rather than the words and symbols for arithmetical numbers.

Assigning numerals to a single word class simplifies English grammar. Numerals, like determiners, were once assigned to different word classes, but modern grammar accepts that the arithmetical properties common to all numerals from zero to infinity are more important than their diverse grammatical properties. The classifications of numerals in the old grammar are illustrated at the end of this section. In modern grammar we need observe only two sub-classes of numerals, cardinal and ordinal.

Cardinal Numerals

The word cardinal comes from a Latin word meaning hinge, and by extension the word came to mean fundamental, chief or principal in the sense that other, secondary things hinged on the principal things.

Cardinal numerals, then, are numerals in their first or principal form:

> one, two, three, four, five . . . ninety-seven, ninety-eight, ninety-nine, 100.

A widely observed practice for writing numerals in standard English prose is to spell out numbers from one to ninety-nine, and to use digits for numbers from 100 upwards. The practice in most British newspapers, journals and many books is to use alphabetical characters from one to nine and digits from 10 upwards. Numerals in thousands or millions show the usefulness of the practice; *17,475,739* is easier to write and to read – even by people who are not highly numerate – than *seventeen million, four hundred and seventy-five thousand, seven hundred and thirty-nine.*

Ordinal Numerals

The word ordinal comes from the Latin *ordinalis*, which means denoting order or position in a series. Ordinal numbers are:

first, second, third, fourth, fifth

and

100th, 101st, 102nd, 103rd, 104th, 105th.

There is a third sub-class consisting only of the adverbials *once, twice* and *thrice*.

The old grammar used to complicate numerals by sub-dividing them into three word classes: adjective, adverb and pronoun. The following example shows three numerals functioning as adjectives:

Mark Mason, the *second* golfer to tee-off, took *six* strokes at the *fourteenth* hole.

The ordinal numeral *second* is an adjective describing the noun *golfer*; the cardinal numeral *six* is an adjective describing the noun *strokes*; the ordinal numeral *fourteenth* is an adjective describing the noun *hole*.

In this example the numerals function as adverbs:

Geoff Gratton, who had won *twice* before on the Blue Pines course, was lying *first* at the end of his round but finished *third* in the tournament.

The numeral *twice* is an adverb modifying the verb *had won*; *first* is an adverb modifying the verb *was lying*; *third* is an adverb modifying the verb *finished*.

The numerals in this example are pronouns:

Forty-two played in the tournament. *Two* equalled the club record of *seventy-three* and a *third* scored *seventy-four*, but the winner was Sean Kelly with a round of *sixty-eight*.

Some of the numerals function *pro*, or on behalf of, nouns such as *golfer* or *competitor* or *player*; some numerals are either the subject or the object of the verbs; and some of the numerals are governed by prepositions. *Forty-two* is the subject of the verb *played*; *Two* is the subject of the verb *equalled*; *seventy-three* is governed by the preposition *of*; *third* is the subject of *scored*; *seventy-four* is the object of *scored*; and *sixty-eight* is governed by the preposition *of*.

VERBS

Verbs form a large class of words that denote varieties of action, change and states of being. Verbs are both content words and function words; they add to the meanings of sentences, and they have more grammatical functions than any other class of words.

A finite verb – that is, a verb with a subject – is normally the minimum grammatical requirement of a standard English sentence. The subject of a finite verb, and thus the subject of the clause or sentence in which the verb appears, is the agent or source of the action denoted by the verb.

The subject can be a noun:

> Authors (noun) write (finite verb)

or a noun phrase, that is, a group of words with a noun as its head word or main word:

> Some modern authors (noun phrase) write (finite verb)

or a pronoun:

> They (pronoun) write.

When the verb expresses a command, the subject can be the implied pronoun *you*:

> Write!

The nature and extent of the action, change or state of being that is denoted by the verb is indicated by the type and form of the verb.

The extent of verbs' influence is affected by several factors; namely, whether the verbs are: regular or irregular, main or auxiliary, transitive or intransitive, finite or non-finite, active or passive in voice, singular or plural in number, or indicative, imperative or subjunctive in mood. The verbs' forms also reveal their tense, through which they express degrees of time.

Regular Verbs

Regular verbs are those to which the inflection -ed is added to form the past tenses (see pages 58–61). The past tenses of the regular verb *walk*, for example, are:

I walked   I have walked   I had walked.

The verb *walk* has a total of four different forms for all tenses and functions:

walk   walks   walking   walked.

Similarly, all other regular verbs have four forms:

add   adds   adding   added

love   loves   loving   loved

zip   zips   zipping   zipped.

Most of the new verbs that are coined or borrowed in English are treated as regular verbs:

anodize, breathalyse, bulldoze, clone, degauss, demote, interface, metricate, overkill, streamline, telephone, televise, transduce, zap, zip.

Irregular verbs

Irregular verbs are those that break the regular pattern outlined in the previous section and that have a different form for the past tense. The irregular verb *think*, for example, changes its form to *thought* in the past tense; the same form, *thought*, is used for three past tenses:

I thought   I have thought   I had thought.

The verb *think* has a total of four different forms for all tenses and functions:

think   thinks   thinking   thought.

Other irregular verbs have two forms for the past tense:

I drank   I have drunk   I had drunk

I drove   I have driven   I had driven

I swam   I have swum   I had swum.

Irregular verbs with two different forms for past tenses have a total of five different forms for all tenses and functions:

drink	drinks	drinking	drank	drunk
drive	drives	driving	drove	driven
swim	swims	swimming	swam	swum.

The most frequently used irregular verb is *be*, which has the forms:

be am are is being was were been.

Past tenses of irregular verbs are often simplified in the non-standard grammar, or folk grammar, that is widely used in Britain. For example, folk grammar has the forms *I have drank* and *she had drove* instead of the standard English forms *I have drunk* and *she had driven*. Folk grammar also invents forms of the past tense that do not exist in standard grammar. In standard English the verbs *burst* and *hurt* keep the same form for past and present tenses, but folk grammar allows the non-standard forms *bursted* and *hurted*.

Standard grammatical forms of other irregular verbs are listed below. With one exception, all the irregular verbs in the list have evolved from Old English or Middle English; the exception is *pay*, from Old French. Forms marked with an asterisk (*) are discussed in more detail on pages 45–6.

IRREGULAR VERBS

arise arose arisen

beat beat beaten

become became become

begin began begun

bid bid bid*

break broke broken

build built built

burn burnt/burned burnt/burned

burst burst burst

cast cast cast

catch caught caught

choose chose chosen

cling clung clung

cost cost cost*

cut cut cut

deal dealt dealt

dig dug dug

do did done

draw drew drawn

dream dreamt/dreamed dreamt/dreamed

eat ate eaten

fall fell fallen

find found found

fling flung flung

fly flew flown

forbid forbade forbidden

forgo forwent forgone

foresee foresaw foreseen

forget forgot forgotten

freeze froze frozen

give gave given

go went gone

grow grew grown

hang hung/hanged
hung/hanged*

heave heaved heaved*

hide hid hidden

hold held held

hurt hurt hurt

kneel knelt knelt

know knew known

lay laid laid*

lean leant/leaned leant/leaned

learn learnt/learned
learnt/learned

let let let

lie lay lain*

light lit lit

lose lost lost

mean meant meant

mistake mistook mistaken

outdo outdid outdone

overcome overcame overcome

pay paid paid

put put put

putt putted putted*

ride rode ridden

ring rang rung

saw sawed sawn

see saw seen

seek sought sought

sew sewed sewn*

shake shook shaken

show showed shown

shrink shrank shrunk

sing sang sung

sink sank sunk

slay slew slain*

sleep slept slept

sling slung slung

slink slunk slunk

sow sowed sowed/sown*

speak spoke spoken

speed sped sped

spell spelt/spelled spelt/spelled

spend spent spent

spill spilt/spilled spilt/spilled

spit spat spat*

spit spitted spitted*

spread spread spread

spring sprang sprung

steal stole stolen

sting stung stung

stink stank stunk

strike struck struck*

string strung strung

swear swore sworn

swell swelled swollen

swim swam swum

swing swung swung

take took taken

teach taught taught

tear tore torn

throw threw thrown

wear wore worn

weave wove woven

weep wept wept

wring wrung wrung

write wrote written

Bid The past tense *bade* and the past participle *bidden* are now archaic.

Cost The form *costed* is used only in the sense of estimated the cost of production.

Hang/hung In standard English usage *hung* refers to inanimate objects: *Portraits have been hung in the gallery. Hanged* refers to persons executed by hanging: *The prisoner was hanged at dawn.*

Heave The past tense form *hove* is now used only in the archaic seafaring phrase, *hove to.*

Lay is the basic form and the present tense of the verb meaning to place on the ground, or to put down on a flat surface, for example, *Hens lay eggs.* The past tenses take the form *laid.* By extension, *lay* can mean simply to place, as in *He laid a bet* or *She is laying paving stones.*

Lie is the basic form and the present tense of the verb meaning to be in a prostrate or recumbent position, for example, *to lie in bed.* The past tense of *lie* is *lay,* as in *He lay in bed until noon.* The past participle of *lie* is *lain,* as in *Litter has lain in the street all week.*

Lie meaning to speak falsely is a regular verb and has the same form, *lied,* for the past tense and the past participle.

Put with one *t* has the same form, *put,* in the present and past tenses, but has two *ts, putting,* in the present participle.

Putt with two *ts* is a regular verb with the form, *putted,* for the past tenses. *Putt* is used only in the sports of golf and shot-putting.

Sew with an *e* is to sew with needle and thread.

Sow with an *o* is to sow corn or oats.

Slay is archaic but has been partly revived by the sub-editors of tabloid newspapers.

Spit meaning to expel saliva from the mouth has the form, *spat,* for the past tenses.

Spit meaning to put meat on a skewer is a regular verb with the form, *spitted,* for the past tenses.

Strike The past tense, *stricken*, is archaic except in expressions like *grief-stricken* and *panic-stricken*.

Main Verbs

A main verb, sometimes known as a principal verb, is normally a single word, shown in italic type in these three examples:

Some authors *write* book reviews for newspapers.

Few novelists *earn* a living from their books alone.

Many journalists now *use* word processors.

The finite verb in each of these three sentences – *write*, *earn* and *use* – is a main verb, a single word with a clear meaning and a distinct grammatical function as the pivotal word between the subject and the object of the sentence. In the first sentence, for example, the subject of the verb is *Some authors*, and the object is *book reviews for newspapers*.

Auxiliary Verbs

An auxiliary verb, colloquially known as a helping verb, is one that precedes a main verb in order to extend or complete the function and the meaning of the main verb. The commonest auxiliary verbs are *be*, *have* and *do*:

Some authors *are writing* book reviews for newspapers.

Few novelists *have earned* a living from their books alone.

The old journalist *does not use* a word processor.

The auxiliary verbs extend the grammatical functions and the meanings of the main verbs so that the full grammatical function is now expressed by the two verbs, auxiliary and main, acting together. When an auxiliary and a main verb act together in this way, the end result is treated as a single verb. The phrase *does not use* in the third sentence shows that an adverb, in this case the word *not*, can appear between the auxiliary verb and the main verb. Similarly:

Journalists *are* now (adverb) *using* word processors.

A main verb can be preceded by more than one auxiliary verb but the end result is a single verb:

Some authors *may have written* book reviews for newspapers.

Few novelists *can have earned* a living from their books alone.

Many journalists *will have been using* word processors for years.

Each group of words – *may have written, can have earned* and *will have been using* – functions as a single verb.

Transitive Verbs

The word transitive means passing across or passing through, and a verb is transitive when the meaning of the sentence passes directly from the subject, through the verb, into the object of the sentence:

Matthew Ray *contested* the Grantown South by-election.

Positron, the rock band, *produced* a new album.

Archaeologists *excavated* an Iron Age settlement.

A transitive verb is a main verb, the meaning of which is incomplete without an object. If we remove the objects from the three sentences above, we are left with statements that are obviously incomplete:

Matthew Ray contested

Positron, the rock band, produced

Archaeologists excavated

and so we know that the three verbs, *contested, produced* and *excavated*, are transitive.

When the transitive main verb is preceded by an auxiliary verb, as it often is, the resulting compound verb is still transitive:

Matthew Ray *will contest* the Grantown South by-election.

Positron, the rock band, *has produced* a new album.

Archaeologists *have excavated* an Iron Age settlement.

Intransitive Verbs

An intransitive verb does not transmit meaning to an object. Instead, the intransitive verb completes the meaning of the sentence without the addition of an object, as this example shows:

Darkness *fell* but the police *persevered*. Stars *glittered* and the moon *shone* as the search *continued*. The chief inspector *shivered*, a sergeant *yawned* and a constable *grumbled*. Their hopes *faded*. Just as dawn *broke* the reinforcements *arrived*. Minutes later the lost child *reappeared* and the search *ended*.

47

Other intransitive verbs include the following, which are grouped according to their meanings rather than alphabetically, in order to show more clearly the intransitive nature of some actions and states of being:

> appear, disappear, seem; emerge, arise, occur; hope, aspire; die, expire, live, exist; dive, fall, slide, slip; laugh, smile, rejoice; giggle, snigger, guffaw; amble, linger, loiter, saunter, stroll; look, gaze, peer, stare; cease, desist; persist, remain; meditate, reflect, philosophize, reminisce, wonder, speculate, hallucinate; retreat; flourish, prosper, succeed, thrive; mutiny, rebel, revolt.

In this area of grammar as in so many others, the English language is highly flexible. Some intransitive verbs can be changed into transitive verbs; the intransitive verb *look*, for example, can be changed into several different transitive verbs by adding different adverbs and prepositions. When words such as *after* or *into*, or phrases such as *down on* or *up to*, are added to the verb *look*, the additional words become part of a new compound or phrasal verb, for example, *look after* or *look into*, *look down on* or *look up to*.

The term compound verb means a verb that consists of, or is compounded from, two or more words; the alternative term, phrasal verb, means a verb that consists of a phrase, that is, two or more words, rather than a single word. By adding prepositions or prepositional adverbs to the intransitive verb *look*, we produce a number of transitive compound verbs:

> look after (care for), look at, look back at; look back on (remember), look down on (literally and figuratively to despise), look for, look forward to, look in on (visit), look into (investigate), look out (items for a jumble sale), look out for (await; beware of), look out on, look over (examine), look through (a lens, or to scan), look to (attend to), look up (a dictionary or an old friend), look up at, look up to (admire).

Each of these compound verbs is now transitive and must be followed by a direct object to complete its meaning:

> When his neighbour went into hospital, Silas Ramsden *looked after* her cat.

> Children *look forward to* their next birthday; old men *look back on* their past.

Finite Verbs

A finite verb is a verb that has a subject. The subject of a verb, and thus the subject of the clause or sentence in which that verb appears, is the factor or agent responsible for the action or activity indicated by the verb:

Rock bands (subject)/attract (verb)/big audiences.

You (subject)/believe (verb)/her.

Members of the committee (subject)/consider (verb)/the planning proposal.

The finite verb can also be used in the past tense and in the future tense:

Anxiety (subject)/undermined (verb, past tense)/the performance.

Students (subject)/will write (verb, future tense)/applications for jobs.

The subject of a finite verb, and thus the subject of the clause or sentence in which the verb appears, is, therefore, the agent or cause of the action or activity. The examples also show that the subject of the verb is normally

a noun: *Anxiety, Students*

a noun phrase: *Rock bands, Members of the committee*

a pronoun: *You.*

Verbs of Command

A common form of statement that breaks this general pattern of subject + finite verb + object is the verb used as a single word of command, or the verb and an adverb functioning together as a command. The element of command is sometimes indicated by an exclamation mark:

Stop! Wait Listen! Get lost! Go away! Stand clear!

Verbs that express direct commands in this way are known as imperatives or are said to be in the imperative mood, and this use of the imperative normally assumes that the subject of the verb is understood:

[You] (subject) stop!

[You] (subject) stand clear!

Non-finite Forms of Verbs

Some forms of verbs are, by definition, not finite; these forms are the infinitive, the present participle and the past participle.

The infinitive form of a verb can be the base form, that is, a single word:

> attract, believe, consider

or it can be the base form preceded by the word *to*:

> to attract, to believe, to consider.

The present participle always ends in *-ing*:

> attracting, believing, considering.

The past participle always takes the form of the verb that is used following the word *have* or *had*. As we have seen, the past participle of regular verbs ends in *ed*:

> attracted, believed, considered.

Irregular verbs, as we saw above, take various forms of past participles:

> drunk, eaten, gone, held, struck, swum, taught.

Split Infinitives

The infinitive verb is said to be split when a word, normally an adverb, appears between *to* and the verb, as in the introduction to the science-fiction series, *Star Trek*: 'To boldly go where no man has gone before.' Many general readers and some grammarians claim that this usage is ungrammatical; most linguists and many grammarians say that it is acceptable in standard English and that authors have been splitting infinitives from Shakespeare's time to the present day. The split infinitive is certainly acceptable and may even be necessary in some sentences. This sentence:

> If you want to fully achieve your ambition you must quickly change your attitude and begin to really work.

uses the split infinitives *to fully achieve* and *to really work*. Objectors would argue that the 'correct' version is:

> If you want fully to achieve your ambition you must quickly change your attitude and begin really to work.

But this version could be ambiguous since *fully* could be read as modifying the verb *want* when it is intended to modify the verb *achieve*, and *really* could be read as modifying the verb *begin* when it is intended to modify the verb *work*. Writers face the dilemma: the split infinitive is acceptable in standard English, but many educated readers believe it is wrong. For purely tactical reasons, then, you may wish to avoid the split infinitive in order to avoid upsetting your readers.

The vital importance of the finite verb in the standard English sentence is illustrated in these examples:

> Free tape of Positron's ten best hits to the winner of the competition.

> Last-minute Christmas spending spree by Saturday shoppers.

> Effort and artistry from Australian xv in a high-scoring match.

Some information is communicated by these statements, but because they contain no verbs the statements are grammatically incomplete and thus unacceptable as written standard English. The first statement reads like a piece of retail advertising copywriting and assumes that the reader will supply the missing information, the finite verb:

> The winner of the competition *will receive* a free tape of Positron's ten best hits.

The other statements could form newspaper picture captions, but if they were to form parts of newspaper reports written in standard English they would have to be rewritten to include finite verbs:

> Saturday shoppers *went* on a last-minute Christmas spending spree.

In a grammatically acceptable but less imaginative sentence we could write:

> There *was* a last-minute Christmas spending spree by Saturday shoppers.

Sentences beginning with the words, *There was* or *It was*, quickly become repetitive:

> *There was* effort and artistry from the Australian xv in a high-scoring match.

A structure like this is preferable:

> The Australian XV *showed* effort and artistry in a high-scoring match.

The subject and the finite verb of the second sentence are more precise, and such a sentence will add variety and energy to your prose style.

Each of the following three statements contains a verb, but because the verbs are in non-finite forms the statements are grammatically incomplete and unacceptable as standard English sentences:

> Amateur archaeologists *to excavate* an Iron Age settlement.
>
> A marina development *proposed* for Cradle Bay.
>
> Light engineering factories *competing* for new orders.

With the addition of a finite verb each statement can be made grammatically complete and thus acceptable as a standard English sentence:

> Amateur archaeologists *are to excavate* an Iron Age settlement
> or
> Amateur archaeologists *will excavate* an Iron Age settlement.
>
> A marina development *is proposed* for Cradle Bay.
>
> Light engineering factories *are competing* for new orders.

The non-finite main verbs have been made finite by adding auxiliary verbs.

Each of the sentences above has only one finite verb, and such sentences are known grammatically as simple sentences. In written standard English, then, the typical simple sentence consists of subject + verb + object.

Together, the verb and the object are sometimes known as the predicate of the sentence; in this context the word predicate means that which is stated or declared. The sentence can then be seen to consist of subject + verb + object, or subject + predicate:

> Anxiety (subject)/*undermined the performance* (predicate).

Active and Passive Voices of Verbs

The grammatical voice of the verb is a semi-abstract concept, but the concept becomes imaginable if you think of a person at a meeting having a voice, that is, the right to express an opinion and to cast a vote. If the person exercises these rights, his or her voice is active or positive, but if the person is not allowed a voice in this sense, the person is inactive or passive. Although the concept of voice is abstract, actual examples of active and passive voices of verbs are easy to identify in other people's writing and easy to use in your own.

Look again at some of the sentences that have already appeared in this chapter:

Matthew Ray *contested* the Grantown South by-election.

Positron, the rock band, *produced* a new album.

Archaeologists *excavated* an Iron Age settlement.

Each verb is a finite main verb, and the voice of each verb is active. The subject of each sentence – *Matthew Ray, Positron, the rock band* and *Archaeologists* – is the source of action in the sentence; the subjects exercise their metaphorical right to speak and, through the finite main verbs, the subjects exert an active, positive influence throughout the sentences. In that sense the entire sentence, not just the verb, can be regarded as active.

Each sentence can be restructured:

The Grantown South by-election *was contested* by Matthew Ray.

A new album *was produced* by Positron, the rock band.

An Iron Age settlement *was excavated* by archaeologists.

Now the subject of each sentence – *The Grantown South by-election, A new album* and *An Iron Age settlement* – is not active but is acted on, and the passivity of each subject is confirmed by the passive voice of the verbs. The entire sentences can now be regarded as passive.

Three differences in the two sets of sentences can be clearly identified. First, the positions of the subjects and the objects are reversed. When *Matthew Ray* is active he is the subject of the sentence; when he is passive he is the object. When *Matthew Ray* is active *the Grantown South by-election* is the object of the sentence; when *Matthew Ray* is passive *the Grantown South by-election* becomes the subject of the sentence. In other words, the subjects of the active sentences become the objects of the passive sentences, and the objects of the active sentences become the subjects of the passive sentences.

The second difference is that the finite main verb in the passive voice is always preceded by an auxiliary verb, and the auxiliary is always the appropriate form of the verb *to be*. In the examples above, the active verb *contested* is changed to the passive *was contested*; the active verb *produced* is changed to the passive *was produced*; the active verb *excavated* is changed to the passive *was excavated*. The same rule applies when the verb is in the present tense or the future tense. For example, the active verb *contests* (present tense) becomes the passive *is contested*. When the present tense is expressed in the alternative active form, *is contesting*, we must still add the appropriate form of the verb *to be* so that the active *is contesting* becomes the passive *is being contested*. If the active verb is in the future tense, *will produce*, the passive form becomes *will be produced*; similarly, *will excavate* becomes *will be excavated*.

The third difference is that the preposition *by* is normally placed immediately after the main verb: *contested by, produced by, excavated by*. In sentences which have no agent nouns, that is, no person or thing doing the action expressed by the verb, the word *by* is omitted:

> The lost child has been found and the police search has been called off.

Stylistically, the passive sentences above are structured in such a way that vital information – the agent or source of the action – is withheld until the end. By delaying information in this way you can sometimes create an element of tension in your sentences and achieve variety in your prose style.

Verbs in the passive voice are always transitive; that is, they are followed or are capable of being followed by a direct object. Intransitive verbs cannot be used in the passive voice. The demonstration passage on intransitive verbs included these lines:

> Darkness fell. Stars glittered and the moon shone. Just as dawn broke the reinforcements arrived. Minutes later the lost child reappeared.

We cannot reverse the positions of the subjects and objects in these sentences because there are no objects; for the same reason we cannot introduce the preposition *by*:

> Darkness was fallen by . . .   Dawn was broken by . . .

Some intransitive verbs from the original demonstration passage could be used in the passive voice, but only by distorting the structure, the style and to some extent the meaning of the original. The active verbs in the sentence:

> The chief inspector *shivered*, a sergeant *yawned* and a constable *grumbled*; their hopes *faded*.

could be changed to passive:

> A shiver *was experienced* by the chief inspector, a yawn *was emitted*

by a sergeant and a grumble *was expressed* by a constable; their hopes *were faded* [by lack of success]

but the result is an absurdly stilted, non-standard sentence.

Verbs of command, that is, verbs in the imperative mood, cannot normally be changed from the active to the passive voice without distorting the original, even when the imperative verbs have direct objects. An added complication is that imperative statements are the equivalent of direct speech – that is, the words that were actually spoken – but a passive statement is normally the equivalent of indirect or reported speech. For example, a passive version of the imperative:

[You] Stop the car!

is not

The car was stopped by him

but

He was ordered to stop the car.

Because the purpose of the imperative is to create a forceful tone that suggests action and energy, a passive imperative is a contradiction.

Singular and Plural Verbs

As we have seen, grammatical number is either singular or plural. The present and past tenses of finite verbs also express grammatical number, which must be the same number as the noun or pronoun that forms the subject of the verb. Thus:

Greenpeace *is* (singular) an international pressure group.

Some pressure groups *are* (plural) also registered charities.

Because the subject of the first sentence, *Greenpeace*, is singular, the verb *is* must also be singular; and because the subject of the second sentence, *Some pressure groups*, is plural, the verb *are* must also be plural.

The same rule applies when the finite verb is in the past tense and in the passive voice:

Oxfam *was founded* to feed the hungry.

Millions of lives *were saved* by Oxfam.

Both Oxfam and Amnesty *have been accused* of political bias.

In the first sentence the subject, *Oxfam*, is singular, and so the passive verb, *was founded*, must also be singular. In the second two sentences the subjects, *Millions of lives* and *Both Oxfam and Amnesty*, are plural, and so the passive verbs, *were saved* and *have been accused*, must also be plural.

When the subject of the sentence includes two nouns or pronouns in the structure *either . . . or, neither . . . nor* the verb must be singular because *either* means one or other of two, and *neither* is the negative form of *either*:

> Either Greenpeace or Friends of the Earth *is* to receive a £50,000 donation.

> Neither Oxfam nor Amnesty *sees* an end to injustice.

Correspondence in number between the subject and the verb of a clause or sentence is known as concord or agreement. The concord required, singular or plural, is normally easy to identify, but when the subject of a sentence is a collective noun, the verb can be either singular or plural. Although the collective noun itself is grammatically singular:

> an archipelago, a constellation, a shoal

it always implies a collection of two or more persons or things. Standard English recognizes this singular/plural duality and allows either a singular or plural verb:

> A school of whales *has been/have been* stranded in the bay all week, and an armada of small boats *is trying/are trying* to drive the whales back to the open sea.

The best practice is to decide whether you wish to emphasize the unity and singularity, or the variety and plurality, of the collective noun. In the following examples the singular verbs treat the collective nouns as single units:

> *An anthology* of war poems *has* just *been* published.

> *A collection* of electronic gadgets *was lying* on the bench.

> Every Wednesday evening *the choir rehearses* for three hours.

By contrast, the plural verbs in these sentences suggest the multiple nature of the subject:

> *A string* of race-horses *were galloping* across the downs.

> The *team*, after six home defeats, *are feeling* demoralized.

> *A group* of first-year students *live* in the same hall of residence.

Concord is optional in these two contexts, but there is a third, apparently similar, context where concord is not optional and where there is sometimes confusion.

Grammatically, the indefinite pronouns *everyone, everybody, anyone, anybody* and *no one* are singular, because *one* and *body* are singular. Standard grammar used to insist not only on singular concord between indefinite pronouns and their verbs, but also between indefinite pronouns and any corresponding personal pronoun in the same clause or sentence. For example, standard English grammar once required:

> Everyone *has* a right to *his* privacy.

> *Is* everybody ready for *his* lunch?

If the indefinite pronoun referred only to women, the pronoun *her* could be used:

> *Does* anyone hope to see *her* words in print?

There was, then, a double concord: between the indefinite pronoun and the singular verb, and between the indefinite pronoun and the corresponding singular personal pronoun.

In colloquial, non-standard, grammar the practice was, and still is, to use a plural pronoun, as in:

> Everyone *has* a right to *their* privacy.

> *Does* anyone *hope* to see *their* words in print?

An exception to this rule is the indefinite pronoun *none*. Although *none* is grammatically singular because it means *not one*, it is often treated as plural and followed by the plural form of the verb and the pronoun:

> The chef looked for his set of knives but none *was/were* where he had left *it/them* and none *was/were* on *its/their* hook/hooks.

In the 1960s and 1970s, when linguists became aware of sexism and the gender debate, they began to use two pronouns, one masculine and one feminine:

> *Does* anyone hope to see *his or her* words in print?
> **and**
> Everyone *has* a right to *his or her* privacy.

But the *his or her* usage is clumsy and highlights the lack of a single unisex or epicene pronoun in English. Linguists began to use the model of *none/their* in standard grammar and of *everyone/their* in colloquial grammar. It is now generally accepted in standard English that the indefinite pronouns *everyone, everybody, anyone, anybody* and *no one*, like the indefinite *none*, can be followed by *their*:

> Everyone *has* a right to *their* privacy.

Although an indefinite pronoun can be followed by the plural *their*, the indefinite pronoun cannot take a plural verb:

> *Are* everybody ready for his/their lunch?

> Everyone *have* a right to his/their privacy.

> *Do* anyone hope to see her/their words in print?

The verb must be singular:

> *Is* everybody ready for their lunch?

> Everyone *has* a right to their privacy.

> *Does* anyone hope to see their work in print?

Tenses of Verbs

The word tense comes from the Old French word *tens*; the modern French word is *temps* (time).

English verbs allow you to express varying degrees of time within the three main time states, or tenses: present, past and future. Each of the time states can be indicated in a tense of the verb that is grammatically simple, that is, the single or shortest grammatical form of the tense in question:

> simple present: I/you/we/they *write*; he/she *writes*

> simple past: I/you/he/she/they *wrote*

> simple future: I/we *shall write*; you/he/she/they *will write*.

Standard English still requires that the personal pronouns *I* and *we* be followed by the future form *shall* and that the other pronouns be followed by the future form *will*.

Each time state can also be expressed by using the present participle of the main verb – the '-ing' form – preceded by the appropriate form of the verb *to be* as an auxiliary to the main verb. Tenses formed in this way are known as continuous or progressive, because the '-ing' form suggests that the action of the verb is continuing:

continuous present:	I *am writing*; he/she *is writing*; we/you/they *are writing*
continuous past:	I/he/she *was writing*; we/you/they *were writing*
continuous future:	I/we *shall be writing*; you/he/she/they *will be writing.*

The past can be expressed in four more tenses, the first two of which are the perfect and the pluperfect. Other grammatical terms are sometimes used for these two tenses, but the words *perfect* and *pluperfect* are the simplest and clearest. In this context the word *perfect* means perfected in the sense of complete; the word *pluperfect*, from Latin, *plus perfectum*, means that the action is in a time state that is even more remote than the perfect tense. The perfect tense is formed by placing *has* or *have* as an auxiliary verb before the main verb; the pluperfect tense is formed by placing *had* as an auxiliary verb before the main verb.

perfect:	I/you/we/they *have written*; he/she *has written*
pluperfect:	I/you/he/she/we/they *had written.*

The other two forms of the past tense are the continuous perfect and the continuous pluperfect. The continuous perfect is formed by taking the '-ing' form of the main verb and placing the auxiliaries *has been/have been* in front of it; the continuous pluperfect is formed by taking the '-ing' form of the main verb and placing *had been* in front of it:

continuous perfect:	I/you/we/they *have been writing*; he/she *has been writing*
continuous pluperfect:	I/you/he/she/we/they *had been writing.*

English verbs do not have separate forms for future tenses; instead, the future is expressed by placing *shall* or *will* as an auxiliary verb before the main verb. As we have seen, *shall* is used with the personal pronouns *I* and *we*; *will* is used with the other personal pronouns. The future, like the past, has several states of time:

simple future:	I/we *shall write*; you/he/she/they *will write*
continuous future:	I/we *shall be writing*; you/he/she/they *will be writing*

future perfect:	I/we *shall have written*; you/he/she/they *will have written*
continuous future perfect:	I/we *shall have been writing*; you/he/she/they *will have been writing*.

Standard English allows even greater subtlety than this in discussing the future; three forms of the present tense of the verb can be used to express futurity:

simple present as future:	I *write* the next chapter tonight.
present continuous as future:	I *am writing* the next chapter tonight.

The third form, a variation of the present continuous as future, is the structure that uses *going* followed by the infinitive of the main verb, *to write*:

I *am going to write* the next chapter tonight.

Yet another, indirect, way of expressing the future is to use the imperative mood of the main verb:

Write the next chapter tonight.

This large number of tenses allows us to discuss time with precision and subtlety. The tenses are summarized below.

Sequence of Tenses of Verbs

PRESENT TENSE

simple present:	I/you/we/they write; he/she writes
continuous present:	I am writing; he/she is writing; we/you/they are writing

PAST TENSE

simple past:	I/you/he/she/they wrote
continuous past:	I/he/she was writing; we/you/they were writing
perfect:	I/you/we/they have written; he/she has written
continuous perfect:	I/you/we/they have been writing; he/she has been writing
pluperfect:	I/you/he/she/we/they had written.
continuous pluperfect:	I/you/he/she/we/they had been writing.

FUTURE TENSE

simple future:	I/we shall write; you/he/she/they will write
continuous future:	I/we shall be writing; you/he/she/they will be writing.
future perfect:	I/we shall have written; you/he/she/they will have written
continuous future perfect:	I/we shall have been writing; you/he/she/they will have been writing.

OTHER FUTURE TENSES

simple present as future:	I write the next chapter tonight.
present continuous as future:	I am writing the next chapter tonight.
to be + going + infinitive:	I am going to write the next chapter tonight.
imperative as future:	Write the next chapter tonight.

Moods of Verbs

In this context the word mood means mode or manner of operation, and the old grammar claimed that verbs had three grammatical moods: indicative, imperative and subjunctive.

The indicative mood includes all normal finite forms of the verb, transitive and intransitive, active and passive.

The imperative mood, as we have seen, is the verb in its command mode of operation.

The subjunctive mood, which has long been ignored or even actively rejected by many educated writers, was said to include verbs that operated in a conditional, hypothetical or wishful mode:

> The chairman demanded that no decision *be taken* without his agreement. Members of the committee would be happier if the chairman *were to resign*. If that *should happen*, [or, If that *were to happen*] his depute would take the chair.

The conditional, wishful nature of the passage allows the use of the subjunctive mood: the subjunctive *be taken* replaces the indicative *was taken*; the subjunctive *were to resign* replaces the simpler indicative, *resigned*; *should happen* or *were to happen* replaces the indicative *happened*. The indicative mood is now accepted in these contexts:

> The chairman demanded that no decision *was taken* without his agreement. Members of the committee would be happier if the chairman *resigned*. If that *happened*, his depute would take the chair.

Even subjunctive forms like *I wish I were* and *If only I were* are now regarded as optional, and the form, *Would that I were*, is archaic. Only in one context is the subjunctive mood still essential:

> God *bless* this ship and all who sail in her.

> Long *live* the king of comedy.

> Let it *be done*. May it *stop* soon.

In effect, the subjunctive survives as a formal, rhetorical and sometimes ceremonial use of language; in that mode of operation the subjunctive is sometimes identical to the imperative:

> Bless this ship, God.   Be done.   Stop soon.

Modal Auxiliary Verbs

The subjunctive mood has largely given way to the indicative, partly because the subjunctive came to be seen as too formal in an increasingly informal society and partly because the systematic teaching of the old, formal grammar ended in the 1960s. There is, nevertheless, still a need to express the moods or modes of action and being – conditional, hypothetical, wishful and others – and this is done by using one of a small group of verbs known as modal auxiliaries.

As the term suggests, these are auxiliary verbs placed in front of main verbs to indicate the mood or mode in which the main verbs operate; the modal auxiliaries also express mood in the sense of the attitude or state of mind of the writer or speaker. The modal auxiliaries are:

> shall/should, will/would, can/could, may/might, must, ought.

Modal auxiliary verbs differ from other verbs in several ways. They exist only in their basic forms; they cannot form the singular present tense by adding the letter *-s*, or the present participle by adding *-ing*, or the past tense by adding *-ed*. Standard English does not permit *shalls*, *mighting* or *oughted*. A partial exception is the verb *will* used in the emphatic sense of to wish:

> The exhausted athlete *willed* himself to complete the marathon.

Modals operate only as auxiliaries and never as main or independent verbs. Although they may sometimes seem to operate independently:

I can, you should, he might, they ought

in every case, again with the possible exception of *will*, the main verb will be clearly implied in the context. For example, in the dialogue:

'Are you coming to the cinema tonight?'

'Do you think I should?'

'Yes, of course. You must.'

the modal auxiliaries *should* and *must* clearly imply *should come* and *must come*.

All modal verbs except *ought* are always followed by the base form of the main verb, that is, the infinitive form without the word *to*:

Emma *can go* to the cinema tonight.

Tim White *must finish* the marathon.

but

You *ought to write* that essay.

In one particular context, as we shall see below, the modal auxiliary verbs:

should, would, could, might

function as the past tense forms of the modals:

shall, will, can, may.

Shall and Will

The main function of the modal auxiliary verbs *shall* and *will* is to indicate the future tense of the main verbs that the modals accompany. *Shall* is normally used after the personal pronouns *I* and *we*; *will* is used after the personal pronouns *you*, *he*, *she* and *they*:

I *shall visit* London later this year.

Emma *will return* from holiday next week.

In the first example above, the modal auxiliary verb *shall*, which follows the first person pronoun *I*, changes the tense, and to that extent changes the meaning, of the main verb *visit*. In the second example the modal auxiliary verb *will*, which follows the third person noun, *Emma*, changes the tense and the meaning of the main verb *return*.

The forms *I/we shall* and *you/he/she/they will* are sometimes reversed to indicate determination or emphasis, and the words may be stressed typographically to highlight the difference:

> I **will** *keep* my promise to write to you.

> You **shall** *travel* with us next year.

These distinctions between *shall* and *will* have been partly eroded, and educated speech and writing now accept the modal auxiliary verb *will* in all the contexts above.

Shall, followed by the pronoun *I* or *we* and the base form of the main verb, is used as the first word of a sentence that implies future action and is part-suggestion, part-question:

> *Shall* I *end* the meeting now?

> *Shall* we *meet* again tomorrow?

When the pronoun is the second person, *you*, the opening word in this kind of sentence is *will*:

> *Will* you *follow* me?

Shall, preceded by the pronoun *I* or *we*, is also used to imply the future in terms of a condition and its consequence:

> If we search long enough we *shall find* the key.

> We *shall freeze* out here in the cold unless we find the key.

When the condition and consequence refer to the second person, *you*, or to the third person *he*, *she* or *they*, then the auxiliary verb *will* is used:

> If she drives carefully she *will arrive* safely.

> They *will* not *get* the money unless they sign the contract.

Should and Would

Should is used to express three subtly different kinds of future possibility. The first example shows the conditional use of *should* with the pronoun *I* or *we*, and *would* with the pronoun *you*, *he*, *she* or *they*:

> I *should be* grateful if you *would remind* him of tomorrow's meeting.

In the second example, *should* is used to suggest a probable future outcome:

If she takes the by-pass road she *should avoid* the town-centre traffic and she *should arrive* before noon.

In this third example, however, *should* implies a less likely outcome:

If you *should see* her before I do, please remind her of tomorrow's meeting.

Should is also used to express duty or obligation:

Since you are a member of the society you *should attend* tomorrow's meeting.

When someone is thought to have failed in their duty, *should* can be used to express disapproval:

They *should have warned* us that they would be late.

Should appears in another context: it modifies statements that might otherwise seem too absolute and it expresses social niceties of courtesy or concern:

I *should like* to begin by thanking the organizers of the meeting.

I *should think* that every member of the society would agree with these proposals.

The modal auxiliary verb *would* is used to express a conditional quality in subtly different ways:

Jack *would like* to practise bowling but he has a part-time job in the supermarket.

If Jack *would* only *agree* to open the bowling it *would strengthen* the team.

It *would* be a waste of talent if he gave up cricket now.

Would, like *should*, is also used to modify statements that might otherwise seem too absolute:

Since Jack never attends training sessions it *would appear* that [or, it *would seem* that] he has lost interest in cricket.

Can and Could

Can and *could* express the ability to do something or the capability of doing it:

Emma *can speak* French fluently now, but on her first visit to France she *could speak* only a few words of the language.

Could, like *should* and *would*, suggests a conditional or future possibility:

> Emma *could learn* to speak Spanish if she wished.

And *could*, like *should*, is used as a mild rebuke:

> She *could have told* us she was going to France again. She *could* at least *have sent* us a postcard when she was there.

Can and *could* are sometimes used, informally, to express permission:

> *Can* I *borrow* the car on Saturday night?

> You *could have* borrowed it last Saturday but we shall need it this week.

In formal standard English, however, permission is expressed through the modal auxiliary verb *may*:

> *May* I *borrow* the car on Saturday night?

> You *may have* the car if we ourselves don't need it.

May is also used to express wishes and curses:

> *May* the saints *preserve* you.

> Long *may* this fine weather *continue*.

> *May* you *rot* in hell!

Both *may* and *might* can be used to express simple possibility:

> We *may/might* need the car ourselves on Saturday.

> The weather *may/might* change in the afternoon.

In other contexts *might* implies a slightly more hypothetical or uncertain quality than *may*. For example:

> Civil engineers *might be* able to reinforce the bridge.

is less optimistic than

> Civil engineers *may be* able to reinforce the bridge.

Might, like *should* and *could*, is sometimes used to express disapproval or exasperation:

> Jack *might attend* a training session at least once a month. He *might have* told us about his part-time job in the supermarket.

Ought and Must

Duty, obligation and necessity are expressed in the modal auxiliary verbs *ought* and *must*. *Ought* normally implies that there is a moral aspect to the statement:

Jack *ought to practise* bowling now that he is in the first XI.

As we noted earlier, *ought* is the only modal auxiliary verb that is followed by the infinitive form of the main verb preceded by *to*. *Ought* is also used in idiomatic phrases that express the likelihood of an expectation being fulfilled or to draw a conclusion about the equivalence of one thing to another:

Ten litres of petrol *ought to be* enough for the journey.

We *ought to arrive* before noon.

Must, on the other hand, indicates strict or absolute necessity:

Jack *must attend* the next training session or he will be dropped from the team.

Drivers *must fasten* their seat-belts.

And *must*, like *ought*, can be used idiomatically to express an expectation that is likely to be realized or to draw a conclusion:

Anyone who crosses the desert alone *must be* very brave or very foolish.

Drivers *must have seen* the burned-out car at the roadside.

Four of the modal verbs have an additional function. When a passage of direct speech is rewritten as indirect or reported speech, the verbs in direct speech move one stage back in time into the appropriate past tense. The modal verbs in the present tense:

shall, will, can, may

must be changed to the past tense

should, would, could, might

as this passage shows:

The Secretary of State said, 'We *may* find it necessary to introduce new legislation on illicit drugs. The advisory committee *will* report next month. I *can* assure the House that I *shall* study the report carefully before I reach a decision.'

In reported speech, the passage should be written:

The Secretary of State said that they *might* find it necessary to introduce new legislation on illicit drugs. The advisory committee *would* report next month. He *could* assure the House that he *would* study the report carefully before he reached a decision.

ADVERBS

Adverbs form a large, flexible and varied class of words that modify, or define more precisely, verbs, adjectives and other adverbs.

Adverbs and Verbs

An adverb can be placed immediately after the verb it modifies:

> Miriam Levy played *confidently* in rehearsal but she performed *nervously* in public.

In this example the adverb *confidently* modifies the verb *played*, and the adverb *nervously* modifies the verb *performed*.

The adverb can be placed some words after the verb it modifies:

> Miriam played the first Chopin sonata *hesitantly*.

The adverb *hesitantly* modifies the verb *played*.

Some adverbs can be placed immediately before the verbs they modify:

> Miriam *always practised* two hours a day.

or they can be placed some words before the verbs:

> *Gradually*, as she played the second sonata, she *overcame* her nerves and *enjoyed* the occasion.

In the last example above, the adverb *gradually* modifies both verbs, *overcame* and *enjoyed*.

When a main verb is accompanied by an auxiliary verb, the adverb is normally placed between the auxiliary and the main verb:

> Miriam had *finally* overcome her nerves and was *actually* enjoying the performance.

In the example above, the adverb *finally* appears between the auxiliary verb *had* and the main verb *overcome*; the adverb *actually* appears between the auxiliary verb *was* and the main verb *enjoying*.

Adverbs and Adjectives

A second function of the adverb is to modify adjectives, and when it is used in this way the adverb is always placed immediately before the adjective. In this example, the adverb *exceptionally* is placed immediately before the adjective *sensitive*, and the adverb *hauntingly* immediately before the adjective *beautiful*.

> Anna Desai gave an *exceptionally* sensitive performance of the *hauntingly* beautiful clarinet solo.

As this example shows, adverbs can be formed by adding the suffix *-ly* to the adjectives *exceptional* and *haunting*; indeed, the majority of adverbs take this *-ly* form. Some words, however, can be adverbs or adjectives, depending on their function in a sentence:

> The concert started *late* because of the *late* arrival of the conductor.
>
> The *high* notes seemed to soar *high* above the audience.

The word *late* appears first as an adverb modifying the verb *started* and then as an adjective describing the noun *arrival*. The word *high* appears first as an adjective describing the noun *notes* and then as an adverb modifying the verb *to soar*. Other words that function both as adverbs and as adjectives include:

> early, daily, fast, hard, little, long, only, wide.

In examples such as these the distinction between adjective and adverb is that the adjective describes or more precisely defines the noun:

> *late* arrival, *high* notes, *daily* practice, *fast* tempo

whereas the adverb describes or modifies the verb:

> He arrived *late*. The note sounded *too high*. She practised *daily*. They played *very fast*.

Adverbs Modifying Other Adverbs

A third function of the adverb is to modify other adverbs. When one adverb modifies another, the first of the two adverbs is usually one that indicates a degree of size, frequency or intensity:

> Miriam plays *supremely confidently* in rehearsal but sometimes performs *remarkably badly* in public. Anna's temperament allows her to behave *sublimely calmly*, so that she seems to play *quite naturally*.

Adverbs that indicate degree in this way are sometimes known as intensifiers because they intensify the adjective or adverb that follows them. Other intensifiers include:

> always, often, frequently, usually, sometimes, occasionally, seldom,

rarely, never, normally, fairly, rather, completely, very, highly, extremely, really, truly, immensely, intensely, largely, particularly, peculiarly, amazingly, astonishingly, abnormally, surprisingly.

Adverbs of degree, like most adverbs, can also modify adjectives. In the examples below, the adverb is in italics:

often anxious, *never* successful, *very* hesitant, *largely* useless, *intensely* angry, *amazingly* fit.

Adverbial Phrases

The adverbial function is sometimes carried out by a phrase; that is, a group of words that does not normally include a finite verb. The adverbial phrases are in italics:

Immediately after the concert the director decided, *quite spontaneously*, that she would take the musicians for a late supper in an Italian restaurant.

Immediately after the concert is an adverbial phrase of time that modifies the verb *decided* by stating when the director decided, and the phrase *quite spontaneously* is an adverbial phrase of manner that modifies *decided* by stating how the director decided. The last two phrases in the sentence, *for a late supper* and *in an Italian restaurant*, can also be considered as adverbials modifying the verb *take*; *for a late supper* indicates the reason or purpose, and *in an Italian restaurant* indicates the place.

Adverbial Clauses

The adverbial function can also be carried out by sub-clauses (see pages 213–225), but in the meantime, the passage below shows some of the ways in which adverbial sub-clauses can be used to extend the circumstances of main clauses.

Leonard Vedley was astonished *when he saw his yacht lying in the car park*. The boat looked *as if a giant had hurled it from the marina*, and Mr Vedley stood there gaping *until Len Masters, manager of the marina, arrived*.

'You won't have heard about the storm *because you were out of town last night*,' said Mr Masters. 'The force of the storm was so strong *that it blew dozens of craft ashore*. It lifted them out of the water *although they were all firmly moored*. I'm afraid your yacht will have to lie *where it is,*' he added, '*while we wait for a heavy crane.*'

The sub-clause *when he saw his yacht lying in the car park* is an adverbial sub-clause of time that modifies, or adds circumstantial detail to, the main clause, *Leonard Vedley was astonished,* by telling us when he was astonished. The sub-clause *as if a giant had hurled it from the marina* is an adverbial sub-clause of manner or method that explains how the boat looked. The adverbial sub-clause of time *until Len Masters, manager of the marina, arrived* tells us how long Leonard Vedley stood gaping.

In the second paragraph *because you were out of town last night* is an adverbial sub-clause of reason that explains why Mr Vedley would not have heard about the storm. The words *that it blew dozens of craft ashore* form an adverbial sub-clause of cause and effect, or result, since they explain the result of the main clause, *The force of the storm was so strong.* The sub-clause of opposition or concession *although they had all been firmly moored* contrasts with its main clause, *It lifted them out of the water.* The sub-clause *where it is* is an adverbial clause of place modifying, or explaining, the main clause *your boat will have to lie,* and finally, *while we wait for a heavy crane* is an adverbial clause of time modifying the same main clause, *your boat will have to lie.*

Each of these adverbial sub-clauses begins with a word that functions as an adverb and that indicates the way in which the sub-clause modifies the main clause by specifying time, manner or method, reason, cause and effect, place or opposition. The introductory adverbs are:

when, as if, until, because, that, although, where, while.

Each adverb also functions as a conjunction, a linking word that joins the main clause to the sub-clause, and because of this dual function – adverb and conjunction – these words can also be classified as adverbial conjunctions. This dual role proves once again the flexible nature of English grammar.

Identifying Adverbs

Because adverbs are such a multi-purpose, highly mobile class of words they are not always easy to identify. The main lesson to be learned, however, is not the grammatical jargon but how to take advantage of the flexibility and dynamism of the English language.

Even so, it is sometimes useful to know the precise function of a word or the relationship between two or more words in a sentence because you will be better able to choose the most appropriate word and give the sentence its most effective structure.

There are broad guidelines that can help you to identify adverbs from other word classes. The section Adverbs and Adjectives (see page 68) shows how adverbs can be distinguished from adjectives. A more general method of identification is to apply the 'Wh?' test, that is, to ask if the word answers the questions *how?*, *when?*, *where?* or *why?*

Words that answer the question *how?* are normally adverbs of manner or method. This group of adverbs includes most of the adverbs of degree – that is, the intensifiers – listed above, and many other adverbs that suggest the method or style of an action:

> alphabetically, badly, genetically, madly.

Words that answer the question *when?* tell us the time at which or the period in which something happened; these words are normally adverbs of time:

> after, before, currently, historically, lately, never, now, previously, soon, suddenly, today, yesterday.

The question *when?* is sometimes answered by an adverbial phrase rather than a one-word adverb. Adverbial phrases of time often begin with a preposition, one of the small class of function words such as *in* or *on* that appear before a noun and indicate the position or place of the noun. Phrases of time include expressions such as:

> at midnight, before daylight, in the afternoon, last June, on a certain date, in 1998, much too late.

Some grammarians argue that the intensifiers of time:

> always, often, frequently, sometimes

answer the question *how?* and are, therefore, adverbs of manner, but it is much simpler and more logical to treat them as adverbs of time.

Words that answer the question *where?* are normally adverbs of place:

> in, out, roundabout, here, there, everywhere.

Adverbial phrases of place, like those of time, often begin with a preposition:

> *inside* a prison cell, *outside* the Grand Hotel, *across* the Arabian Sea, *under* an apple tree.

When we ask the question *why*? we strike an inconsistency in English grammar because the question *why*?, unlike the other 'Wh?' questions, cannot be answered by a one-word adverb of reason or purpose. The following adverbs:

> as, because, for, since, so, consequently, therefore

suggest only the beginning of a reason but do not answer the question. Instead, we need an adverbial phrase or an adverbial clause to explain the reason for, or the purpose of, an action. In the next two examples the words in italics are adverbial phrases:

> Musicians from the National Youth Orchestra went to the restaurant *for a late supper*.

> Flights had to be cancelled *because of the strike by air traffic controllers*.

Adverbial sub-clauses of reason and purpose are explained in detail in Chapter 6. In the meantime, examples are in italics in the two sentence below:

> Oscar worked longer hours *so that he could send money home to his family*.

> *Because he was homeless*, he slept in the park.

Comparison of Adverbs

Those adverbs that have the same forms as the corresponding adjectives can be compared in exactly the same way. Regular adverbs take the forms:

POSITIVE	COMPARATIVE	SUPERLATIVE
fast	faster	fastest
high	higher	highest
slow	slower	slowest

Irregular adverbs include:

badly/ill	worse	worst
well	better	best
little	less/lesser	least
much	more	most

Other adverbs, including all those ending in -*ly*, are compared:

curiously	more curiously	most curiously
furiously	more furiously	most furiously
luxuriously	more luxuriously	most luxuriously.

PREPOSITIONS

Prepositions form a comparatively small, frequently used class of function words. The prefix *pre-* in the word *preposition* means before, and prepositions are normally positioned before nouns, noun phrases or pronouns, which are then said to be grammatically 'governed' by the prepositions in the sense that the prepositions are directly related to, and influence the meaning of, the nouns, noun phrases and pronouns.

In this sentence:

> Spectators stood *around the boundary*.

the word *around* is a preposition that adds detail to the noun *boundary*. The end result, *around the boundary*, is a preposition phrase. In this example:

> Batsmen struggled *against the accurate fast bowler*.

the preposition *against* is directly related to the noun phrase, *the accurate fast bowler*. The noun phrase becomes part of the preposition phrase *against the accurate fast bowler*. And in the sentences:

> *Between them*, the two batsmen made only ten runs. *With the bright sunlight behind him*, the bowler's deliveries were unplayable.

the preposition *between* refers to the pronoun *them*, and the preposition *behind* refers to the pronoun *him*. The second sentence in the example above opens with two preposition phrases, *With the bright sunlight* and *behind him*, so that the end result is the extended preposition phrase *With the bright sunlight behind him*.

As the last example shows, prepositions govern pronouns grammatically by requiring the pronouns to take the objective, or accusative, case: *them*, not *they*; *him*, not *he*.

Several prepositions indicate position in the additional sense of place or location:

> *from* the city shops, *to* the mountain tops, *through* the open door, *on* the pebbled shore.

Prepositions that indicate place in this way are:

> across, along, above, among, at, behind, below, beside, between, beyond, down, in, inside, into, near, off, out, outside, over, towards, under, up, upon, with.

Some prepositions indicate direction and movement:

> *from* Penzance, *across to* France, *through* the spray, *against* the swell, *round* the Bay, *towards* La Rochelle.

Prepositions also indicate time:

> *Before* the match *on* the last Friday *in* June he felt nervous but *after* the first over he relaxed. *By* the tenth over he had scored twenty-seven runs and *at* the end of the innings he was not-out for fifty-three. *Until* that game his highest score had been forty-one.

The examples above show that the typical preposition phrase consists of:

> preposition + determiner + noun
>
> or
>
> preposition + determiner + noun phrase
>
> or
>
> preposition + determiner + pronoun

There are two variations on this pattern. The simpler of the two is one in which the prepositions are not single words but compounds of two or more words:

> *out into* the monsoon rain; *up above* the flooded plain.

Other compound prepositions include:

> along with, at the head of, at/to the rear of, away from, in advance of, in front of, in from, in out of (the rain), in through, away from, on top of, out from, out from under, out in, out into (the garden), out of, out through, over and above, up above.

The second variation is the one in which the preposition appears at the end of a clause or a sentence. Sentences ending with prepositions were once dismissed as bad English usage, but there is no objection to this kind of sentence structure:

> What do you want this hammer *for*?
>
> Which channel is the programme *on*?
>
> This is the town I was born *in*.

Who was that student you were talking *to*?

These sentences can be restructured so that they do not end with prepositions, but the resulting sentences are not 'more grammatical' or better than the originals:

For what do you want this hammer?

On which channel is the programme?

This is the town *in which* I was born.

Who was that student *to whom* you were talking?

Prepositions sometimes assume an adverbial function. Although the difference between the two word classes, preposition and adverbial preposition, is of interest to grammarians rather than to other writers, it is a difference that can be detected quite simply: prepositions are directly related to nouns, noun phrases or pronouns; adverbial prepositions are directly related to verbs.

In these lines from the nursery rhyme:

Jack fell *down* and broke his crown
And Jill came tumbling *after*

the word *down* refers directly to the verb *fell*, and *after* refers directly to *came tumbling*, and so *down* and *after* are adverbial prepositions.

The difference between the two word classes is illustrated in these three pairs of sentences, in which example (a) has the preposition and example (b) the adverbial preposition:

1 (a) Jenny the news-girl sets off *before* dawn.
  (b) She delivers fifty newspapers *before* she goes to school.

2 (a) Jenny whistles as she walks *along* the deserted streets.
  (b) On most mornings she sees Freddie's milk-float purring *along*.

3 (a) Jenny waves as the milk-float sails *past* her.
  (b) Freddie shouts 'Good morning' as he drives *past*.

In 1(a) the preposition *before* governs the noun *dawn*; in 2(a) the preposition *along* governs the noun phrase, *the deserted streets*; in 3(a) the preposition *past* governs the pronoun *her*. In 1(b) the word *before* is an adverbial preposition modifying the verb *delivers*; in 2(b) the adverbial preposition *along* modifies the present participle *purring*; in 3(b) the adverbial preposition *past* modifies the verb *drives*.

The change in word class from preposition to adverbial preposition – like those similar changes from adjective to adverb and from conjunction to adverbial conjunction – is a reminder of the fluid nature of English grammar. The changes also highlight the strange status of the English adverb. Some adverbs, especially those ending in -*ly*, are easily identified, but others seem uncertain of their role. It is much more important for students and writers to use words appropriately and effectively than to classify them grammatically.

CONJUNCTIONS

Conjunctions form a small class of function words; that is, words that are as important for their grammatical effect or function as they are for their meaning.

Some conjunctions are known as coordinating conjunctions because they link or coordinate two or more similar linguistic units. The coordinating conjunctions are:

> and, but, or, both . . . and, either . . . or, neither . . . nor, not only . . . but also.

The units that are linked by conjunctions can be single words:

> Neither *Upper* nor *Lower* Sallow has tourist accommodation.

The units can be phrases:

> The nearby village of Parsemer has not only *a country house hotel*, *Curtminster Grange*, but also *an eighteenth-century coaching inn*, *The Bullyard*.

Clauses, too, can be coordinated by conjunctions, and when two clauses are linked in this way both clauses are main clauses, and the sentence is known grammatically as compound. In the examples below the oblique line separates the two clauses:

> Either you stay overnight at Parsemer/or you drive on to the city of Grantown.

> Aldridge Tower at Upper Sallow is derelict/but Thornham Hall in Lower Sallow is still inhabited.

You can use coordinating conjunctions to illustrate points of similarity, comparison and contrast, and by using pairs of conjunctions:

> both . . . and, either . . . or, neither . . . nor, not only . . . but also

you can achieve the effect of equilibrium by balancing one fact or set of facts against another.

As we saw under Adverbial Clauses (pages 70–71), another group of conjunctions, known as adverbial conjunctions or subordinating conjunctions, operate differently. Their function is not only to link two or more clauses in a sentence but also to show that one or more of the clauses is subordinate to a main clause. A sentence with a main clause and one or more sub-clauses is known grammatically as complex, and complex sentences are discussed in Chapter 6.

INTERJECTIONS

Interjections, the smallest of the word classes, have the exclamatory function of expressing emotion. The word *interjection* means thrown in or thrown into in the sense that the word suddenly appears in its context. They are more often used in speech or in written dialogue representing speech than in written standard English. Because of this and because they refer to the speaker's agitated state of mind rather than to external reality, interjections sometimes have an incoherent, comic-strip quality when they appear in written English:

> ah, aha, aargh, golly, gosh, hey, hoy, huh, hurrah, och, oh, ooh, oops, oi, ouch, ow, wow.

Interjections are often part of a longer exclamation:

> Ah, the concert was wonderful!
>
> Hey, switch it off!
>
> Oh, I've deleted the wrong file.

Expressions such as *Wait! Stop it! Jump! Go. Hold on*, with or without the exclamation mark, are not interjections but examples of verbs in the imperative mood.

2 Punctuation

Punctuation affects not only the structure, rhythm, tone and style of a piece of prose but also the meanings of sentences. Although it remains more fluid than other features of standard English, particularly spelling, semantics and grammar, there are clear principles of punctuation, the effect of which is to make punctuation a little code within the greater code of written standard English. If you ignore the little code, you risk being ignored or at best misunderstood by readers.

Punctuation and Meaning

The main purpose of punctuation is to clarify the meaning of what you write. This statement, for example, seems contradictory:

> I understood everything he said but I didn't understand a word.

Apart from the apostrophe to indicate the missing letter *o* in *didn't*, there is no internal punctuation in the sentence. But if the statement is rewritten as two sentences:

> 'I understood everything,' he said. But I didn't understand a word.

we see that, although the syntax or word order remains the same, the identities and the relationship of the two people involved have changed; there is now the speaker, *he*, who understood everything, and the narrator, *I*, who understood nothing. There is also the structural division into two sentences, but it is mainly the added punctuation, particularly the use of inverted commas to mark direct speech, that solves the riddle.

In this illustration the effect of the punctuation is equally important:

> The *Clarion* editor said the designer is a fool.

> The *Clarion* editor, said the designer, is a fool.

The punctuation creates opposite meanings in these otherwise identical sentences. In the first sentence the editor denounces the designer; in the second, with the addition of the two commas, the designer denounces the editor. Here again the difference becomes clearer still if quotation marks are used:

> The *Clarion* editor said, 'The designer is a fool.'

> 'The *Clarion* editor,' said the designer, 'is a fool.'

Punctuation, then, can be used to clarify the identities and roles of the people you write about. It can even be used to determine the order of physical reality:

> Below, the city lights were shining.

> Below the city, lights were shining.

Both sentences use the same words in the same word order, but the sentences mean distinctly different things. The first sentence implies that the city lights are seen from above, from an aircraft, perhaps, or a hillside, whereas the second sentence implies that the lights are shining beneath the city, as if in a mine or in underground bunkers. This difference in meaning is created simply by changing the position of the comma.

Here is another way in which punctuation can change the meaning of a sentence:

> Vitesse Bordeaux Football Club spent £7 million, more than any other club, on transfer fees last year.

> Vitesse Bordeaux Football Club spent £7 million more than any other club on transfer fees last year.

The first sentence means that the club spent a total of £7 million on transfer fees, and that no other club spent as much. The second sentence means that the club's expenditure on transfer fees was £7 million more than any other club's expenditure, but the club's total transfer budget is not stated.

Faulty punctuation can cause ambiguity and absurdity, the effect of which is to divert the reader's attention from your intended meaning to your faulty prose style, which can undermine your authority and credibility as a writer. *A little-used car*, for example, is not the same as *a little used car*; nor are *long-suffering spectators at a low-scoring match* the same as *long suffering spectators at a low scoring match*. The limits of absurdity are reached in a sentence like this:

> The Australian athlete won the marathon one minute after he collapsed.

Punctuation marks remove the ambiguity and clarify the meaning:

The Australian athlete won the marathon. One minute after – he collapsed.

Although that last example is a contrived one, it confirms that punctuation is often an essential aid to meaning, and for that reason punctuation and punctuation marks are discussed in some detail.

Punctuation, Prose Rhythm and Style

Punctuation affects the rhythm as well as the meaning of what you write. As we shall see in the discussion of paragraph structures, and in particular the discussion of narrative pace, prose rhythm can affect the tempo, the tone and thus the overall style of your prose.

Prose rhythm is created mainly by the length and the internal structuring of sentences, and by the length and pronunciation of words; any word of two or more syllables is in itself a rhythmic unit. But rhythm is also directly affected by punctuation because every punctuation mark except the hyphen introduces a pause in the flow of communication. It follows, then, that every piece of prose has a rhythm. Lightly punctuated prose normally reads more smoothly and fluently than densely punctuated prose. The rhythm may sometimes change from one paragraph, or even from one sentence, to another, or it may be so confused or uncontrolled that it forms no clear pattern, when it is described as dysrhythmic. Even so, rhythm is an inevitable property of everything you write.

Rhythm is sometimes so important that the semantics of a piece of prose – that is, the meanings of the words used in a passage – can be overridden by the punctuation and the syntax. We can see this in the one-sentence paragraph:

> The man, who walked with a limp, jumped into the front passenger seat, and, before he had time to fasten his seat-belt, or time even to close the door, the driver of the car, which was a black Ford saloon, accelerated fiercely, sped along the High Street, screeched round the corner into Edward Street, and then, with a noisy gear change, raced out of town.

Despite using the words *jumped*, *before he had time*, *accelerated fiercely*, *sped*, *screeched* and *raced*, the sequence fails to convey an impression of speed and urgency because the sentence is convoluted, uses multiple embedding and has internal punctuation of thirteen commas, each of which interrupts the flow of the sentence.

The end result is not one of speed but of an absurdly faltering 'stop-go' progress.

By reducing the number of internal punctuation marks we reduce the number of pauses in the sentence so that the rhythm becomes faster and more fluent. The tempo can be further increased if the single convoluted sentence with its many sub-clauses is rewritten as a succession of shorter sentences, the effect of which is to create a faster rhythm.

> The limping man jumped into the front passenger seat of the black Ford saloon. Before he had time to fasten his seat-belt or even close the door, the driver accelerated fiercely. The car sped along the High Street and screeched round the corner into Edward Street. With a noisy gear change, the car raced out of town.

One long, convoluted sentence is replaced by four shorter sentences with little internal punctuation. The second version of the paragraph achieves the effect of speed as much through the lighter punctuation and simplified syntax as through the meanings of the words.

Your prose will always create rhythmic effects. The passage above shows that rhythm reinforces the meaning of a piece of prose and that rhythmic effects are achieved mainly through syntax and punctuation. It is essential, then, that you control the effects through your understanding of syntax and punctuation. Two more passages illustrate the methods of control.

The first example takes the form of a long, densely punctuated sentence:

> Experienced archaeologists, all of them members of the National Archaeological Society, which was founded – after vigorous campaigning – thirty years ago by Dr Jenny Somerford (who is still, despite her other commitments, president of the society), will excavate the site, thought to be an Iron Age burial mound, provided, that is, the site owner gives permission.

Although the diction of this sentence is undemanding, the density of the punctuation, all of which is technically correct, creates a ponderous tone and a rhythm that is fragmented and yet plodding. Too much information is crammed into the one sentence; the use of embedded clauses – that is, statements, like this, inserted into other statements – becomes repetitive; and the dense punctuation scheme emphasizes rather than disguises the repetitive structure of the clauses and the overload of information. The sentence yields its meaning more clearly when a lighter punctuation scheme is applied, despite the volume of information in the original version:

> Experienced archaeologists, all of them members of the National Archaeological Society, which was founded after vigorous campaigning thirty years ago by Dr Jenny Somerford, who is still, despite her other commitments, president of the society, will excavate the site thought to be an Iron Age burial mound provided, that is, the site owner gives permission.

The punctuation is now much lighter but the fragmented, embedded nature of the sentence structure is still an obstacle to fluency and intelligibility; the embedding also delays unnecessarily the completion, and thus the meaning, of the first part of the sentence.

An even more effective response is to recognize that a mass of information such as this becomes more intelligible to the reader when it is broken down into shorter units of communication, that is, into shorter sentences, and rearranged in a more logical sequence:

> Experienced archaeologists, all of them members of the National Archaeological Society, will excavate the site provided the site owner gives permission. The site is thought to be an Iron Age burial mound. The society was founded thirty years ago after vigorous campaigning by Dr Jenny Somerford, who is still president of the society despite her other commitments.

A second passage, similar to the first in length and volume of information, uses an even lighter punctuation scheme.

> Farmers in the Northwest say that the fall in livestock prices could force them out of business. Prices for cattle and sheep have been falling for some months but last week's 15 per cent drop is the biggest single fall. Some farmers are turning to tourism and letting their fields as caravan parks. A few have approached property developers with proposals for out-of-town shopping centres and housing estates.

The division into four sentences makes the information easier to assimilate. This, along with the absence of any internal punctuation, which would interrupt the flow of words and meaning, produces a brisk rhythm and a supple prose style that is similar to the prose of good journalism.

Few readers will notice the craftsmanship that underlies a prose style like this because most readers have no special interest in, or understanding of, the craft. Another reason for readers failing consciously to notice the craftsmanship is that writers often choose to make simplicity – or the illusion of simplicity – part of their overall design. When you achieve this simplicity of style your message transmits itself as if effortlessly from the page into the minds and thoughts of your readers, and it is this kind of skill that turns the writer's craft or art into a mystery to non-specialist readers. They may not be able to explain the experience, but they are intuitively aware that something is happening to them, that the writer or musician or painter is casting some kind of spell.

To turn from the mysteries of craftsmanship to the specific use of punctuation marks may strike you as an anticlimax, but punctuation is one of the factors that determine prose style, and if you want your prose to be effective you should look at the guidelines in the pages that follow.

THE FULL STOP

The functions of the full stop, which is sometimes known as the period, are to mark the ends of sentences and to indicate abbreviations. Since the first of these functions is illustrated throughout this book, particularly in the chapters on sentence structure, no specific examples are needed here.

The Full Stop and Abbreviations

The second function, to mark abbreviated words, is observed by some editors and publishers but ignored by others. For example, some publishers print a full stop after every abbreviated word in a person's title:

> V.C. (Victoria Cross), O.M. (Order of Merit), Rt. Rev. (Right Reverend), Rt. Hon. (Right Honourable), F.R.S. (Fellow of the Royal Society), M.A. (Master of Arts).

Some editors and publishers insist on the full stops even in such well-known abbreviations as Mr. (Mister) and M.P. (Member of Parliament). Other editors and publishers omit the abbreviations in these cases and in all others.

Until recently it was standard practice to include the full stop after the initial letters of a person's first names:

T.S. Eliot, H.W. Fowler, R.S. Thomas

but this agreement has broken down, and some publishers now omit these full stops.

Most publishers omit the full stops from the abbreviated names of well-known organizations:

BBC, BP, NATO, RAC, RSPCA, UN

although some publishers still include the full stops.

There used to be a simple general guideline that the full stop was omitted only when the abbreviation ended with the same letter as the full word – *Mr*, *Mrs*, *Dr*, *vols* – but the guideline is widely ignored. The only unanimous agreement among British editors and publishers is the omission of full stops after the abbreviations N (north), S (south), E (east), W (west) and C (central) in London postal districts.

As a result of this lack of agreement, the use or non-use of the full stop for abbreviated words and the form that the abbreviation takes are no longer questions of right or wrong but of house style (see page 130) or personal preference.

THE COMMA

The comma is now the multi-purpose punctuation mark in standard English, and its current use is an indication not only of changing practices in punctuation but also of the changing concept of what makes a standard English sentence. Until the late nineteenth century writers used the semicolon where today we normally use a comma, and a comma where no punctuation is needed today. In Robert Louis Stevenson's 'Markheim', a psychological and sometimes melodramatic study of a murderer, the author, who lived from 1850 to 1894, writes:

> The face was robbed of all expression; but it was as pale as wax, and shockingly smeared with blood about one temple.

Although punctuation is an essential aid to the meaning of a piece of prose, patterns of punctuation – the marks actually used by writers – change over time. Current practice is to use lighter punctuation schemes than those used in previous centuries, but there are still many contexts where commas are essential to the meanings of sentences.

Commas and Adverbials

A comma is often needed when a sentence opens with an adverb, an adverbial phrase or an adverbial sub-clause, that is, an opening form of words indicating opposition, time or place, reason or purpose, manner or method, or cause and effect.

The introduction to this chapter included these two examples:

> Below, the city lights were shining.

> Below the city, lights were shining.

The word *Below* and the phrase *Below the city* are both adverbial because they describe, or modify, the verb, *were shining*, by stating where the shining took place. In the first example the comma separates *Below* from the rest of the sentence and shows that the city was seen from above; in the second example the separating comma shows that the unit is *Below the city* and not *Below the city lights*. Many other introductory words must be followed by a comma in order to make their meaning clear:

> Normally, spoken English is less formal than written English.

In the sentence above, the word *Normally* is an adverb that describes, or modifies, the verb *is*, and the sentence means that it is customary for spoken English to be less formal than written English. Without the comma after the word *above*, the sentence immediately preceding this one could be misread as 'In the sentence above the word *normally* . . .', that is, the sentence before the one we are discussing. In the same form of words without the comma:

> Normally spoken English is less formal than written English.

Normally describes, or modifies *spoken*, which is the past participle form of the verb *speak*, and the sentence means English as it is normally spoken is less formal than written English. The second meaning is not the same as the first.

Some introductory adverbial phrases, especially phrases denoting time and place, reason and purpose, and cause and effect, can also be misleading if they are not followed by commas.

> At the weekend matches were postponed players were disappointed and supporters frustrated.

Without commas after *weekend* and *postponed*, the first half of the sentence suggests that postponed players attended the weekend matches. Similarly:

Shortly after the snow[,] warning, lights suddenly went out.

In the morning, milk[,] was frozen in the bottles.

The false comma in the square brackets shows how these phrases could be misread. Other introductory phrases that must be treated in the same way are some slightly colloquial expressions like *Above all*, *After all* and *Curiously enough*. Once again the false comma is shown in square brackets:

Curiously[,] enough, highly trained athletes are subject to injury and viral infection.

Many introductory phrases containing non-finite forms of verbs must be followed by commas. One non-finite form is the simple infinitive. For example, the infinitive, *to show*, in the phrase, *to show good will*, must be punctuated:

To show good will, the chairman bought a round of drinks.

Other introductory phrases that use the infinitive form of the verb are *To begin with*, *To start with* and *To end with*, all of which must be followed by a comma in structures such as this:

To begin with, the sprinters tested their starting-blocks.

A second non-finite form of the verb is the present participle, which always ends in *-ing*. A missing comma or a misplaced comma, as shown in square brackets, can create absurdity in examples such as this:

After eating, some directors[,] began to smoke cigars.

A slight variation is the introductory phrase, *According to*:

According to the *Clarion*, supporters[,] agree with the directors' decision.

A third non-finite form that needs a comma is the one that combines the present participle with the past participle, for example, *having* (present participle) *won* (past participle):

Having won[,] the race, the sprinter felt elated.

Having won, the sprinter[,] felt elated.

The phrases, *Having won the race* and *Having won*, must be punctuated with commas.

A comma is usually optional after an adverbial sub-clause that opens a sentence, but a comma is essential when the introductory sub-clause ends with a verb and the verb is followed immediately by a noun in the main clause. A comma is then part of the meaning of these sentences. In this sentence:

> Since Barbara left (sub-clause),/her house has been a melancholy place (main clause).

the adverbial sub-clause ends with the verb *left*, and the main clause opens with the pronoun and noun, *her house*. If the comma were omitted, the opening of the sentence could be read as *Since Barbara left her house*, which is not the same thing. In this example:

> If she does not return (sub-clause),/her family and friends will be distressed (main clause).

the sub-clause ends with the verb *return*, and the main clause opens with the pronoun *her* and the nouns *family and friends*. If the comma were omitted or misplaced, then the sub-clause could be misread as *If she does not return her family and friends*, and the drama would be reduced to farce.

Notorious pitfalls are adverbial sub-clauses like *As you know*, *As I said* and *As we can see*, because they can result in misreadings like:

> As you know the President of France[,] is in London today.

Instead of

> As you know, the President of France is in London today.

The 'As you know' structure can lead to genuine ambiguities like this:

> As you know the people object to the marina proposal.

If the comma is placed after *people*, then the sub-clause is *As you know the people*, and the main clause is a command: *[You] object to the marina proposal*. If the comma is placed after *know*, the sub-clause is *As you know*, and the main clause is a statement: *the people object to the marina proposal*.

Commas and Descriptive Sub-clauses

Two other kinds of sub-clause must be punctuated with commas. Commas are sometimes needed to define who or what is being discussed by the sub-clause, as we shall see in the discussion of sub-clauses in complex sentences (pages 205–8). In this sentence:

> The Sri Lanka bowler who took six wickets was named the man of the match.

the implication is that the noun *bowler* is one among several other bowlers, but when the sub-clause is marked off by commas:

> The Sri Lanka bowler, who took six wickets, was named the man of the match.

then it is clear that only one bowler is being considered.

Another kind of descriptive sub-clause that must be punctuated with commas is one that describes the entire main clause:

> Cradle Bay Sea Angling Club has a new club-house, which is welcome news to the members.

> Members of the Sea Angling Club agreed to a higher subscription fee, which pleased the club treasurer.

A slightly colloquial version of the sub-clause omits the word *which* and the verb *is*, but still needs the comma:

> Cradle Bay Sea Angling Club has a new club-house, [which is] welcome news to the members.

Commas in 'And' and 'But' Clauses

Compound sentences sometimes need a comma between the two main clauses. A compound sentence, as we shall see in Chapter 6, is a sentence with two main clauses joined by a conjunction, most often the conjunction *and* or *but*.

When two clauses joined by *and* have the same subject or the same opening phrase, a comma is not normally required:

> Cradle Bay Sea Angling Club was established fifty years ago and [Cradle Bay Sea Angling Club] has over 300 members.

> At midnight the alarm was raised and [at midnight] the lifeboat was launched.

When the subjects of the two clauses joined by *and* are different, or when the two clauses are designed to create a contrast, a comma reinforces the difference or the contrast by introducing a slight pause:

> All through the night the search continued, and in the morning an upturned boat was found.

Commas may be needed to clarify the meanings of other sentences linked by *and*:

> Four young anglers applied to the club secretary, and the committee approved their applications.

> The four anglers received their membership cards on Tuesday, and on Friday they set out for a day's fishing.

Without the commas, part of the first sentence could be misread as *applied to the club secretary and the committee*, and part of the second sentence misread as *received their membership cards on Tuesday and on Friday*.

A clause that opens with the conjunction *but* always implies a difference or a contrast, and this adversative quality is reinforced by the slight pause created by a comma:

> The four young anglers were enthusiastic, but they had little experience of sea angling.

> Older members of the angling club warned them of bad weather, but the young men merely laughed.

Commas and Terms of Address

Commas must be used when you address a person or describe a person in certain ways.

One form of address is direct and often uses the person's name:

> Ah, Miller, you are just the man I'm looking for.

> Please telephone or write to us, Barbara.

Sometimes a general term of address is used:

> All aboard, ladies and gentlemen, for the *Skylark* cruise.

> Gather round, my friends, and hear the news.

This way of using a noun, or the pronoun *you*, is known grammatically as the vocative case. The word *vocative* means calling out or calling to, and a useful way of remembering the vocative, and the necessary comma or commas, is to imagine the word *Oh* or *Ah* immediately in front of the name. If the comma is not used, the noun may change from the vocative case to the objective case, with ambiguous results:

> Keep moving Emily. Give up Fred. Hang on Jack.

instead of the correctly punctuated:

> Keep moving, Emily. Give up, Fred. Hang on, Jack.

Another way of referring to a person is to use a descriptive phrase that is equivalent to the person's name. People are often identified in two ways in the same sentence:

> Mr Godfrey Pendleton, editor of the *Daily Clarion*, still takes part in the annual fun run.

Mr Pendleton is identified first by name and then by an equivalent descriptive phrase, *editor of the Daily Clarion*, which indicates his professional identity. Equivalent phrases like this are in apposition to the word or phrase that most closely identifies the person. In this context, the term in apposition means placed alongside.

Animals and inanimate objects can be identified in the same way:

> Malus Sylvestris, a three-year-old grey, won the two o'clock race at Doncaster.

> Mill House, the Hughes family's holiday cottage, was vandalized.

Commas are often used to mark off the reporting verb, that is, a verb such as *said* or *replied*, and to identify the speaker in a sentence, whether the verb is reporting direct or indirect speech. Direct speech is discussed on pages 103–6. Examples in indirect, or reported, speech are:

> Miller was just the man he was looking for, he said.

> Miller, he insisted, was ideal for the task.

> After all, he added, Miller was an expert.

Commas and Parenthesis

A person or a thing can be described and defined by statements that are clearly additional to the main description. This additional information is often given in parenthesis, which means beside the main information. Parentheses (the plural form of the word) can be punctuated by commas, by brackets or by dashes.

Parenthetical statements are similar in structure and function to statements in apposition (see above). The main difference is that a statement in apposition is always an equivalent descriptive phrase, another way of stating the person's identity, whereas the statement in parenthesis can add any kind of information. If we look again at the sentence:

> Mr Godfrey Pendleton, editor of the *Daily Clarion*, still takes part in the annual fun run.

we see that the phrase, *editor of the Daily Clarion*, is part of the man's identity and is thus in apposition to his name, Mr Godfrey Pendleton. If we restructure the sentence:

> Mr Godfrey Pendleton, who still takes part in the annual fun run, is editor of the *Daily Clarion*.

the sub-clause punctuated by commas, *who still takes part in the annual fun run*, is not part of the man's identity but is in parenthesis. Similarly, in the sentence:

> Mr Leonard Vedley, who has just bought a new yacht, is the developer of the Cradle Bay Marina.

the sub-clause, *who has just bought a new yacht*, is in parenthesis, that is, it is useful additional information but not part of the man's identity.

Commas and Lists

One of the simplest functions of the comma is to separate two or more items in a list. The items can be single words:

> A strike by air traffic controllers affected flights to France, Portugal, Spain and Italy.

> Students yawned, coughed, grimaced, writhed and squirmed with boredom.

The list can consist of phrases:

> As they drew up outside their holiday cottage, the Hughes family saw the signs of vandalism: uprooted plants, broken windows, a smashed door panel and black paint daubed on white-washed walls.

A comma is usually optional between the second-last item in the list and the word *and*, but in some lists a final comma is an aid to the meaning. In this sentence:

> She wrote cheques payable to Bayne & Duckett, Marks & Spencer, and Martin & Frost.

the final comma reinforces the difference between the ampersand (&) and the word *and*.

THE SEMICOLON

The main function of the semicolon today is to separate two or more main clauses in a compound sentence, especially when the sentence does not use the conjunctions *and* or *but*. A passage from Swift's *Gulliver's Travels* shows how punctuation and syntax have changed since Swift's book was first published in 1726:

> That he had once, by way of Experiment, privately removed a Heap of these Stones from the Place where one of his Yahoos had buried it: Whereupon, the sordid Animal missing his Treasure, by his loud lamenting brought the whole Herd to the Place, then miserably howled, then fell to biting and tearing the rest; began to pine away, would neither eat nor sleep, nor work, till he ordered a Servant privately to convey the Stones into the same Hole, and hide them as before; which when his Yahoo had found, he presently recovered his Spirits and good Humour; but took Care to remove them to a better hiding Place; and hath ever since been a serviceable Brute.

The passage is, in fact, a single sentence but it covers a complete narrative sequence that would normally be written as a paragraph of several sentences in current standard English. Swift uses the semicolon where we would use a comma, a colon or even a full stop. We now favour shorter sentences and a lighter but more systematic use of punctuation marks, including the semicolon:

> Jean-Paul Chambery is manager of Vitesse Bordeaux Football Club; Jerzy Novak is manager of Cracow Solidarnoz.

Replacing the conjunction with the semicolon breaks the continuity of the sentence and introduces a pause, the effect of which is to create a deliberate juxtaposition, a direct contrast or counterbalancing of the two clauses:

> Vitesse is one of the richest clubs in France; Solidarnoz is one of the poorest clubs in Poland.

A different kind of equilibrium is achieved when the sentence is extended to three main clauses:

> Jean-Paul Chambery's career as a player was cut short by injury; Jerzy Novak won fifty-three caps for Poland; both men are expert football strategists.

The combination of the semicolon and the syntax produces a distinctive effect; other choices of punctuation and syntax would produce different effects. For example, when the conjunctions *and* or *but* are used in these sentences the result is acceptable, both grammatically and stylistically:

> Jean-Paul Chambery is manager of Vitesse Bordeaux Football Club, and Jerzy Novak is manager of Cracow Solidarnoz.

but the sentence loses the abruptness of the contrast brought about by the semicolon.

Another structural option is to rewrite a compound sentence as a complex sentence; that is, one of the main clauses can be reduced to a sub-clause, and a necessary linking device – the word *whereas* in the sentence below – can be inserted:

> Vitesse is one of the richest clubs in France whereas Solidarnoz is one of the poorest clubs in Poland.

Here too the result is acceptable, but once again the deliberate abruptness of the original is replaced by a smooth continuity.

In a compound sentence punctuated by semicolons, each of the clauses can normally function as an independent sentence, but the similarity of the ideas in the clauses creates a thematic unity that calls for a single sentence. The end result is sometimes a creative tension between the continuity of ideas that links the clauses and the pause or separation created by the semicolon. If the clauses were rewritten as separate sentences, the resulting sentences might seem too short, staccato and contrived:

> Chambery's career as a player was cut short by injury. Novak won fifty-three caps for Poland. Both men are expert football strategists.

When you use the semicolon in that balanced way you achieve a distinct effect. The semicolon can also be effective in sentences that are designed only to maintain narrative progress:

> In the last minute of the game Eddy Tissac tackled hard and won the ball; he struck an inch-perfect pass to Claude Montereau, the Vitesse striker; Montereau's fiercely driven shot went head-high past the Solidarnoz goalkeeper.

This passage would be effective and would generate a slightly quicker narrative pace if it were written as three short sentences. By writing it as one sentence punctuated by semicolons we achieve a similar tempo as we cut abruptly from one incident to the next; we also achieve a unity by showing that each of the sharply defined incidents is part of a longer narrative sequence.

One other function of the semicolon is to punctuate detailed items in a list in which the items are already punctuated internally by commas:

> Vitesse Bordeaux's board of directors is dominated by three men: Charles Auriol, Chairman, and chairman of three other companies in and around Bordeaux; Henri de Loches, great-grandson of a founding director of the club; and Jacques Cateraggio, the Corsican-born banker.

Each item in the list above is an extended phrase; semicolons may also be needed when the items in the list are clauses:

> A large area outside Wembley, the neutral ground chosen for the final, was like a street market. One man was selling scarves, rosettes, pennants, and balloons in Vitesse Bordeaux colours; thirty yards away another salesman had the same items in Cracow Solidarnoz colours; mobile snack bars offered tea, coffee, Bovril, hamburgers, hot dogs, pies and crisps; the man in the Automobile Association caravan was conducting a half-hearted membership drive; ticket touts were testing the laws of supply and demand.

The list forms one long sentence, *One man was . . . supply and demand*, consisting of five extended items, each one a main clause. The unity of the single sentence gathers the detailed imagery of each clause into a composite picture.

This five-clause structure is effective but it is not the only way of presenting the information. If you had already used extended lists punctuated by semicolons in your essay or report, you would look for a different syntactic option in order to give variety to your prose.

In the passage above, the first two main clauses could be rewritten as a complex sentence with one main clause and one sub-clause:

> One man was selling scarves, rosettes, pennants, and balloons in Vitesse Bordeaux colours, while thirty yards away another salesman had the same items in Cracow Solidarnoz colours.

The third clause could form one short, grammatically simple sentence:

> Mobile snack bars offered tea, coffee, Bovril, hamburgers, hot dogs, pies and crisps.

And the fourth and fifth clauses could be edited into one compound sentence by inserting the conjunction *and*:

> The man in the Automobile Association caravan was conducting a half-hearted membership drive, and ticket touts were testing the laws of supply and demand.

These variations show that even minor changes of punctuation and syntax produce different rhythmic and structural effects. The differences create a variety that adds energy and interest to your prose.

THE COLON

The colon has finally assumed one main function. It is now used as a device to mark the introduction of some form of illustrative or explanatory material: a quotation, a list of items or an explanation. The promise of information in the opening statement is followed by the colon, which introduces a slight pause before the information is given.

In British newspapers the colon is the standard punctuation mark that is placed between the reporting verb, that is, a verb denoting speech, and the words that are actually spoken. The reporting verb can introduce a statement, a question, a command or an exclamation:

> The sports editor of the *Daily Clarion* demanded: 'Why didn't you interview Chambery after the match?'

> Pete Gardelli, the young sports reporter, said: 'There wasn't time for an interview because I had to meet the deadline for the first edition of the *Clarion*.'

In newspaper practice the colon need not appear immediately after the reporting verb but it must appear immediately before the quotation:

> Jean-Paul Chambery, manager of Vitesse Bordeaux, roared as he entered the dressing room: 'Magnifique! Merveilleux! Parfait!'

The information that appears before the colon is reported, or indirect, speech; the information that appears immediately after the colon is direct speech. The punctuation of direct speech is discussed on pages 103–6.

A variation on this use is when the colon is preceded by a general statement and followed immediately by the list of items or examples:

> For the next test match, the selectors have named a squad of twelve: Wyatt (captain), Alder, Aylmer, Butts, Earnshaw, Flaxman, Fry, Jowett, Loveridge, Otway, Pullman and Wilkes.

The list that follows the colon can consist of phrases as well as single words, as we saw in the section on the comma:

> As they drew up outside their holiday cottage, the Hughes family saw the signs of vandalism: uprooted plants, broken windows, a smashed door panel and black paint daubed on the white-washed walls.

The colon always marks a strong structural division within a sentence, the effect of which is to introduce a pause and to add emphasis to the information that follows the pause. When the two sentences above are rewritten without the division and without the colon, the result is less emphatic:

> The selectors have named Wyatt (captain), Alder, Aylmer, Butts, Earnshaw, Flaxman, Fry, Jowett, Loveridge, Otway, Pullman and Wilkes in the twelve-man squad.

> As they drew up outside their holiday cottage the Hughes family saw that the signs of vandalism were uprooted plants, broken windows, a smashed door panel and black paint daubed on the whitewashed walls.

In a third variation the colon marks the structural division between a statement, often a statement of purpose or intent, and an explanation of that statement:

> Fran Prasana had to face the facts: with so slight an artistic talent she could never be a successful painter.

> Fran's choice was clear: she could complete her course at art college or join Upstart Genes.

This third variation includes a sub-division in which the colon is used as the pivotal point in a sentence that is deliberately structured to create some form of tension – ironic, comic or epigrammatic – through the deliberate juxtaposition, on either side of the colon, of the two halves of the sentence:

> You needn't sell your soul to the devil in order to play this piece: you could try practising instead.

> I won't visit the dentist: I'll wait for the tooth fairy.

> A little humility can be charming: too much is sickening.

This last structure should be used sparingly because the rhetorical contrivance of such sentences focuses the reader's attention more precisely. Your sentence must be effective to survive such scrutiny.

THE QUESTION MARK

Written standard English allows questions to be phrased in a variety of ways, and a question mark, sometimes known as an interrogation mark, must be placed at the end of a question, no matter what form the question takes.

The most obvious form is the direct question:

> Have you seen the Camera Club's annual exhibition?

Writers sometimes wrongly omit the question mark at the end of longer or more detailed questions, probably because the idea at the end of the train of thought is so far from the initial idea that they forget that the sentence is a question:

> Have you had a chance to see the Camera Club's annual exhibition, which was formally opened by the picture editor of *The Times* last Friday and which runs for the next three weeks in Wellington Hall?

These sentences must be punctuated with question marks because the questions are put directly. Exactly the same form of words, with the addition of inverted commas, would be used if the questions were spoken in direct speech. When the same information is written indirectly, not as an interrogative statement but as a plain, or indicative, statement, no question mark is needed:

> Cherry Greville asked her colleague Margot Salles if she had seen the Camera Club's annual show.

> Margot Salles questioned the standard of some of the portrait photographs in the exhibition.

> Cherry demanded to know why Margot was criticizing something she had not seen.

Each sentence has an interrogative reporting verb, that is, a verb that poses a question: *asked, questioned* and *demanded*; but the verbs appear in sentences that are structured as plain statements in what is grammatically the indicative mood. The three sentences above are giving information rather than asking for it, and it is only when a sentence asks for information that it should end with a question mark. The difference between giving and asking for information, between indicative and interrogative statements, can be demonstrated by rewriting the three statements above as questions. Inverted commas are used to illustrate the direct nature of the questions:

> Cherry Greville asked her colleague Margot Salles, 'Have you seen the Camera Club's annual show?'

> 'Do you think the portrait photographs are up to standard?' Margot Salles asked.

> 'Why are you criticizing something you haven't seen?' Cherry demanded.

A common way of asking questions, especially in spoken English, is to make an indicative statement followed by tag question, that is, a short question that is tagged, or added, to the plain statement:

> You haven't seen the exhibition, have you?
>
> The portraits are rather weak this year, don't you think?
>
> Some of the landscapes are beautiful, are they not?

Each of the tag questions above is also a Yes/No question which, as the name indicates, can be answered with the word *Yes* or *No*.

The Yes/No question is a particular version of what is sometimes known as a closed question, that is, a question that calls for a strictly factual response:

> Who took the photograph of the River Nile at dusk?
>
> How many of his own photographs is the president exhibiting this year?

In contrast with the closed question is the open question, which always invites a fuller response:

> How did Cherry Greville shoot her sports photographs?
>
> Why did the committee restrict each club member to a maximum of six prints this year?

The open questions above are also 'Wh' questions, the slightly colloquial but correct term for questions beginning with the words *Who, What, Why, Where, When* and *How*. 'Wh' questions are normally open questions because they call for reasoned or detailed responses.

Rhetorical Questions

The rhetorical question is unlike the other forms of question discussed so far because it is not a request for information. The rhetorical question can take the form of a simple social exchange:

> How do you do? Isn't it a lovely day?

or a more challenging form of exchange:

> Do you think I'm doing this for my health?
>
> Just who do you think you are?

A variation on this form of rhetorical question is the colloquial or folk philosophy of:

> What's it all about? Who would have thought it?

In heightened language the rhetorical question can be genuinely philosophical or poetic:

> How did we fall so far from the bright morning?

Although it seldom requires a precise answer, the rhetorical question must always be punctuated with a question mark. Sentences that are grammatically indicative, that is, plain statements, often function as questions and should be punctuated with question marks:

> Margot finally went to the Camera Club exhibition last night?

> She said she liked the portraits? Surely not?

> You mean to say she wasn't impressed by any of those strange, haunting landscapes?

The use of the question mark here, like the use of the exclamation mark after some indicative statements, is determined by the context, the nature of the dialogue, or the state of mind and quality of voice – the metaphorical written voice – of the writer. The question mark gives the written word the rising intonation of doubt, incredulity or opposition that would be apparent in the spoken word.

THE EXCLAMATION MARK

The main function of the exclamation mark in written standard English is to indicate the kind of heightened emotion that would be expressed in speech; the written symbol suggests the tone and volume of the spoken word in moments of anger, surprise, exhilaration or self-pity. On the other hand, in informal writing such as personal letters or holiday postcards the exclamation mark often replaces the written word and becomes the equivalent of the spoken phrase, 'You know what I mean?' or 'Just imagine.' There is, then, a distinct difference between the formal use of the exclamation mark in standard English and its colloquial use in non-standard English.

In standard English the exclamation mark is, of course, used to indicate exclamations:

> What a farce! How stupid! You're fired!

Exclamations often take the form of commands:

> Wait for me! Don't jump! Get out!

The initial exclamation can be followed by a slightly longer one:

> What a farce! Hamlet split his tights and Ophelia lost a false tooth in a fit of the giggles!

An exclamation can take the form of an invocation, that is, an actual or metaphorical attempt to invoke or appeal to someone:

> Oh, God! Let this be a comedy!

The emotion that prompts the invocation is similar to the emotion that prompts the solemn oath:

> I swear by all the saints that this is true!

The exclamation mark is optional after the solemn oath above, but it is essential in the not so solemn oath, that is, a curse:

> May you rot for ever!

Some editors insist that the exclamation mark should be used only in the contexts outlined above, but it can also be used to punctuate indicative statements, that is, sentences that use the normal finite form of the verb, if the statements express heightened emotion:

> He was covered in blood!

> Vitesse Bordeaux won the cup!

> I've just seen the ghost of Rose de Silva!

One other context justifies the use of the exclamation mark: the commonplace and yet complex remark that is uttered in exasperation or incredulity and is at one and the same time a statement, a question and an exclamation:

> The match begins in ten minutes and you've left the tickets at home!

> Anna Desai won the national scholarship and turned it down!

But an example like this:

> You can imagine what the musical director will say to Anna at the next rehearsal!

strays across the dividing line between the standard and non-standard, or formal and colloquial, use of the exclamation mark. Although the dividing line between standard and non-standard English is sometimes faint, two simple tests can be used to decide whether the exclamation mark is justified.

The first, rather subjective, test is to ask how the written words would sound if they were spoken. If you are sure that the words would be spoken in a tone that was more emphatic than normal and at a louder volume than normal, the exclamation mark may be justified. The second test, more objective and more reliable than the first, is to ask if the exclamation mark is being used as a substitute for words rather than as a punctuation mark. Consider these examples:

> You can imagine how embarrassed Anna Desai will feel when she has to explain!

> Just after midnight, and ten miles from the nearest town, we ran out of petrol!

> Sam did his usual demolition job on the sherry trifle!

In each sentence the exclamation mark is an appeal to the reader to supply the missing information. The words alone communicate a meaning, but the addition of the exclamation mark is a signal that invites the reader to cooperate by imagining what has been left unwritten. This kind of informal invitation is part of the common currency of friendship, but the writer of standard English cannot assume the sympathy of the reader and must not expect the reader to do the work that should be done by the writer.

Even in casual writing, the frequent colloquial use of exclamation marks soon makes the prose style hollow and mannered, more notable for its punctuation than its content and substance. And the use of double or treble exclamation marks is a desperate measure that makes the prose style not only mannered but hysterical.

INVERTED COMMAS

Inverted commas form a sub-code within the wider code of punctuation because their functions and the rules governing these functions are more specific than those of other punctuation marks. Inverted commas are exactly what their name implies: commas turned upside down. They are sometimes known as quotation marks because their main function is to indicate that the words they enclose are being quoted directly from a speech or a written source. When the spoken or written word is quoted in this way, the passage in inverted commas is known as direct speech.

A second function of inverted commas is to indicate that the words enclosed are merely alleged and not necessarily true, or that the words are not the views of the writer. A third function is to punctuate the titles of essays, articles, poems and short stories.

Quotations

The general practice of book publishers in Britain is to use single inverted commas to punctuate quotations from the spoken word or from written texts; the general practice of newspaper publishers is to use double inverted commas. Either method is acceptable as long as it is practised consistently. The need for consistency will also determine what additional punctuation mark you use to separate reported, or indirect, speech from the direct speech in the quotation. Book publishers generally use the comma; newspaper publishers use the colon.

As the examples in this book show, inverted commas are not needed when the quotation is set in a different type size or type style from, and with wider margins than, the surrounding text. These typographical differences are normally enough to identify the quotation, but inverted commas will be used in the examples in this section of the book.

When a speaker or a written source is being quoted for the first time in your report or essay, you should identify the speaker before you quote his or her words. For example, if you write:

> 'The students in question, all ten of them, are members of Central University Literary Society. They say they were following the Wordsworth Trail but got lost in the dark. They parked their minibus in a lay-by and took to the fells, but only two of the students had any experience of fell-walking and none of the party had the right equipment,' said Don Stanton, leader of the Fells Rescue Unit.

you risk irritating your readers by making them wait for the vital information that gives the speaker's identity and the credentials that give authority to his statement. Instead, you should write:

> Don Stanton, leader of the Falls Rescue Unit, said, 'The students in question . . . the right equipment.'

The example above shows that when a quotation is a full sentence, or the main part of a sentence, the first word inside the inverted commas is spelled with a capital letter, and the final punctuation mark at the end of the sentence – a full stop, a question mark or an exclamation mark – is inside the closing inverted comma. Here is a typical example, which also shows the punctuation before the quotation:

> A spokesman for Central University said, 'We apologize for the foolish behaviour of the men students.'

When the quotation is part of a longer sentence – for example, when the direct speech is surrounded by reported speech – a punctuation mark is needed immediately after the inverted commas as well as the full stop at the end of the sentence:

> What the university spokesman actually said was, 'We apologize for the foolhardy behaviour of the men students', in his statement.

Although the quotation is itself a sentence, the quotation cannot be punctuated with a full stop because it is part of a longer sentence and a sentence should have only one full stop. The comma after *students* is placed outside the inverted comma so that the quotation is punctuated as an embedded statement.

With other end-punctuation marks – the question mark and the exclamation mark – the practice is different. In this example:

> The reporter asked, 'Will the university take disciplinary action against the students?' when he interviewed the university spokesman.

the question mark refers only to the quotation, not to the complete sentence, and so the question mark must be placed inside the closing inverted comma. Similarly, in this example:

> 'Disciplinary action? Don't talk such rot!' snapped the spokesman.

the exclamation mark applies only to the quotation and not to the complete sentence, and so the exclamation mark must be placed inside the closing inverted comma. These examples show that when the quotation is part of a longer sentence, the quotation can be punctuated with a question mark or an exclamation mark – but not a full stop – inside the closing inverted comma; the full stop can be used only at the end of the complete sentence.

A sentence can normally take only one full stop but it can take more than one question mark:

> Why did the reporter ask, 'Will the university take disciplinary action against the students?' when he telephoned the university spokesman?

Two question marks are needed because two questions are being asked, one by the words in direct speech and the other by the statement that surrounds the direct speech.

Quotations within Quotations

When the surrounding statement itself is in direct speech, that is, when the complete sentence consists of a quotation within a quotation, two question marks are still needed:

> 'Why did the reporter ask, "Will the university take disciplinary action against the students?" when he spoke to me this morning?' the spokesman wondered.

But note what happens to the question marks when the end of the internal quotation coincides with the end of the sentence which is itself a quotation:

> The Vice-Chancellor of Central University said, 'When that reporter spoke to you are you sure that he asked, "Will the university take disciplinary action against the students?" '

The question mark can be placed inside the double inverted commas, as above, or inside the single inverted comma, but not both. Two question marks cannot be used alongside each other because a convention of standard English is that the same punctuation mark cannot appear twice at the end of a sentence. A double question mark: . . .?"?' would look absurd, as would two exclamation marks or two full stops.

When two quotations end simultaneously at the end of a sentence, and when both quotations are indicative statements rather than questions or exclamations, the full stop should be placed between the single and the double inverted commas because that is where the complete sentence ends:

> The *Clarion* reporter said, 'I'll use that first quote you gave me, "We apologize for the foolhardy behaviour of the ten students".'

Each of the last three examples above shows how to punctuate a quotation within a quotation by using single and double inverted commas. Because the preferred style in this book is single inverted commas, we must use single inverted commas to open and close the first quotation and double inverted commas for the quotation within the quotation. Here is another example of the technique:

> Godfrey Pendleton, editor of the *Clarion*, said, 'I like your whiff of irony, "They wandered lonely as a cloud", in your piece on the lost students.'

Since the complete sentence ends with the word *students*, the full stop is placed immediately after *students* and inside the closing inverted comma. The editor's complete statement is:

> 'I like your whiff of irony, "They wandered lonely as a cloud", in your piece on the lost students.'

Since the line from Wordsworth, "I wandered lonely as a cloud", is a quotation within a quotation, the line must be punctuated with double inverted commas to distinguish it from the editor's own words:

'I like your whiff of irony in your piece on the lost students.'

The quotation within the quotation is doubly differentiated by the commas after *irony* and *cloud*.

Quotations and Paragraphs

When a speaker or a written source is quoted for the first time, you should open a new paragraph. When a direct quotation from one speaker extends over two or more paragraphs, the opening inverted comma is repeated at the start of each new paragraph, but the inverted commas are not closed until the end of the complete quotation:

> Don Stanton, leader of the Fells Rescue Unit, said, 'Around midnight last night a hill farmer telephoned the police to say that he could hear the sound of chanting and bursts of wild laughter drifting across the fells. He told the police he thought it sounded like a coven of witches and warlocks at some midnight ritual.
>
> 'The police called me and asked if I could guide them over the fells. It's a tricky route at the best of times and dangerous in the dark.
>
> 'We heard the noise from half a mile away: rhythmic chanting and bursts of wild laughter, just as the farmer said. Nearer, the chanting seemed somehow familiar. And then we realized . . . Poetry! The students were reciting poetry!'

Similarly, when you are quoting two or more speakers in conversation with each other, or when a new speaker is quoted, you must open a new paragraph:

> Police Sergeant Harry Mercer said, 'Right, lads. What's the celebration?'
>
> ' "Bliss was it in that dawn to be alive, But to be young was very heaven!" ' a student recited in a loud and slightly slurred voice.
>
> 'Wordsworth?' said Don Stanton. 'Wordsworth never set foot on these fells.'
>
> 'But we thought . . .' said a second student. 'I mean, we thought . . .'
>
> The first student said to the second, 'You dozy daffodil! I told you we should have turned left at Cockermouth.'

Inverted Commas, Allegations and Ironies

A second, less precise, use of inverted commas has evolved from the first. This second function is less precise because the inverted commas are not used to indicate a direct quotation from a speaker or a written source but to distance the writer from the words in inverted commas. In effect, the writer is using the punctuation marks to show that the words inside them are what other people, but not the writer, might say or think:

> Don Stanton's favourite 'leisure' activity is climbing mountains on his own in midwinter.

The effect of the inverted commas is to show that the writer thinks that mountain-climbing is not a genuine but merely an alleged or so-called leisure activity.

In dissociating ourselves from another person's words there is sometimes a temptation to ridicule the person, and so the inverted commas can imply sarcasm or irony:

> He feels 'crowded' if he sees as much as another set of footprints in the snow.

The writer invites the complicity of the reader in ridiculing the person.

A variation on this use of inverted commas, and a device used by sub-editors who write the headlines in tabloid newspapers, is to use the inverted commas to point up a nickname, a catch-phrase or a particularly bad pun:

> Don 'Mr Snowman' Stanton leads midnight rescue
>
> It's 'snow' joke when Don takes to the hills
>
> Have an 'ice' day, Mr Stanton
>
> 'Freeze' a jolly good fellow

These last examples expose the dangers of this use of inverted commas: the prose style quickly becomes mannered because it draws attention to the writer's self-conscious attempt at cleverness in a way that resembles the misuse of the exclamation mark. Some readers will see that the punctuation is a device to mask the lack of substance. Readers may also find the prose ambiguous. Nicknames can be used contemptuously as well as affectionately, irony is a difficult mode that can elude even the attentive reader or may be misinterpreted as sarcasm, and sarcasm will always antagonize some readers.

Inverted Commas and Titles

Single inverted commas are used by most British book publishers and editors to punctuate the titles of essays, articles, poems, short stories and articles in magazines. The titles of longer or complete works – books, plays, magazines, newspapers and films – are set in italic type. In this reference, for example:

Edwin Muir's 'Sick Caliban' in *One Foot in Eden*

'Sick Caliban' is the title of a poem and *One Foot in Eden* the title of the book of poems in which 'Sick Caliban' appeared. We need a standard system for punctuating the titles of shorter works; without a standard there would be these and other absurdities: Philip Larkin's Coming, W.H. Auden's Missing, Norman Cameron's In the Queen's Room, Stevie Smith's Not Waving but Drowning and Siegfried Sassoon's Falling Asleep.

The use of inverted commas has become standard practice. It is useful in distinguishing life from art: Raymond Carver's Venice is not the same as his poem 'Venice', nor is Edward Thomas's Sussex in the South Country the same as his chapter 'Sussex' in *The South Country*. The practice is useful too when the title of a collection of short stories, essays or poems is taken from a single work in the collection: the essay 'Fires' in the collection *Fires* by Raymond Carver, or the short story 'May We Borrow Your Husband?' in the collection *May We Borrow Your Husband?* by Graham Greene. The combined use of unpunctuated words, single inverted commas for shorter works and italic type for longer works allows you to distinguish a character whose name forms the title of the story, novel, poem, play or film from the story in which the character appears, for example, Lispeth in Rudyard Kipling's short story 'Lispeth' in the collection *Plain Tales from the Hills*, or the secret agent in Joseph Conrad's *The Secret Agent* or Hamlet in *Hamlet*.

Musical titles can be punctuated in the same way, with inverted commas used for the titles of shorter items and italics for the titles of longer or complete works:

Elgar's 'Nimrod' is one of the most popular portraits in his *Enigma Variations*.

Trick Fraser plays a long drum solo in 'Parallax' on *Lunar Landscapes*, the new compact disc by Upstart Genes.

THE APOSTROPHE

The problems caused by apostrophes are problems of scale. Apostrophes seem to make such fine distinctions in the meanings of words and to demand such precise attention that some writers see them as finicky and unnecessary while others see them as little irritants to be ignored, but the distinctions that apostrophes make are real. The sentence:

> The band's on stage. (The band is on stage.)

is different from the phrase:

> the bands on stage (two or more bands on stage)

and different yet again from:

> The band's live performance on stage is more exciting than its tapes.

Some words:

> cant, hell, ill, its, shell, well, were

change their meanings when an apostrophe, and in one case a capital letter, is added:

> can't, he'll, I'll, it's, she'll, we'll, we're.

These differences can be explained in sets of guidelines for the two functions of the apostrophe: first, to mark contractions and omissions such as *can't* for *cannot*, *he'll* for *he will* and *we're* for *we are*; second, to mark the possessive case of nouns (see pages 111–17).

Apostrophes for Contractions and Omissions

Many of the most widely used contracted words are combinations of pronouns and verbs:

> I'm/I am, you're/you are, he's/he is, she's/she is, we're/we are, they're/they are.

These written forms with the apostrophe represent spoken forms. The standard unit of spoken English is a cluster of words uttered as a continuous sound with no interval between the individual words; the intervals appear between the clusters of words. The contracted written forms are representations of this fused quality of spoken English, and as such they are not normally used in written English. Although current written standard English is less formal than it was fifty years ago, these contracted words are still unacceptable unless the writer is deliberately creating a casual, colloquial tone. This passage shows the contrasting tones:

> Leonard Vedley's a persuasive businessman. Some councillors said they'd oppose the plan for the Cradle Bay Marina, but now they've changed their views. They'll support the plan because they're sure it's a sound investment that'll improve the town.

When the contracted words are written in full, the tone – and to that extent the meaning – of the passage becomes rather more formal:

> Leonard Vedley is a persuasive businessman. Some councillors said they would oppose the plan for the Cradle Bay Marina, but now they have changed their views. They will support the plan because they are sure it is a sound investment that will improve the town.

One other use of the apostrophe is sometimes seen:

> Britain enjoyed an economic surge in the late 1980's but suffered a recession in the early 1990's.

Although the apostrophe in *1980's* and *1990's* is accepted, it is unnecessary and confusing: unnecessary because there is no contraction or omission, and confusing because the apostrophe could be mistaken for a possessive apostrophe. The expressions *1980s* and *1990s*, without apostrophes, are simple plurals, formed in the standard way by adding the letter *s* to the singular *1980* and *1990*. There is no need for the apostrophe.

The possessive apostrophe is used correctly in a statement such as:

> The Austin Mini was a 1960s' success story.

The phrase, *a 1960s' success story*, means a success story of or belonging to the 1960s.

The apostrophe to mark a contraction or omission may be used in such expressions as:

> House prices soared in the '80s.

> By the early '60s television was the most popular medium of mass communication in Britain.

in which the apostrophe marks the missing century number, 19. The simple plural form, *in the 1980s* or *in the 1960s*, needs no apostrophe.

A similar use of the apostrophe appears in:

There are two c's and two m's in 'accommodation', and there are two i's in 'liaison'.

The expressions, *c's*, *m's* and *i's*, are neither contracted nor possessive. They are simple plural forms, but because they will certainly cause confusion if they are written with no punctuation – cs, ms and is – the apostrophe is justified. There are two other options in this case. One is to place the letter of the alphabet inside inverted commas, or quotation marks, with the letter *s* outside the inverted commas:

There are two 'c's and two 'm's in 'accommodation'.

The other is to print the specified letter of the alphabet in italic type or bold type, with the letter *s* in medium or normal type:

There are two *c*s and two *m*s in *accommodation*. (italic)

There are two cs and two **m**s in **accommodation**. (bold)

Apostrophes and Possessive Nouns

The apostrophe that marks the possessive case of nouns, the possessive apostrophe, is the only relic of case endings, or inflections, in nouns. We have already noted that nouns and pronouns in Old English changed their forms according to their grammatical functions in sentences. Many masculine and neuter nouns had a possessive singular form, that is, the form meaning *of* or *belonging to*, ending in *-es*:

cyninges	of the king/the king's
weres	of the man/the man's
scipes	of the ship/the ship's
huses	of the house/the house's

In Middle English, the language of Chaucer (*c*.1345–1400), other case endings began to disappear, but the possessive *-es* ending remained and was applied to feminine as well as masculine and neuter nouns. Chaucer's *Canterbury Tales*, for example, has 'The Prioresses Tale' and 'The Seconde Nonnes Tale'. In Modern English the nouns are punctuated Prioress's and Nun's.

By Shakespeare's time (1564–1616) the practice was changing. In the edition of Shakespeare's *The Winter's Tale* published in 1623, the possessive *-es* ending is applied to women: *Ladyes* and *Ladies* for *lady's*, and *Queenes* for *queen's*; it is applied sometimes to children: *Boyes* for *boy's* and *Sonnes* for *son's*: but not to men: *my Lords tricks, my Fathers honour'd friend* and *the Kings Brother in Law*. (These examples also show that almost all nouns were then spelled with an initial capital letter, and that hyphens were not then used, as they are today, in compound words such as *brother-in-law*.) The apostrophe is consistently used in *The Winter's Tale* to indicate contractions and omissions, as in *honour'd, Hee'le* for *he will, You'le* for *you will* and *let me have't* for *let me have it*. By contrast, the possessive apostrophe is rare; even the title of the 1623 edition of the play was printed as *A Winters Tale*.

A seventeenth-century variation – *my Master his table* for *my master's table* and *Mr Heminges his word* for *Mr Heminges's word* – did not survive, probably because printers began to use the possessive apostrophe in the course of the seventeenth century.

By the beginning of the eighteenth century the possessive apostrophe was standard practice. In the 1721 edition of *Fables, Ancient and Modern* by John Dryden (1631–1700), the possessive -es ending has disappeared and singular possessive nouns are indicated as they are today, by an apostrophe followed by an s, ('s): *your Grace's accession, the old Gentleman's Excuse* and *Chaucer's Stories*. And Dryden, or his printer, writes the title, *The Wife of Bath's Tale*, in italic type, where Chaucer's early publishers had written the unpunctuated title, The Tale of the Wyf of Bathe.

Clearly, the possessive apostrophe was first introduced to mark the missing letter *e* in the old -es case ending, and by indicating the missing case ending the apostrophe itself became the case ending.

The key to the use of the apostrophe to indicate possession is to decide if the noun is possessive, that is, if there is something of or belonging to that noun. You then note whether the noun is singular or plural.

Singular Nouns

If the noun in the possessive case is singular, add an apostrophe and the letter *s* ('s) to the end of the word.

> a car's tyres, the manager's tracksuit, a bus's windscreen, a glass's rim, Miriam's piano, Mike's computer, Thomas's ambition, Evans's mortgage, Smith's salary, Jones's overdraft.

The singular form of a noun may consist of more than one word: Arms & Armour Press, for example, is one publisher; Marks &

Spencer is one company. These examples observe the same rule for the singular form of the possessive; the apostrophe s ('s) is added to the end of the name of the organization to indicate the possessive case:

> Arms & Armour Press's latest book, Marks & Spencer's chief executive.

Hyphenated words in the possessive case are punctuated in the same way:

> the Attorney-General's ruling, the vice-captain's benefit year, his brother-in-law's party.

When the possession refers to two persons or two things, the same rule applies. For example:

> Miriam and Anna's concert performance

means a single concert performance by Miriam and Anna together, for example, a sonata for clarinet and piano. The words *Miriam and Anna* are treated as if they are a single unit, and the 's is added to the end. But the phrase:

> Miriam's and Anna's concert performance

means a performance by Miriam and a separate performance by Anna. Similarly:

> the house and garage's insurance policy

means one policy covering both the house and the garage. But:

> the house's and the garage's insurance policy

means that each building, the house and the garage, is separately insured.

Another variation to be noted is this:

> a painting of Winston Churchill

means that Winston Churchill is the subject of the painting. But with the addition of the 's:

> a painting of Winston Churchill's

the phrase means that Churchill was the painter, not the subject of the painting. Similarly:

> a wild story of Dylan Thomas

means a story about one of Dylan Thomas's escapades, whereas

> a wild story of Dylan Thomas's

113

means a story written by Thomas.

The rule for the vast majority of singular nouns in the possessive case is: add 's to the end of the word.

Exceptions to this rule are those singular nouns that look and sound plural, for example:

> gallows, measles, scissors, trousers, acoustics, ethics, hysterics, logistics, mathematics, politics.

These words will look and sound awkward and will inevitably cause confusion if they are punctuated with 's:

> gallows's platform, trousers's pockets, hysterics's cure, politics's rewards.

You should avoid the 's and rephrase according to the context:

> the platform of the gallows, the pockets of the trousers/the trouser pockets, a cure for hysterics, the rewards of politics/political rewards.

The same objection of awkwardness of sound and appearance applies to that group of nouns derived from Greek and ending in -is in the singular:

> antithesis, basis, diagnosis, hypothesis, paralysis.

Here again you must avoid the awkwardness of:

> the diagnosis's results, the paralysis's cause

and instead use a form of words that fits the context:

> the result of the diagnosis, the cause of paralysis.

The plural form of these -is words ends in -es, and again the 's must be avoided. Instead, you should write:

> the results of the diagnoses, the causes of paralyses.

A notable sub-group is authors' personal surnames ending in s, for example, Burns, Dickens, Graves, Hughes, Keats, Thomas and Yeats. The convention is that the s at the end of the surname is followed by an apostrophe and another s:

> Burns's songs, Dickens's novels, Robert Graves's autobiography, Ted Hughes's poems for children, Keats's sonnets, Edward Thomas's essays, Yeats's poems and plays.

Plural Nouns
If the possessive noun is plural and does not end in the letter s, add 's to the end of the plural form of the word. For example, the plural

of *child* is *children*, and so the possessive plural is *children's*; the plural of *sheep* is *sheep*, and so the possessive plural is *sheep's*. Examples of the possessive case formed from plurals that do not end in *s* include:

> children's comics, men's habits, women's rights, aircraft's pilots, deer's habitat, geese's eggs, news media's messages, plateaux's structures.

When the plural form of the noun does end in *s*, as most English plurals do, add only the apostrophe after the existing *s*:

> players' entrance, students' grants, nurses' duties, doctors' prescriptions.

When the plural refers to two or more members of the same family, and the family surname does not end in *s*, the same rule applies; you add the apostrophe after the *s*. For example, if the family name is Smith, Brown or Jackson, two or more members of these families are the Smiths, the Browns or the Jacksons and the possessive cases are punctuated:

> the Smiths' house, the Browns' house, the Jacksons' house.

The phrase *the Smiths' house* means the house of or belonging to two or more Smiths.

When the family surname does end with the letter *s*, form the plural by adding *-es* and the possessive plural by adding the apostrophe after the final *s*. For example, if the family name is Evans, two or more members of the Evans family are the Evanses; if the name is Hughes the plural is Hugheses; if the name is Jones the plural is Joneses. The possessive plural forms of these family names are:

> the Evanses' mortgage, the Hugheses' holiday cottage, the Joneses' overdraft.

Some writers and editors feel that these possessive plural forms of family names – *Evanses'*, *Hugheses'*, *Joneses'* – look and sound awkward; a simple alternative is to use the possessive singular case of the word *family*, which is *family's*:

> the Evans family's mortgage, the Hughes family's holiday cottage, the Jones family's overdraft.

Self-styled purists sometimes object to expressions such as

> Edinburgh's Holyrood Park, London's Bloomsbury Square, Australia's Sir Don Bradman, New Zealand's Sir Richard Hadlee

claiming that these are false possessives, unacceptable in standard English, and that the correct expressions should be

> Holyrood Park, Edinburgh; Bloomsbury Square, London; Sir Don Bradman of Australia; Sir Richard Hadlee of New Zealand

> or

> the Australian, Sir Don Bradman; the New Zealander, Sir Richard Hadlee.

But there is no logical objection to the expressions, *Edinburgh's Holyrood Park* and *Australia's Sir Don Bradman*; the phrases are formed correctly and their meanings are perfectly clear. The objectors offer the stylistic argument that the usage is colloquial or inelegant, but standard English has long had the almost identical usage:

> Edinburgh's parks, London's squares, Australia's greatest batsman, New Zealand's greatest bowler.

The objection is too late because the usage is now firmly established in educated speech and writing; and on questions of style it is educated usage that makes an expression acceptable.

Apostrophes and Personal Pronouns

As we saw in the chapter on pronouns, one of the few absolute rules in English language is that the possessive case of personal pronouns never takes an apostrophe. The spellings are:

> yours, his, hers, ours, theirs, its

Similarly, the word *whose*, the possessive case of the relative pronoun *who*, is never spelled with an apostrophe.

Confusion sometimes arises from the spellings of the words *its* and *it's*, and *whose* and *who's*. The distinction between each pair was explained on pages 28–9, and you may wish to look again at the explanation and examples given there. To avoid all possibility of mis-spelling *it's* and *its*, *who's* and *whose*, you should adopt this simple procedure. When you mean *it is* you should write *it is* and not *it's*; when you mean *who is* you should write *who is* and not *who's*. Then you can never be wrong. The full forms of these contracted words – *it is* for *it's* and *who is* for *who's* – are also the preferred forms in standard English.

Here is a passage showing the possessive apostrophe. First, the passage without the apostrophes:

> *Oliver Twist* and *Great Expectations* are cinemas most success-
> ful adaptations of Dickenss novels. The novels effectiveness in the
> cinema stems from their dramatic plots, their atmospheric loca-
> tions, and above all their large casts of contrasting characters.
> Olivers innocence and vulnerability, for example, contrasts with
> Sykess brutality and Fagins cunning. The central contrast in *Great
> Expectations* is between Pips younger and older selves.

The passage should be punctuated as follows:

> *Oliver Twist* and *Great Expectations* are cinema's most successful
> adaptations of Dickens's novels. The novels' effectiveness in the
> cinema stems from their dramatic plots, their atmospheric locations,
> and above all their large casts of contrasting characters. Oliver's
> innocence and vulnerability, for example, contrasts with Sykes's
> brutality and Fagin's cunning. The central contrast in *Great Expecta-
> tions* is between Pip's younger and older selves.

The possessive form of *Sykes* can be spelled *Sykes'* or *Sykes's*.
Because the words *plots, locations, casts, characters* and *selves* are
simple plurals and not possessives, they do not take apostrophes.

THE HYPHEN

All punctuation marks except the hyphen introduce some form of
break, separation or division in a piece of writing; the hyphen is
the only punctuation mark that serves as a linking device.

The horizontal stroke of the hyphen should be shorter than the
length of the dash (see pages 123–5), but some modern keyboards
use the same symbol for both punctuation marks. You can indicate
the difference simply by keying in the hyphen as if it were one of
the letters of the compound word, as in *low-key*, with no space
between the two words. You indicate the dash by keying in an additional space – like this – before and after the dash so that the words
on either side of the horizontal stroke are separated.

Hyphens and Word Formation

The main function of the hyphen is to link two or more words into
one compound or hyphenated word. Those old favourites *a man
eating tiger* for *a man-eating tiger* and *the vice captain* for *the vice-
captain* illustrate the function. Few readers would interpret the
unhyphenated versions as a man eating a tiger or as a captain of

vice, but many readers would be aware of the unintended absurdity and, as we have already seen, the readers' awareness can undermine the writer's authority.

Compounds of more than two words are formed in exactly the same way: *three-year-old* child, *fifty-four-year-old* lecturer, *brother-in-law* and *mother-in-law*, *foot-and-mouth* disease.

Some words, like *brother-in-law* and *mother-in-law*, are permanently hyphenated, as are two-digit numbers such as *fifty-four*, *twenty-one* and *ninety-seven*. As we have seen, numbers of 100 and more are easier for the reader as well as the writer when numerals rather than alphabetical characters are used (see pages 39–41).

Words beginning with certain prefixes often have a hyphen between the prefix and the word:

> anti-hero, ex-directory, ex-president, neo-Nazi, pan-American, post-war, Post-Impressionist, pre-Conquest, pre-election, vice-captain, vice-chancellor.

Two prefixes can be used, but the result may seem clumsy:

> ex-vice-captain, pre-by-election.

The prefix *ex* should not be used in phrases like *ex-British Prime Minister* or *ex-German Chancellor* because these forms of words could be interpreted as a Prime Minister who is no longer British and a Chancellor who is no longer German. Safer forms of words are *a former Prime Minister of Britain* and *a former Chancellor of Germany*. The prefixes *de* and *re* are sometimes hyphenated to the root form of the word in order to avoid awkwardness or confusion in pronunciation or spelling:

> de-afforestation, de-ice, re-educate, re-entry.

A single letter of the alphabet forms the prefix in

> T-bone, U-turn, X-ray, Y-chromosome.

Other permanently hyphenated words include:

> Anglo-Saxon, Attorney-General, bee-keeping, cross-examine, double-barrelled, fox-hunting, heart-rending, spine-chilling.

Standard English also includes many ready-made, adjectival phrases to cover a wide variety of occasions:

> blow-by-blow, cut-and-dried, door-to-door, down-and-out, down-to-earth, face-to-face, fly-by-night, free-for-all, happy-go-lucky, out-of-the-way, ready-to-wear.

Other words can be hyphenated to express more specific ideas:

> six-wicket victory, two-goal lead, blood-spattered rugby shirt, free-range hens, oven-ready chickens, pre-election promises.

Specific hyphenation is a remarkable phenomenon. The compound words can be formed from so many grammatical combinations and can appear in so many different contexts that they form an endless source of variety, energy and creativity in English word formation. The meaning of the compound word is always different from the meanings of its constituent parts, and the grammatical form and function of the compound often differs from the form and function of its constituents.

The hyphen's power to transform meaning and grammar can be illustrated in the compound *soft-pedal*. When the words are used separately, as in *the soft pedal of a piano*, *soft* is an adjective describing the noun *pedal*, but when the words are hyphenated the *soft* component becomes an adverb and *pedal* becomes a verb. The compound word, the verb *to soft-pedal*, can then be used literally, meaning to reduce the volume of sound from a piano, or meta-phorically, meaning to treat gently.

The examples that follow show how new words and new gram-matical functions can be created by the hyphen. Nouns can be formed by hyphenating an adjective and a noun:

> double-bass, half-term, side-show, single-decker;

by hyphenating an adverb or a preposition and a noun:

> by-product, off-chance, out-worker, under-manager;

by hyphenating two nouns, for example, the agent nouns denoting a person's occupation or activity:

> child-minder, fire-fighter, house-mother, piano-tuner;

and non-human nouns:

> death-wish, road-map, shelf-life, time-switch;

by hyphenating a noun and a verb:

> air-drop, face-lift, ski-lift, wind-break;

or a verb and a noun:

> flick-knife, go-cart/kart, hang-glider, slip-knot;

and by hyphenating a verb and an adverb:

> break-in, change-over, drop-out, flare-up.

New adjectives can be formed by hyphenating two other adjectives, one of which may take the form of the past participle or present participle of a verb:

> flat-footed, heavy-handed, fast-talking, high-flying;

by hyphenating a noun and an adjective, including adjectives formed from past participles and present participles:

> accident-prone, duty-free, goal-hungry, word-blind, beer-stained, grief-stricken, oil-fired, dope-peddling, mind-bending, soul-destroying;

by reversing the order to hyphenate an adjective and a noun:

> first-rate, second-hand, short-range;

by hyphenating an adverb and a past participle adjective:

> fully-fashioned, hard-bitten, ill-advised, short-lived;

by hyphenating a preposition and a noun:

> in-house, off-peak, on-line, up-country.

Verbs can be formed by hyphenating an adverb and a verb:

> cross-examine, quick-freeze, out-think.

New verbs can be formed by hyphenating existing verbs:

> dive-bomb, freeze-dry, kick-start, shrink-wrap.

There are also the compounds of verb-conjunction-verb in *park-and-ride*, which is a mix of private and public transport; and verb-adverb + verb-adverb in *roll-on roll-off* car ferries.

Adverbs, some of which can also function as adjectives, can be formed by hyphenating an adverb or a preposition and a noun:

> above-board, off-shore, on-stream, up-market.

At present, some of these words – *index-linked, freeze-dry, shrink-wrap* – are neologisms, that is, words that are fairly new in the language; others – *up-market, roll-on roll-off* – are colloquialisms, that is, words that are current in popular speech or writing but may not have found their way into standard English. Some observers deplore these word formations, but most of them were formed to identify new phenomena in a constantly changing world. The English language, like life itself, is in a state of continuous evolution, and standard English dictionaries include many thousands of words that were once new, or colloquial, or slang, or foreign. Part of the evolutionary process is that, once the hyphenated word has been accepted as standard English, the hyphen is often dropped so that the two words form a single word.

The examples above show that the hyphenating process can be applied to most word classes, with the notable exception of pronouns. Adverbs too, especially those ending in *-ly*, are resistant to compounding. A standard English convention is that the word *well* used as an adverb is not normally hyphenated but *well* used as an adjective is hyphenated. In this sentence:

Arthur Miller's plays are well known.

the word *well* is an adverb modifying the verb *are known*. But in this sentence:

Arthur Miller is a well-known playwright.

the compound word *well-known* is an adjective that describes the noun *playwright*.

A process that takes as many forms as this is difficult to define or summarize, but the attempt must be made. The hyphenated, or compound, word can be formed from two or more words, or from one word and one or more prefixes. The meaning of the hyphenated word is different from the meanings of its component words; otherwise, there would be no need for the hyphenated word.

The grammatical function – noun, verb, adjective, adverb – of the hyphenated word will always differ from one of its component words and may differ from all of its components.

In most hyphenated words, the first component defines or describes the second component. In the word *income-tax*, for example, *income* describes the kind of tax. In the phrase, *high-income tax proposal*, the word *high* describes the word *income*, so that the proposal applies only to high incomes.

The passage below illustrates some of the ambiguities and absurdities that can arise when hyphens are wrongly omitted.

The long suffering, rain soaked spectators had hoped for an action packed game but the Vitesse Bordeaux Cracow Solidarnoz final was a low scoring match with too much time wasting.

Bordeaux supporters were finally rewarded by a last minute goal by Claude Montereau. The twenty two year old striker took an inch perfect pass from the mud spattered Eddy Tissac, the hard working mid field player. Montereau's fiercely driven shot went head high past the goalkeeper.

Swiss born Jean Paul Chambery, the Vitesse manager, was

delighted. His pre match plan and his well chosen words at half time had brought about the breakthrough and the long awaited victory.

And here is the passage with the hyphens added:

The long-suffering, rain-soaked spectators had hoped for an action-packed game but the Vitesse Bordeaux-Cracow Solidarnoz final was a low-scoring match with too much time-wasting.

Bordeaux supporters were finally rewarded by a last-minute goal by Claude Montereau. The twenty-two-year-old striker took an inch-perfect pass from the mud-spattered Eddy Tissac, the hard-working mid-field player. Montereau's fiercely driven shot went head-high past the goalkeeper.

Swiss-born Jean-Paul Chambery, the Vitesse manager, was delighted. His pre-match plan and his well-chosen words at half-time had brought about the breakthrough and the long-awaited victory.

The combinations of adverb and verb in *finally rewarded* and *fiercely driven* are not hyphenated.

Hyphens and Word Division

The second function of the hyphen is to indicate that a word has been broken at the end of a line of text. The break is simply for the purpose of line spacing or typesetting; the word remains a single word. Problems of word division seldom arise in hand-written manuscripts because the writer normally takes the word over into the next line, but for writers who use word processors and wish to justify their texts by having vertical margins on the right as well as the left side of pages, the following guidelines can be applied.

Words of one syllable should not be hyphenated because the result would be absurd. Some printers and publishers prohibit the hyphenating of proper nouns such as personal names, partly out of respect for the name and partly to avoid even the minor confusion of *Arm-/our, Boy-/den, Long-/man, Man-/sell*.

When a word of two or more syllables is broken at the end of a line, the break should come between one syllable and another. When one or more syllables is a prefix or a suffix the break is clear. For example, the two-syllable word *freedom* would be broken as *free-/dom*, and the three-syllable word *disgraceful* as *dis-/graceful* or *disgrace-/ful*. When the syllables are less obvious, the breaks should be determined by the pronunciations and the meanings of the words; for example, *com-/plicate, illus-/trate*.

The words *com-/plicate* and *illus-/trate* follow the convention established and still observed by most printers and publishers that the break should normally be made after a vowel and before a consonant, except where the result is awkward, ambiguous or absurd; for example, *parti-/ciple, criti-/cism* and *pri-/mary*, but *dis-/connect*, not *disco-/nnect*, and *minis-/ter*, not *mini-/ster*.

Another convention is that when a verb doubles its final consonant to form the present participle, as in *appal/appalling, drop/dropping, grovel/grovelling, run/running*, the hyphen is placed between the two consonants: *appal-/ling, drop-/ping, grovel-/ling, run-/ning*. But when the root word already ends in a double consonant, the break comes after the double consonant: *add-/ing, bless-/ing, dwell-/ing, purr-/ing, sniff-/ing*.

THE DASH

The dash is one of the punctuation marks that make the reader consciously aware of the structure and content of the sentence in which they appear. The dash breaks the general stylistic rule that punctuation should be unobtrusive in shaping the meaning and the rhythm of a piece of prose. Instead, the dash interrupts sentences in such a dramatic way that it invites the reader's attention, and because the attentive reader is likely to be more discerning, the writer must use the dash with particular care.

One of the three functions of the dash is similar to the parenthetical function of brackets and commas: to mark off a piece of additional, supplementary information. Dashes do this best when the additional information creates a shift in the narrative focus of the sentence. In a normally structured sentence such as:

> Radio Norgate, the independent local station that began to broadcast only last month, repeated the storm and flood warning in hourly news bulletins throughout the night.

the parenthetical statement, *the independent local station that began to broadcast only last month*, is correctly punctuated with commas. But when the sentence is restructured:

> Radio Norgate – the independent local station began to broadcast only last month – repeated the storm and flood warning in hourly news bulletins throughout the night.

the abruptness of the parenthetical statement justifies the use of dashes. The information inside the dashes often forms a sentence within a sentence, as it does in the second example.

Consider another example. The parenthetical statement in this sentence is correctly punctuated with commas:

> Tenants in sheltered housing in the Seagate area of the city, an unsuitable site for the elderly and infirm, had to be evacuated at midnight.

But when the sentence is restructured:

> Tenants in sheltered housing in the Seagate area of the city – Why was such an unsuitable site chosen for the elderly and infirm? – had to be evacuated at midnight.

the abruptness of the parenthesis, which is now a sentence asking a question within a longer sentence, justifies the dashes.

A second use of the dash, this time as a single punctuation mark, is to introduce a mildly dramatic or ironic pause in order to indicate a change of direction or tone in a sentence:

> City councillors held an emergency meeting and agreed to build new flood barriers – when funds allowed.

The drama can take the form of anticlimax:

> On the morning after the storm Mr Leonard Vedley found his new yacht – in the marina car park.

The third function of the dash is to separate a list or catalogue of items from the words that follow. A colon, as we saw, introduces a list; a dash concludes it.

> Yachts, cabin cruiser, sailing dinghies, power boats, lobster boats – dozens of craft were torn from their moorings in the marina.

> Seagate, Port Street, Fisherman's Row, Marina Parade, Vedley Close – all were flooded at the height of the storm.

These are the only contexts that justify the use of the dash, and even in these contexts the dash will seem contrived and disruptive unless it is used sparingly. When the dash is wrongly used it quickly reduces a passage of continuous prose to a series of rough jottings that read like preliminary notes rather than a finished piece of writing:

> Radio Norgate repeated the storm warning – every hour throughout the night. At the height of the storm – around midnight – fifteen-

foot waves struck Cradle Bay Marina – and the neighbouring streets. Grantown Fire Brigade – and the police – evacuated elderly tenants, some of whom were dressed for the storm – others wore only their nightclothes.

BRACKETS

Round and square brackets are forms of parenthesis, which means a placing beside. Some parenthetical statements – asides, interjections, opinions, sudden recollections, an abrupt departure from and return to a train of thought – can be enclosed in round brackets or punctuated by commas or dashes, as we saw in previous sections. Round brackets and square brackets are used to enclose a piece of information in order to show that the nature of the enclosed information is different from the surrounding material. Both sets of brackets, round and square, indicate that the writer is making a change in narrative focus.

Round brackets mark off information that is not an essential part of the main text but is closely related or supplementary. The information enclosed by round brackets can be anything from a single word to several sentences. In journalism, for example, round brackets are used to indicate a person's age:

> Rose de Silva (37), the novelist and critic, was killed in a climbing accident in the Scottish Highlands yesterday.

They are widely used in literary and historical studies to state a person's year of birth and death:

> W.H. Auden (1907–73) and Louis MacNeice (1907–63) are joint authors of *Letters from Iceland*.

When the bracketed information forms only part of a sentence, the full stop at the end of the sentence should be outside the closing bracket:

> Brackets indicate that the writer is making a change in narrative focus (see Narrative Viewpoint in Chapter 6).

When the bracketed information forms a complete sentence or more than one sentence the full stop should be inside the closing bracket:

> One of the first poems Auden wrote after emigrating to the United States in 1939 was 'In Memory of W.B. Yeats'. (MacNeice, who remained in Britain, published a critical study of Yeats in 1941, the

year MacNeice joined the BBC as a drama producer.) Auden's elegy marks the end of an era as well as the end of a great writer's life.

Square brackets indicate a greater and more specific shift in narrative focus. They should be used only to mark an addition to, or a comment on, an author's original text. For example, the editor of someone's notebooks or diaries would indicate his, the editor's, comments like this:

> I have decided to accept E.P.'s [Edwin Palfrey's] challenge to a race across three Scottish peaks. We have agreed to set off from the MacGregor Arms inn at seven tomorrow morning. [These are the last words Rose de Silva wrote before her death.]

One of the commonest uses of square brackets is around the Latin word *sic*, which means such or so, and indicates that the word or words immediately before [*sic*] may seem unusual or even wrong but are the words actually used by the writer who is being quoted:

> A red boy [*sic*] marked the site of the wreck.

> John Ireland (1879–1962) was a thoroughly English [*sic*] composer.

Brackets, especially square brackets, must be used sparingly because too many shifts in the narrative focus of a piece of prose, as well as the physical marks – ( ) and [ ] – on the page, create a fragmented, faltering effect. For the same reasons of style and concern for your reader you should try to avoid using brackets within brackets because it can produce an effect like the multiple embedding of clauses. The following passage develops the Auden–MacNeice theme, but here the subject is the poetry of W.H. Auden and occasional references are made to Auden's contemporaries.

> One of the first poems Auden wrote after emigrating to the United States (with Christopher Isherwood (1904–86) the novelist) in 1939 was 'In Memory of W.B. Yeats' (first published in the *London Mercury* in April 1939). MacNeice, who remained in Britain, published a critical study of Yeats in 1941, the year MacNeice joined the BBC as a drama producer. MacNeice's own radio plays (see *The Dark Tower*, 1947) attracted critical acclaim. Auden's elegy on Yeats marks the end of an era as well as the end of a great writer's life.

The passage reads like a parody of an academic style of writing, but by reducing the use of brackets and integrating the information into continuous prose a more fluent style and a more intelligible statement is achieved.

One of the first poems Auden wrote after emigrating to the United States in 1939 with the novelist Christopher Isherwood (1904–86) was 'In Memory of W.B. Yeats', which was first published in the *London Mercury* in April 1939. MacNeice remained in Britain and published a critical study of Yeats in 1941, the year MacNeice took up the post of drama producer with the BBC, where his own radio plays, published as *The Dark Tower* in 1947, attracted critical acclaim. Auden's elegy marks the end of an era as well as the end of a great writer's life.

THE ELLIPSIS

The word *ellipsis*, which is derived from Greek, means leave out, and the main function of the ellipsis is to indicate a missing word or words in a sentence or paragraph.

An ellipsis can indicate that a spoken statement is left unfinished by the speaker, whose words simply tail away:

'The road to Kiln Acres,' he repeated. 'It's . . . Well . . . I mean . . .'

A slight variation on this function uses the ellipsis to indicate hesitations in a person's speech rather than missing words:

He said the Kiln Acres issue was . . . difficult. He needed time . . . to think.

Writers of fiction should not need to explain which function, to indicate missing words or to indicate hesitation, their ellipses serve; in a novel or short story the function should be self-explanatory, and the author's intervention could disrupt the narrative flow. But in non-fiction the writer should tell the reader exactly how the ellipsis is being used:

'The road to Kiln Acres,' he repeated. 'It's . . . Well . . . I mean . . .' His words tailed away.

He said the Kiln Acres issue was . . . difficult. He needed time . . . He paused again. Time, he said, to think.

Readers may need an explanation of how the ellipsis is being used because there is another variation on the use of the ellipsis: to show that a spoken or written statement has been edited down to an abridged version of the original. When it is used in this way to indicate a substantial omission, the ellipsis should be placed at the end of a sentence or paragraph, not at the beginning:

> Sarah Harding, Secretary of Kiln Acres Action Group, said that the
> area was no longer a derelict site. There had been natural regenera-
> tion in the three years since the brickworks had been demolished and
> the rubble cleared . . .
>
> Kiln Acres, Ms Harding continued, was now a habitat for plants
> and creatures found nowhere else in the area. Two varieties of wild
> orchid grew there, fritillary and hairstreak butterflies had returned,
> and pipistrelle bats had begun to colonize the old ash trees.

The ellipsis can be typeset in different ways, but writers must be
consistent in the way they use it. It can be treated as a word, and
a space can be inserted before and after the ellipsis, as in the four
short examples above. Or it can be typeset as if it were a letter of
a word, with no space before or after:

> Well. . . I mean. . .

When the ellipsis appears at the end of a sentence it can be treated
as a complete end-punctuation mark, as in all the examples above.
Alternatively, a full stop can be added, with a space between the
ellipsis and the full stop: . . . .

CAPITALS

The use of capital, or upper case, letters involves a different set of
principles.

Capitals must be used for the first letter of the first word in a
sentence. As we saw in the section on the use of inverted commas,
capitals must also be used for the first letter of the first word quoted
in direct speech, unless the quotation is merely a word or a phrase.
For example, this quotation must open with a capital letter:

> Derek Bly said, 'My brother was astonished when he passed his
> driving test at the first attempt.'

But a capital letter is not needed when the quotation is as brief as
this:

> Derek Bly said his brother was 'astonished' when he passed his
> driving test at the first attempt.

The section on nouns showed that capitals must be used for proper
nouns. For example, capitals are used for personal names and for
the particular office held by a named person:

> Maria Riesgal, Director of the National Youth Orchestra

Jean-Paul Chambery, Manager of Vitesse Bordeaux Football Club.

As these examples show, capitals must also be used for the names of specific organizations. Once the organization's name has been given in full and with initial capital letters, a reduced form of the name can be used without capital letters:

Maria Riesgal is Director of the National Youth Orchestra. The orchestra will tour Australia and New Zealand next year.

Specifically named geographical features are also proper nouns, and capitals must be used for all continents and countries, counties and cities, lakes and rivers, mountains and valleys:

Antarctica, Shropshire, New York, Ben Nevis.

Here again, once the feature has been named in capitals, it can be referred to as the *continent*, the *county*, the *city* or the *mountain*, in small, or lower case, letters.

Two more groups of proper nouns are days of the week and months of the year:

the first Monday in October, every Saturday in August.

Seasons of the year are spelled as common nouns, without initial capitals:

spring, summer, autumn, winter.

Most abbreviations are spelled with capitals. This applies to organizations:

AA, BBC, NATO, UNESCO, YMCA

to terms of address, degrees or distinctions:

BSc, Dr, FRC, MP, OBE, VC

to chemical elements and compounds:

Al, C, H, O, H_2O, TNT, $ZnCO_3$

and to some acronyms, that is, words made from the initial letters of the full names:

AIDS, NAAFI, NATO, UFO, VAT.

Other acronyms have been assimilated into standard English as common nouns and are spelled in lower case letters:

radar (radio detection and ranging), laser (light amplification by stimulated emission of radiation), scuba (self-contained underwater breathing apparatus), sonar (sound navigation and ranging).

Abbreviations for weights and measures are normally spelled with lower case letters:

m, cm, mm, km, ft, sq yds.

HOUSE STYLE

House style is the term used for the guidelines drawn up by a company or organization to standardize those aspects of English usage that can be written and presented in different ways. A seemingly simple matter like a date, for example, has eight variations when the month and the year are written in full:

24 June 1999; 24 June, 1999; 24th June 1999; 24th June, 1999; June 24 1999; June 24, 1999; June 24th 1999; June 24th, 1999

and another variation when the month is given as a number and the year abbreviated to the last two digits, as in *24.6.99*. In the United States the preferred style is to have the month first – *6.24.99*.

Similarly, a person's name can take several forms:

Miss Francesca Prasana; Ms Francesca Prasana, Miss Fran Prasana, Ms Fran Prasana, Francesca Prasana, Fran Prasana, Miss F Prasana, Ms F Prasana

with additional variations if a full stop is placed after the abbreviations *Ms* and *F*.

Publishers of books, magazines and newspapers produce written sets of rules, known as style books, that specify the publishers' preferred usage. The purpose of the style book is to change variable factors into constant factors to achieve uniformity of usage by the various editors in a publishing house or the reporters on a newspaper, and consistency of usage by each individual writer. Through uniformity and consistency the writer can bring clarity to areas that would otherwise be confusing for employees of the publishing house and for the reader.

The need for consistency is not confined to publishers and large organizations. Each piece of writing, whether it is a letter, essay or report, must be internally consistent in terms of hyphenation, capitalization and punctuation. The aim of house style, clarity, should be the aim of every writer.

With or without the full stop, some abbreviations can be ambiguous: *St* is both Saint and Street, *Dr* both Doctor and Drive, and the capital letter *C* means one hundred, century, Celsius, centigrade, the musical key-note and the element carbon. The meaning of an abbreviation is normally clarified by the context in which the abbreviation appears, but if you are in doubt you should write the words in full.

3 Spelling

Spellings were fixed or standardized by the time Samuel Johnson published his *Dictionary of the English Language* in 1755, and the spellings of almost all the words that have entered the English language since then are also fixed. There are exceptions. Some foreign words that have not been fully anglicized still have variant spellings: *amuck, amock, amok; guerilla, guerrilla; harem, hareem, harim; orang-utan, orang–utang, orang-outang; veranda, verandah*. A few long-established words also break the pattern by having variant spellings: *acknowledgement, acknowledgment; connection, connexion; enquire, inquire; inflection, inflexion; jeweler, jeweller, jewelry, jewellery; judgement, judgment*. There are also the variants, such as: *burned, burnt; dreamed, dreamt; spelled, spelt; mis-spelled, mis-spelt, misspelled* and *misspelt*.

But these exceptions form only a tiny minority of the vast lexicon of English words. A result of such firmly standardized spelling is that errors are more easily identified than deviations from almost any of the other standards that make up written standard English. Readers may be uncertain about the standards that apply in grammar, semantics, syntax and punctuation, but many will spot a spelling error instantly, and anyone can check a spelling by looking up the word in a dictionary.

Words and the correct spellings of words are the common property of all literate persons, readers as well as writers. Because of this, and because spelling errors are avoidable, they attract more censure than deviations from other standard features of English. A few spelling errors in any piece of writing – an essay, a newspaper article, a local government report – will undermine the authority of the writing, the writer and the organization the writer represents. If the reader's spelling ability is better than the writer's, the reader is not only entitled to question the writer's authority in a particular piece of writing but to question the writer's fitness to practise at all.

The fact that the English language has more words than any other language is a source of variety and strength. At the same time, the very size of the English lexicon means that no one can memorize the spelling of every word. This is a problem only for those writers who do not use dictionaries. Several publishers produce reliable, inexpensive dictionaries, including spelling dictionaries, which give the various forms of words: irregular forms of plural nouns, adjectives derived from nouns, and the present and past participle forms of verbs as well as the base forms. A spelling dictionary soon confirms that English spelling is based on a variety of principles and sometimes on none.

Old English, the Germanic language spoken by the Anglo-Saxons, was a phonetic language in the sense that each letter of the alphabet symbolized a sound. Because all letters were sounded and none was silent, there was a direct correspondence between the written and the spoken word, but as Old English began to assimilate words from other languages – at first, a few words from Latin, a few more from the Old Norse of the Vikings and then, after the Norman invasion of 1066, hundreds of words from Old French – the phonetic links between speech and writing began to break down.

When English emerged as the national language of England in 1362, it had assimilated so many French words that it was no longer a Germanic language. The process of assimilation continued until the words originating in Old English were greatly outnumbered by words that were borrowed or derived from French, Latin and Greek.

Most of the loan words have been fully anglicized in spelling and pronunciation, but the process has been inconsistent, and the non-English origins of some words are still detectable. The inconsistency can be illustrated by considering a few words borrowed from, or modelled on, French.

The pronunciation of the noun suffix *-ment*, originally from French, has been fully anglicized in hundreds of English nouns – for example, *announcement*, *employment*, *government* – but the word *denouement* retains its French pronunciation.

Another French suffix, *-age*, has been fully anglicized in *baggage* and *carriage*, largely but not finally anglicized in *garage*, but remains obviously French in *camouflage*, *dressage*, *entourage*, *massage* and *sabotage*. The pronunciation of a third French suffix, *-ette*, as in *brunette*, *cassette*, *etiquette* and *silhouette*, has been anglicized as *-et*, but the spelling remains recognizably French, or at least not English.

133

Modern English continues to borrow from other languages. From French we have adopted *au pair*, *discothèque*, *piste* and *quiche*; from German: *delicatessen*, *diktat*, *gestalt* and the military terms *blitz*, an abbreviation of *blitzkrieg*, and the acronyms *flak* (*Fliegerabwehrkanone*, pilot defence-gun) and *Gestapo* (*Geheime Staatspolizei*, Secret State-police); and from Japanese: *bonsai*, *karate*, *kung fu* and *origami*. Japan's economic influence has drawn some attention to Japanese culture and language. *Glasnost* and *perestroika*, two Russian words widely used in English in the late 1980s and early 1990s, seem to have been temporary borrowings and have not been assimilated.

The English language also continues to derive new scientific, medical and technical words from Latin and Greek: *cryogenics*, *cybernetics*, *microsurgery*, *nanometrics*, *quadriplegia* and *tomography*. Scientific word formation has been a highly organized process ever since the Swedish scientist Carl Linnaeus invented the Latin binomial ('double name') nomenclature system of classifying plants and animals in the eighteenth century. Today the language of science, or rather, the languages of sciences, are international and exist almost independently of standard English.

While the borrowings and derivations continue, English spelling will remain inconsistent, sometimes anglicizing a word fully, sometimes partly and sometimes not at all. One visible effect of this is that the spellings of more and more words are divorced from their pronunciations. A phonetic writing system can be decoded by 'sounding out' the characters, but a purely phonetic system cannot possibly cope with *cue*, *queue* and *Kew*; with *main*, *Maine* and *mane*; or with the *ough* sounds of *bough*, *cough*, *dough*, *hiccough*, *lough* (the Irish equivalent of the Scots *loch*), *thorough* and *through*.

Our adoption of words from different languages at different historical periods explains another feature of English spelling. The language has hundreds of homophones, words that sound similar but are spelled differently and have different meanings, for example, *palate*, *pallet* and *palette*. *Palate* entered Middle English from Latin *palatum*; *pallet* emerged in late Middle English from the Anglo-French word *paillete*, meaning straw; *palette* existed in Old French but did not enter English until the 1620s.

There are other reasons for the discrepancy between spelling and pronunciation. The English alphabet has twenty-six characters, each of which represents a sound, but these twenty-six characters cannot represent all the sounds that a single person makes in speaking the language; and the alphabet cannot represent all the sounds of all the words in the English lexicon with consistency and clarity.

English pronunciation, unlike spelling, has never been standardized but varies according to region and time. Even the form of spoken English known variously as received pronunciation, the Queen's or King's English, Oxford English and BBC English is not fully standardized but varies from one social or professional group to another and from one generation to another. The received pronunciation of a formally trained actor differs from that of a member of the Royal family; and the received pronunciation of a younger generation of actors differs from that of an older generation, as you can clearly detect from the soundtracks of British films from different periods.

Pronunciation is, in fact, infinitely variable. Every person has a uniquely distinctive voice, a range of sounds that form a phonetic pattern as intricately individual as the visual pattern of human fingerprints. English spelling is a compromise between the simplicity of the twenty-six-character alphabet and, on the other hand, the vastness of the English lexicon and the infinite variety of speech.

SPELLING PATTERNS

Despite the inconsistencies of English spelling, several clear patterns exist. One pattern is that the plurals of nouns ending in a consonant and the letter *y* are formed by dropping the *y* and adding *ies*:

> charity/charities, rarity/rarities, biography/biographies, choreography/choreographies.

If the singular form of the noun ends with a vowel and the letter *y*, the plural is formed simply by adding the letter *s*:

> holiday/holidays, stowaway/stowaways, jockey/jockeys, turkey/turkeys, convoy/convoys, newsboy/newsboys.

A common, easily memorized rule for the long *e* sound written as *ie* is: *i* before *e* except after *c*, and a simple mnemonic for this is *a piece of pie*. Words spelled with *ie* include:

> achieve, belief/believe, chief, grief/grieve, hygiene/hygienic, piece, pier, pierce, retrieve, siege, thief.

Immediately after the letter *c*, the long *e* is spelled *ei*:

> conceit, conceive, deceit/deceive, receipt/receive.

Exceptions to the *ie* rule are *seize* and *weird*.

Another guideline involving the letter *e* is this: when the *e* is silent at the end of the word and the word is extended by adding a suffix that begins with a vowel, the silent *e* is dropped. Thus:

> ache/aching, shake/shaking, adore/adorable, endure/endurable, nerve/nervous, serve/service.

But when the suffix begins with a consonant, the silent *e* at the end of the word is retained:

> boredom, wholesome, looseness, useless, astutely, stately, pavement, basement, tasteful, wasteful.

No spelling rule is absolute, and so once again there are exceptions. If the *e* at the end of the word marks a soft *c* or *g*, then the *e* is retained even when the suffix begins with a vowel:

> manageable, noticeable, courageous, outrageous.

The small group of verbs ending in *-inge* observe two different patterns in forming the present participle. *Singe* and *swinge* retain the *e* so that they can be distinguished from *sing* and *swing*:

> singe/singeing, sing/singing, swinge/swingeing, swing/swinging

but the other '-inge' verbs drop the *e* in the present participle:

> cringe/cringing, impinge/impinging, infringe/infringing, tinge/tinging.

Some rules apply to words ending with consonants. When the word is a monosyllable ending with a single vowel and a single consonant, the single consonant is normally doubled if the suffix begins with a vowel:

> dam/damming, dim/dimming, slam/slamming, slim/slimming, sad/sadder, plod/plodder, grit/gritty, wit/witty.

Similarly, if the word is two or more syllables and ends in a single vowel and a single consonant, and if the stress or accent is on the last syllable of the word, the single consonant is doubled if the suffix begins with a vowel. The rule sounds complicated but the reality is clear:

> abhor/abhorred/abhorrence, occur/occurred/occurrence, commit/committed/committal, rebut/rebutted/rebuttal, distil/distilled,

compel/compelled,   instal/install/installed,   forget/forgettable, regret/regrettable.

Partial exceptions are the verbs *confer*, *infer*, *inter* and *refer*. They follow the standard pattern by doubling the letter *r* for the present and past participles:

conferring/conferred, inferring/inferred, interring/interred, referring/referred

but the nouns have only a single *r*:

conference, inference, interment, reference.

With the consonant *l*, if the word ends with a single vowel and a single *l*, and if the suffix begins with a vowel, the *l* is doubled:

criminal/criminally,   national/nationally,   snivel/snivelling/ snivelled, swivel/swivelling/swivelled, patrol/patrolling/patrolled, pencil/pencilling/pencilled, council/councillor, counsel/counsellor.

A similar guideline is that adjectives ending in *-ial* double the *l* when the word takes the adverbial form:

artificial/artificially, judicial/judicially.

Here again the pattern is a guide rather than an absolute rule, and there are several exceptions. Adjectives ending in a single *l* which take the noun forms *-ism* and *-ity* keep the single *l*:

cannibal/cannibalism, symbol/symbolism, national/nationalism/ nationality, sentimental/sentimentality.

A large sub-class of words that are frequently mis-spelled are the adjectives ending in *-ful*. The single adjective *full* is spelled with a double *l*, but adjectives that have *-ful* as their suffix end with a single *l*; the associated *-ly* adverbs have a double *l*:

artful/artfully, hurtful/hurtfully.

The two *-ful* adjectives, *skilful* and *wilful*, need special attention. The nouns *skill* and *will* are spelled with a double *l*, but the double *l* becomes single in the adjectives *skilful* and *wilful*. The single *l* of the adjective ending in *-ful* becomes a double *l* in the *-ly* adverbs *skilfully* and *wilfully*:

skill/skilled/skilful/skilfully, will/willed/wilful/wilfully.

The spelling of the verb *fulfil* should also be noted. The base form of the verb is *fulfil* but the present and past participles are spelled *fulfilling* and *fulfilled*; the noun is *fulfilment*.

The small sub-class of abstract nouns ending in -*our* sometimes cause confusion because the -*our* is reduced to *or* followed by -*ous* in the corresponding adjective:

> amour/amorous, clamour/clamorous, humour/humorous, labour/ laborious, odour/odorous, rancour/rancorous, rigour/rigorous, valour/valorous, vigour/vigorous.

Laborious breaks the pattern by having the additional letter *i*.

Another group of nouns that can cause confusion are those that end in -*ice*, which changes to -*ise* in the corresponding verb:

> advice/advise, device/devise, practice/practise;

similarly:

> choice/choose, licence/license, prophecy/prophesy.

Some of the words that are most often mis-spelled are listed below.

abscess	analysis	benefited
abysmal	annihilate	benefiting
accessible	anonymous	besiege
accommodate	antibiotic	bigot
acknowledge	appal	bigoted
acoustic	appalling	bourgeois
acquaintance	apparent	boutique
acquire	Arctic	braille
acquisition	argument	breathalyser
acquit	ascend	brief
acquittal	asphyxiate	brochure
address	assassinate	Buddhist
adolescent	assessment	bulletin
advertisement	assignment	buoy/buoyant
aggravate	attendant	bureaucracy
aggressive		business
alignment	balloon	by-election
allege	banana	bypass
a lot (many)	bankruptcy	
allot (distribute)	beautiful	caffeine
allotted	beginning	calculator
allotment	behaviour	calendar
all right	believe	calibre
already	beneficial	calorie
analyse	benefit	campaign

cannabis
carbohydrate
carburettor/carburetter
cassette
casualty
ceiling
census
changeable
character
chauffeur
chief
chrysanthemum
clientele
colleague
committee
commuter
comparative
complementary
complimentary
concealment
conceit
condemn
conscience
conscientious
conscious
consensus
consignment
coolly
coronary
correspondence
courageous
cynic

deceive
decipher
definite
dehydrate
delicatessen
descendant
develop
dialogue

diarrhoea
discipline
discreet
discrete
disguise
dissatisfied
dissuade
draft
draught
drought
dynasty

earnest
eccentric
ecstasy
effervescent
efficient
eighth
eightieth
eligible
embarrass
encyclopedia/
   enclyclopaedia
enrol
envelop (verb)
envelope (noun)
equip
equipped
escalator
espionage
exaggerate
excel
excellent
excite
exercise
exhilarate
existence
expansive
expensive

Fahrenheit

faithful
faithfully
fascinate
fatal
fatally
fatality
fatigue
favourite
February
ferocious
feud
fibre
fibreglass
fiery
flammable
fluorescent
foyer
freight
frequent
fulfil
fulfilled

gardener
garrulous
gauge
ghetto
gimmick
glamorous
glamour
gnarled
goodbye
gorilla
guerrilla/guerilla
gossip
gossiping
gouge
government
graffiti
grammar
grief
grotesque

gruesome
* guarantee
guardian

* haemorrhage
hallucination
hallucinogen
harass
harassment
haulage
* havoc
hazardous
height
hemisphere
heroin
heroine
hierarchy
hi-fi
hijack
hilarious
hindrance
holocaust
honorary
honour
humorist
humorous
humour
* hygiene
hypnotist
* hypocrisy
* hypocrite
hypodermic
hysterical

icecream
icicle
idiosyncrasy
idyllic
illegible
illicit
imitate

impasse
impetuous
impetus
imprisonment
inaccessible
inaccurate
incognito
incommunicado
inconceivable
incredible
incredulous
independent
indictment
ineligible
inexhaustible
innocent
inoculate

jeopardy
juggernaut

kaleidoscope
kidnap
kidnapped

lacquer
lager
launderette
ledger
legionnaire's disease
leukaemia/leukemia
liaise
liaison
libel
libellous
licence (noun)
license (verb)
licensee
loose (adjective)
loosen (verb)
loosened

lose (verb)

malign
manageable
manoeuvre
marijuana
marvel
marvellous
mayonnaise
medieval/mediaeval
meteorology
meter (noun, e.g.,
    water meter)
meter (verb, to
    measure)
metre (rhythm;
    39.37 inches)
midday
migraine
millionaire
mimic
mimicked
mimicry
minuscule
miscellaneous
mischief
misdemeanour
model
modelled
monetary
mortgage
motorcycle/motor
    cycle
moustache
mystify

negligible
ninetieth
noticeable

obsession

occasion

occasionally

occur

occurred

occurrence

omit

omitted

ophthalmic

opportunity

orthopaedic

oscillate

oscilloscope

outrageous

overdraft

overrate

overreach

overrun

panacea

panic/panicked

paralysis

parliament

pasteurize

pastime

patrol

patrolled

peaceable

pedal (a bicycle)

peddle (drugs)

penicillin

perceive

permit

permitted

personal

personnel

physiology

physiotherapist

picnic

picnicked

plaintiff (noun)

plaintive (adj)

pneumatic

pneumonia

poltergeist

polythene

possess

practice (noun)

practise (verb)

precede

precedent

predecessor

prejudice

prerogative

privilege

profession

propaganda

prophecy (noun)

prophesy (verb)

protein

pseudo

psychiatry

psychology

quarrel

quarrelled

queue

queued

rabbi

rabbis (plural)

rabies

racial

racially

racketeer

radios (plural)

ransack

rebel

rebelled

rebellious

receipt

receive

recipe

reconnaissance

reconnoitre

recur

recurrence

refer

reference

referred

refuel

refuelled

regret

regrettable

regretted

rehearsal

rehearse

relief

reminisce

rendezvous

repentance

repertoire

repetitive

reprieve

reservoir

restaurant

resuscitate

retrieve

rhyme

rhythm

ricochet

rigorous

rigour

risotto

rissole

rivet

riveted

rocket

rocketed

sabotage

saccharine

sacrilege

sacrilegious

sadden
safeguard
satellite
schizophrenia
seismic
seize
separate
separation
serviceable
sheikh
sheriff
shield
shriek
shy/shyer/shyest
shyly
siege
sieve
skilful
skilfully
slay
sleigh
sleight-of-hand
sleuth
slyly
sombre
spaghetti
squalor
staccato
stiletto
stilettos
straight
strait
strait-jacket
strait-laced
stupor
subterranean
successful
suddenness
superannuation
superintendent
supersede

surveillance
susceptible
symmetrical
synchronize
syndicate
synonym
synthetic
syringe

taboo
tariff
tattoo
taxi
taxiing
technology
teetotaller
televise
temperature
tenancy
tenant
terrestrial
therapeutic
therefore
thief
thinness
thorough
threshold
throughout
tobacco
total
totally
traffic
trafficked
tranquil
tranquillizer
tranquilly
transcend
transmit
transmitter
transparent
traumatic

treacherous
trek
trekking
tremor
trespass
trousers
trousseau
turquoise
tycoon
tyranny
tyrant

unconscious
underdeveloped
underprivileged
underrate
unduly
unequal
unequalled
unforgettable
unfortunately
uninterrupted
unnecessary

vaccinate
vacuum
variegated
vegetarian
veil
vein
vendetta
veneer
vengeance
veto
vetoed
vicious
vigorous
vigour
virus
viruses
voluntary

wagged
waive
wave
wallop
walloped
warrant
weird
welcome
welfare
whereabouts
wherewithal
whole

wholly
wield
withhold
wonderful
wondrous
woollen
wreak
wreath (noun)
wreathe (verb)
writhe
wrought-iron

X-ray

yacht
yield
yogurt/yoghourt

zealous
zigzag
zigzagged
Zionism
zoology

4 Vocabulary

Readers of this book are likely to have a personal vocabulary of from 100,000 to 150,000 words, including variants of the same word, for example, *walking* and *walked* as variants of the word *walk*. Your vocabulary is sometimes known as your personal lexicon, that is, your personal store of words, or as your idiolect, that is, your uniquely individual store and use of language.

LANGUAGE CHANGE

All living languages evolve, and some of the most obvious changes in the English language in its continuous process of evolution are in the vocabulary. In his *Dictionary of the English Language*, published in 1755, Samuel Johnson gave these definitions:

> *to hack*: To hackney; to turn hackney or prostitute
>
> *jogger*: One who moves heavily and dully
>
> *mouse*: The smallest of all beasts; a little animal haunting houses and corn fields, destroyed by cats

Modern dictionaries state that *to hack* also means to gain unofficial access to a computer file; that a *jogger* is a person who runs for pleasure or for fitness; that one meaning of *mouse* is a device that complements or overrides the keyboard of a computer. The addition of a new meaning to an existing word can be defined as re-designation.

Johnson also gave these definitions:

> *micher*: A lazy loiterer, who skulks about in corners and by-places, and keeps out of sight; a hedge-creeper
>
> *woundy*: Excessive. A low bad word

These two words appear in some modern dictionaries but *micher* is noted as a dialect, that is, a non-standard, word, and *woundy* as obsolete and archaic. Johnson probably described *woundy* as *A low bad word* because it is a contraction of the blasphemy, *By Christ's wounds*.

Some words disappear from current speech and writing while other words are re-designated to carry new meanings. But society changes at such a pace that re-designation alone is not enough to deal with all the new discoveries, ideas and customs. New words are needed. The section on hyphens in Chapter 2 showed that new words can be formed by hyphenating two or more existing words. This section considers some of the other ways in which new words enter the English language.

FOREIGN WORDS IN ENGLISH

Most of the words we now use were adopted or derived from foreign languages. Words that are adopted directly into English, with little or no change in the forms of the words, are sometimes known as borrowings or loan words, which are odd terms since the words will not be returned to the original languages; indeed, most of the words have been anglicized to the extent that they no longer seem foreign.

English borrowed foreign words for various reasons. Sometimes the foreign word signified an object, or a concept, that did not exist in English, like the Latin words:

font, pope, school, street, wine

that the Anglo-Saxons adopted. Some words entered the language as a result of cultural contact and exchange, like that of the Anglo-Saxons and the Vikings from around the year 900 when the two peoples began to live in peace in England. Norse nouns that entered the English language from that period include:

dunt, fellow, law, leg, skin, skull.

Many of the French words that entered English after 1066 were imposed on the English language as part of the process of linguistic and cultural imperialism that followed the military imperialism. French words from this period include:

loyal, royal, voyage, baptism, glory, saviour, mercy, victory.

Most of the foreign words in English, or words that were once foreign, are borrowed or derived, that is adapted, from French, Latin and Greek and have been so completely assimilated into English that their non-English origins are usually forgotten, but from non-European languages we have adopted many words that still look and sound foreign. British imperialism imposed the

English language on large parts of the world, and in the post-imperial age the process continues through British and American commerce, the printed word, the communications and entertainment industries, and tourism. In this centuries-long process the English language in turn has adopted words from the indigenous languages.

From native Americans we borrowed:

> moose, racoon, skunk, squaw, tomahawk, wigwam;

from Arabic:

> almanac, arsenal, assassin, calibre, harem/hareem/harim, hashish, nadir, zenith, zero;

from Hindi:

> bungalow, dinghy, dungarees, juggernaut, pyjamas, veranda/verandah;

from Persian:

> azure, bazaar, caravan, shawl, tulip, turban;

from Chinese:

> kowtow/kotow, tea, ketchup, mah-jong/mah-jongg;

from Aboriginal Australian:

> boomerang, budgerigar, didgeridoo, kangaroo, kookaburra;

and from Malay:

> amuck/amock/amok, kapok, orang-utan/utang/outang, sago, sarong.

A person's wardrobe could be made up of loan words. The French language gives us:

> beret, blouson, cagoul/cagoule, cravatte/cravat, culottes, pants (from pantalon).

Inuit, or Eskimo, languages give us *anorak* and *parka*; German gives *dirndl*; Flemish *duffel/duffle*; Japanese *kimono*; and, as we saw above, Hindi gives *dungarees* and *pyjamas*, and Malay *sarong*.

Plural Forms of Foreign Nouns

The plural forms of some foreign nouns present some interesting inconsistencies. The fact that there are alternative spellings for some foreign words:

harem/hareem/harim, orang-utan/orang-utang/outang

shows that these words have not yet been fully anglicized, but even when words seem to be firmly established in English there can still be uncertainty about the spellings of the plural forms.

Some words borrowed from Latin have a singular form ending in -*um* and a plural form ending in -*a*:

addendum/addenda, erratum/errata, memorandum/memoranda

but some words in this group have been partly anglicized so that an English plural form ending in *s* and a Latin plural form ending in *a* are both used in educated speech and writing:

gymnasiums/gymnasia, maximums/maxima, minimums/minima, referendums/referenda, stadiums/stadia.

The plural forms of two other words in the same group, *media* and *data*, are now widely misused for the singular forms, *medium* and *datum*. A reason for the misuse is that both plurals, *media* and *data*, came to be used as collective nouns and so were regarded as singular in number, *media* for the news media and *data* for sets of information. Now *media* is sometimes wrongly used as a synonym for *television*.

Latin nouns with the singular form ending in -*x* and the plural in -*ices* have also been anglicized so that either plural form is acceptable, although *indices* is the preferred plural spelling in mathematics:

apex, apexes/apices; appendix, appendixes/appendices; index, indexes/indices.

Latin nouns ending in -*us* remain tricky; some have been completely anglicized, some partly anglicized, and some not at all:

focus, focuses/foci; nucleus, nuclei; opus, opera; syllabus, syllabuses/syllabi; terminus, termini; virus, viruses.

Most Greek nouns with a singular form ending in -*is* have the plural ending -*es*:

analysis, analyses; basis, bases; crisis, crises; emphasis, emphases; synopsis, synopses; thesis, theses.

The misuse of the plural forms of two Greek nouns, *criteria* and *phenomena*, is similar to the misuse of *data* and *media*, and for the same reason: *criteria* and *phenomena* are sometimes seen as collective, singular nouns. The correct singular forms are *criterion* and *phenomenon*.

Foreign nouns with the singular form ending in -o can have the plural form ending in -s, -es or -i. Many of these nouns are borrowed from Italian, some are borrowed from Spanish and a few from Portuguese, but there is no consistency in the plural forms in English. Italian nouns, for example, include:

> fresco, frescos/frescoes; graffito, graffiti; inferno, infernos; manifesto, manifestos/manifestoes; volcano, volcanoes.

Even in Italian musical nouns there are these variations:

> oratorio, oratorios; piano, pianos; piccolo, piccolos; tempo, tempos/tempi; virtuoso, virtuosos/virtuosi.

Spanish nouns present the same kind of inconsistency:

> cargo, cargoes; lasso, lassos/lassoes; potato, potatoes; sombrero, sombreros; tornado, tornadoes.

And Portuguese nouns are equally inconsistent in English:

> buffalo, buffaloes; commando, commandoes; flamingo, flamingos/flamingoes.

French singular nouns ending in -eau are also inconsistent in the plural; some endings have been partly anglicized to -s while others retain the French -x:

> bureau, bureaux/bureaus; gateau, gateaux; plateau, plateaux/plateaus; tableau, tableaux.

Unless you have a photographic memory for these variations you should use a spelling dictionary.

WORD FORMATION BY PREFIXES AND SUFFIXES

Less colourful and thus less obvious than foreign borrowing is word formation by affixes. As we saw in the sections on nouns and adjectives, an affix is a short verbal element, normally less than a full word, added before or after a root word. An affix added before the root word is a prefix; an affix added after the root word is a suffix. The simplicity of the process partly masks its importance as a source of new words; this section, therefore, will explain and illustrate some of the main patterns within the overall process of word formation by prefix and suffix.

Prefixes

A small number of positive and negative prefixes give large numbers of verbs, nouns and adjectives. The prefixes *en-* and *in-* add the positive sense of encouraging or instilling:

VERB	NOUN	ADJECTIVE
engage	engagement	engaged/engaging
inspire	inspiration	inspired/inspirational.

The same effect is achieved by the prefixes *em-* and *im-*, which sometimes replace *en-* and *in-* when the root word begins with the letters *b*, *p* or *m*:

embarrass	embarrassment	embarrassed/embarrassing
implant	implantation	implanted

The negative prefixes *de-* and *dis-* appear in:

VERB	NOUN	ADJECTIVE
derail	derailment	derailed
disobey	disobedience	disobedient

Other negative prefixes are *anti-*, *mis-*, *non-* and *un-*. *Anti-* appears in nouns, adjectives and adverbs: *antibiotics* (noun), *anticlockwise* (adjective and adverb), *antisocially* (adverb). *Mis-* appears in nouns, adjectives, verbs and in a few adverbs: *mistake* (noun and verb), *mistaken* (adjective), *mistakenly* (adverb). *Non-* can be added to large numbers of nouns and adjectives, as in: *nonpayment*, *non-alcoholic*, and to a few adverbs, for example, *nonsensically*. *Un-*, as we noted above, is used mainly with adjectives and verbs: *unfair* (adjective), *unfasten* (verb), with some nouns: *unconsciousness*, *unhappiness*, and a few adverbs: *unconditionally*.

Several Latin and Greek prefixes give us words for numbers:

PREFIX	MEANING	WORDS
mono-, uni-	one, single	monopoly, unison
bi-, di-, duo-	two, twice	bilingual, diagonal, duet
tri-	three	triangle
quad-, tetra-	four	quadruped, tetrameter
quin-	five	quintuplet
hexa-, sex-	six	hexagon, sextet
sept-	seven	septennial

Vocabulary

PREFIX	MEANING	WORDS
oct-, octa-, octo-	eight	octave, octopus
nona-	nine	nonagenarian
dec-, deci-	ten	decimal
cent-, hec-, hecta-	hundred	century, hectare
kilo-, mil-	thousand	kilometre, millimetre
giga-	billion	gigawatt

Other Latin and Greek prefixes indicate quantity, size or scale:

PREFIX	MEANING	WORDS
micro-, mini-	small	microscope, miniature
maxi-, mega-	large, great	maximum, megalomaniac
hyper-, super-	over, beyond	hyperbole ('hype'), superhuman
sub-	under, less	submarine, sub-human
ultra-	beyond,	ultrasound, ultraviolet

Some prefixes are occasionally used loosely in an attempt to impress readers or listeners; for example, an entertainer may be described as a *megastar*, a shopping area as a *hypermarket*, and a new gadget as *ultramodern*.

Prefixes can indicate place, position or relationship:

PREFIX	MEANING	WORDS
ad-, pro-	to, towards	advance, proceed
retro-	back	retrospect, retro-rocket
intra-	inside	intravenous
inter-	between, among	international, intermingle
extra-	outside	extraterrestrial
equi-, iso-,	equal	equilibrium, isobar
auto-	self, alone	autobiography
homo-	same	homonym, homosexual
hetero-	other, different	heterodox, heterosexual
dia-, per-, trans-	through, across	diameter, percolate, transport
pan-	all	panorama
para-	alongside	parallel, para-medical

PREFIX	MEANING	WORDS
cata-	down, away	catacomb
ante-, pre-	before	antenatal, premeditated
post-	after	posthumous
tele-, telos-	far	telescope

The following Latin and Greek prefixes indicate specific subject areas. Some of the examples show that Latin and Greek are still sources for new words in medicine, science and technology:

PREFIX	MEANING	WORDS
aero-	air	aerodynamic, aerosol
anthropo-	man	anthropology
bio-	life	biology, biography
eco-	habitat	ecology
electro-	electricity	electronics
fluor-, fluo-	flow	fluorescent, fluoride
haemo-, hemo-	blood	haemorrhage
neuro-	nerve	neurotic
optic-, opto-	sight	optician
phil-	love of	philanthropy
proto-	first	prototype
psycho-	mind	psychology
pyro-	fire	pyrotechnics
socio-	society	social
spectro-	sight, image	spectrograph
techno-	art, craft	technical, technology
therm-, thermo-	heat	thermometer

The literal meaning of the prefix *eco-* is house, and is the basis of the word *economy*, which once meant household management.

Suffixes

Many of the suffixes in English modify rather than transform the meanings of the root words. For example, the suffixes *-able* and *-ment* extend or vary the meaning of the root word *agree*:

agreeable, agreement; in contrast, the prefix *dis-* placed before the root word *agree* produces a word with the opposite meaning: *disagree*. Dozens of suffixes operate in this modifying way, from *-acy*, *-ator* and *-ation* to *-ous*, *-urgy* and *-yte*.

One important group consists of the medical suffixes:

SUFFIX	MEANING	WORD
-algia	pain	neuralgia
-ectomy	cutting out	appendectomy
-itis	disease, inflammation	appendicitis, tonsillitis
-lysis	loosening	paralysis
-oma	tumour	carcinoma
-osis	condition	thrombosis
-scopy	examination	radioscopy

Some suffixes are used in general as well as medical terms, and in extending the use of the suffixes *-phil, -philia, -path, -pathy, -stat* and others, the derivation from Greek or Latin is occasionally confused:

SUFFIX	MEANING	WORD
-arium	place for	aquarium
-cide	kill	homicide
-gram, -graph, -graphy	writing	diagram, autograph, geography
-mania	madness, obsession	maniac, kleptomania
-naut, -nautic	sailor, voyager	astronaut
-path, -pathos	feeling, disease	empathy, sympathy, pathology
-phil, -philia	lover of	Anglophile
-phobia	dread	agoraphobia
-scope	look, examine	microscope
-sphere	ball, globe	hemisphere
-stat	standing	thermostat

Finally, a small number of suffixes appear in many hundreds of English words. The suffix *-ism* covers a wide range of words indicating beliefs, theories, processes and characteristics:

baptism, hooliganism, modernism, optimism.

A similar range of human activities can be expressed in words ending with the suffixes -logy and -ology, both of which originally meant words, and have come to mean the study of a given subject:

>archaeology, demonology, mythology, zoology.

Related to the -isms and the -ologies are the agent nouns, the -ists and the -ologists, that is, the people involved in the -ism or the -ology:

>atheist, bigamist, pacifist, specialist, biologist, pathologist, psychologist, terrorist.

One of the attractions of prefixes and suffixes is that they can be adapted to meet new developments. In science and medicine, for example, we now have:

>antibiotics, computer graphics, interferometry, microbiology, neurosurgery, superconductivity, thermonuclear energy, tomography, ultrasonics.

When Greek and Latin prefixes and suffixes are applied to new developments in social affairs or in human behaviour, the application is often less precise, and in some neologisms the application is simply wrong or at best whimsical. The expressions *bikeathon* and *swimathon*, which are modelled on *marathon* and *pentathlon*, are amusing inventions. The neologisms *chocoholic* and *workaholic* are modelled on the word *alcoholic*, and they too are amusing if we note that the suffix in *alcoholic* is not -*oholic* but simply -*ic*.

Some neologisms capture a new development so neatly that the words assume wide currency. For example, the expressions *sexism* and *sexist*, and *ageism* and *ageist* are so effective in expressing the ideas of discrimination on the grounds of sex or age that the new words may find a permanent place in standard English. So too could some of the hundreds of words that are coined every year: *biohazard, destabilize, disinformation, Eurocurrency, user-friendly, hyperinflation, megadeath, multi-task, optoelectronics, prequel, superovulation, telemarketing.*

Eponyms

The word eponym means giving the name of a person to a place or an institution, and by extension the word has come to include objects and actions named after persons. Among the most obvious eponyms are place names; throughout the world there are thousands of streets and buildings and hundreds of towns that are named after eminent persons: explorers, politicians, generals, millionaires. Some commonplace, everyday eponyms are *cardigan*, the item of clothing named after James Thomas Brudenell, seventh Earl of Cardigan, who led the charge of the Light Brigade in the Crimean War; *balaclava*, named after the site of the battle in the Crimean War; *wellingtons*, the boots named after Arthur Wellesley, first Duke of Wellington; *sandwich*, from John Montagu, fourth Earl of Sandwich, who was said to have been so obsessed by gambling that he had food in the form of sandwiches brought to him at the gaming table; *mackintosh*, also *macintosh*, from Charles Macintosh, who patented the waterproof material from which the coats were once made; and *stetson*, the wide-brimmed hat designed by John Batterson Stetson for use in the American west and adopted later in Australia.

Eponyms are fairly common in the fields of science and technology. In botany, for example, there are hundreds of eponymous plants, some of the best known being *bougainvillaea*, named after Louis Antoine de Bougainville, *dahlia*, named after Anders Dahl, and *fuchsia*, named after Leonhard Fuchs. In one botanical area alone, the names of different kinds of maple tree, there are the following:

EPONYM	PERSONAL NAME
Miyabe's maple	Kingo Miyabe
Lobel's maple	Mathias de l'Obel
Van Volxem's maple	Van Volxem
Trautvetter's maple	Ernest von Trautvetter
Heldreich's maple	Theodore von Heldreich
Père David's maple	Armand David
Forrest's maple	George Forrest

From the study of electricity we have:

EPONYM	PERSONAL NAME
farad	Michael Faraday
hertz	Heinrich Hertz
joule	James Prescott Joule
maxwell	James Clerk Maxwell

EPONYM	PERSONAL NAME
ohm	Georg Simon Ohm
volt	Alessandro Volta
watt	James Watt

Eponyms show the direct influence of people on the English language. When eponyms are widely used, the words become fully assimilated into the language so that the proper nouns, the persons' names, become common nouns and can also be used as adjectives. Examples of this are the adjective *geiger* in the term *geiger counter* from the name Hans Geiger, and the adjective *diesel*, as in *diesel engine* and *diesel fuel*, from Rudolf Diesel. Other, more specialist, eponyms retain their scientific or technological air and are unlikely to be assimilated fully into the language: *gauss*, a term used in electro-magnetism, *gauss's law* and *gaussmeter* from Karl Friedrich Gauss, the German scientist.

Some eponyms meet a temporary need and gain wide currency, only to disappear when the need disappears or is met in some other way. British pilots in the Second World War used the affectionate slang term, *Mae West*, for their inflatable life-jackets; Mae West was a large-bosomed American stage and film actress. The word *becquerel*, a unit of radioactivity named after the French physicist Antoine Henri Becquerel, was widely used by the news media in reporting the radiation leaks at the nuclear power station on Three Mile Island in Pennsylvania, USA, in 1979, and at Chernobyl in Ukraine in 1986.

ACRONYMS

The same simple test applies to acronyms, which are words formed from the initial letters of other words. The more widely used the acronyms are, especially in the news media, the more likely they are to be assimilated into the language and then written and pronounced as independent words. An example of this is *AIDS* (sometimes *Aids*), Acquired Immune Deficiency Syndrome, which entered the English language in the 1980s; in doing so it displaced the slightly older acronym *AID*, Artificial Insemination by Donor. *AIDS* was quickly adopted as a word in its own right, but the retrovirus associated with AIDS, *HIV*, Human Immunodeficiency Virus, is still pronounced as three letters rather than as a single word.

The word acronym itself entered the English language in the 1940s along with several acronyms associated with the Second World War:

ACRONYM	FULL NAME
asdic	Allied Submarine Detection Investigation Committee
radar	Radio detection and ranging
sonar	Sound navigation and ranging

Another acronym dating from this period, *Pluto*, *P*ipe *l*ine *u*nder *t*he *o*cean, was an ingenious choice by the scientists and engineers who devised the underwater link, because Pluto was the Greek god of the underworld. But Pluto was also the name of a Walt Disney cartoon dog, and some people made the association with the animated cartoon figure rather than with classical mythology. The later dog acronym, *Fido*, *F*og *I*nvestigation and *D*ispersal *O*peration, is a method of clearing fog from airport runways.

These words from the 1940s partly explain the attraction of acronyms:

ACRONYM	FULL NAME
NAAFI	Navy, Army and Air Force Institutes
WAAF	Women's Auxiliary Air Force
WREN	Women's Royal Naval Service

In each case the acronym seems less formal, more human and much easier to remember, to say and to write than the full name. Indeed, it was this tendency to humanize and simplify that led to the false acronym *WREN*, which does not follow from the full name, *Women's Royal Naval Service*. Other examples of this simplifying tendency are *laser*, *l*ight *a*mplification by the *s*timulated *e*mission of *r*adiation; *maser*, *m*icrowave *a*mplification by the *s*timulated *e*mission of *r*adiation; and from astronomy, *quasar*, *quas*i-stell*ar* radio source. Two acronyms that appeared in the 1980s are *CAT* and *PET*, *c*omputerized *a*xial *t*omography and *p*ositron *e*mission *t*omography, non-invasive scanning techniques for gaining three-dimensional views of the interior of objects, including the human body and brain. *CAT* and *PET* are less intimidating and more 'user-friendly' or 'patient-friendly' than the full names.

Today, acronyms appear in a wide range of contexts. There are the international organizations:

ACRONYM	FULL NAME
GATT	General Agreement on Tariffs and Trade
NASA	National Aeronautics and Space Administration
NATO	North Atlantic Treaty Organization
UNO	United Nations Organization

There are the computer terms:

CAD	Computer-aided Design
CAM	Computer-aided Manufacture
RAM	Random Access Memory
ROM	Read Only Memory

There are colloquial terms, some of which were devised for particular social or political occasions and may not survive in the language: *Nimby*, *Not in my back yard*, a term used by objectors to planning proposals for roads or buildings; *OMOV*, One Member One Vote, the movement in the Labour Party to replace block voting by trades unions; *Quango*, *Quasi-autonomous non-government(al)* organization, a term applied to semi-independent bodies like the Arts Council; and there are pressure groups, some of which choose names that can be reduced to memorable, quotable and 'user-friendly' acronyms such as *ASH*, Action on Smoking and Health.

Acronyms, like other words in English, have evolved in inconsistent ways. As we saw with *AIDS*, some terms of two or more words are reduced to acronyms and written and pronounced as independent words while others, for example, *HIV*, are reduced to initial letters, which are then pronounced separately. A similar inconsistency appears in financial acronyms in Britain: *VAT*, *value added tax*, and *MIRAS*, *mortgage interest relief at source*, are written and pronounced as acronyms, but *PAYE*, *pay as you earn*, is pronounced as four separate initial letters. *AIDS*, *VAT* and *MIRAS* are usually written entirely in upper case, or capital, letters, and are thus proper nouns; *radar*, *sonar*, *laser* and *scuba* are written in lower case letters and are thus common nouns.

The attraction of acronyms is that they simplify, or seem to simplify, complex terms; they also represent a kind of word formation that adds variety and energy to the English language.

PART TWO

5 Choosing The Right Word

When we have a particular interest in a subject – computers, photography, rock music – we readily assimilate words and phrases associated with that subject into our personal vocabulary; the keener our interest in a subject, the more likely we are to acquire the vocabulary. The assimilation is sometimes an unconscious or semiconscious process; we are so absorbed in the subject that we are not aware that we are learning the vocabulary of that subject.

Your vocabulary will be similar to the vocabularies of other people in your age group or people who have been brought up in similar social circumstances and who have had a similar education. Simple proof of this common knowledge is that many readers will see that the five short statements below are likely to have come from a regional or local newspaper:

(a) Two first-half goals by Glasborough Rovers dashed Wallfield United's hopes for the league title.

(b) Prices fell sharply at Deanvale this week. Cattle were down to 102.5p a kg (−6.5 from last week).

(c) Beechmount Players' Christmas revue, *The Icing on the Cake*, had the audience helpless with laughter on opening night last Saturday.

(d) Three Cradle Bay children were seriously injured on Monday when the school bus in which they were travelling overturned on Marina Road.

(e) Upstart Genes' 'Schizophrenia', their controversial follow-up to 'The Beginner's Guide To Death', has been banned by the BBC.

The subject matter is not specified in any of the statements above, and yet we know what the subjects are because each statement includes words drawn from the vocabulary of a particular subject. Statement (a) refers to a football match, or a similar team game; statement (b) to a weekly livestock market; (c) to an amateur theatre group's Christmas production; (d) to a news report of a road accident; and (e) to a new recording by a rock group. Each of the five subject areas is discussed in a recognizable range of words, a range that is sometimes known as a register.

We acquire many such registers without being consciously aware of the process of acquisition: through reading and listening, through taking part in sport or spectating, and through conversation. The learning process becomes a conscious one when we are required to make a formal study, especially of subjects that we find uninteresting at school, in higher education or at work. And we are even more aware of register when we discuss a subject with someone who knows much less about it, or much more, than we do, or when we come to write about the subject, because we must then formulate our understanding into thoughts and words. On occasions such as these we become aware that the extent of our vocabulary is the extent of our ability to communicate with others. We cannot discuss a subject effectively if our personal vocabulary, or the vocabulary of the person we are talking to, does not include enough words from the register of the subject. In a wider sense, the limits of our personal lexicon are not only the limits of our ability to communicate but also the limits of our understanding.

The bulk of our personal lexicon will remain fairly constant through most of our adult life. Some words and phrases will be forgotten, while others will be acquired in ways already outlined: formally, at school, in higher education or at work; informally, by reading and listening, through sport or leisure, and through conversation.

Only you can be responsible for your own vocabulary, but you will find the responsibility easier to exercise if you use a dictionary. What matters is not the total number of words you can memorize but your ability to use words effectively in your own speech and writing. Of particular importance is your ability to understand the words used by those people – politicians, advertising copywriters, some journalists and some teachers – who are trying to change your mind.

NEUTRAL AND EMOTIVE WORDS

People who try to change your mind sometimes make a calculated use of emotive language; that is, they use words in a deliberate attempt to arouse emotions that may influence your thoughts and actions. Advertising agencies working for charities and pressure groups try to arouse our compassion or moral indignation in the hope that we will donate money or join the pressure group; politicians appeal to our self-interest or to a partisan sense of patriotism in order to win our votes; tabloid newspapers constantly invite our admiration or revulsion for the characters in a daily melodrama that confuses fact and fiction; advertisements for cars try to lure us into fantasies of power; advertisements for toiletries and cosmetics try to create a sense of personal inadequacy that will be replaced by physical beauty if we use the advertised products.

An obvious example of the emotive use of language is in the reporting of wars. A neutral war correspondent may use the neutral term, 'guerrilla forces', to refer to irregular troops; a war correspondent who identifies with these forces may describe them as 'gallant freedom-fighters'; an opposing war correspondent may describe them as 'bloody terrorists'. In this and in many other contexts an awareness of the emotive use of words is of fundamental importance to you as a reader: if you are not aware of the emotive content of a piece of writing then you could be more easily influenced by the writer into accepting his or her biased viewpoint.

It is equally important that you as a writer should be aware of your own use of emotive diction for this reason: if you cannot control the emotion, the emotion may control you. When you become agitated or excited in presenting your point of view, your powers of reason are sometimes overwhelmed by emotion to such an extent that you overstate and thus misrepresent your real views: 'All Conservative politicians are corrupt', 'All Labour politicians are liars', 'Upstart Genes is the best rock band in the world', 'Positron's music is absolute rubbish'.

An occasional loss of control is understandable because a writer cannot be completely in command of his or her emotions at all times, but you should try to be aware of those topics that arouse your emotions: politics, nationality, social issues, sports teams, different forms of music. Lack of awareness of your own sympathies or prejudices can lead you into ludicrous exaggerations that could undermine your authority as a writer. When the emotion is uncontrolled it may lead not only to grotesque overstatements like those in the previous paragraph but also to a form of linguistic inflation that leads to linguistic bankruptcy. For example, if you describe a defeat in sport as a *national disaster*, *tragedy* or *catastrophe*, you inflate the currency of these words; if you then had to describe a war or a famine that kills thousands of people, you would have to use the words you had already used to describe the sports event, and in that sense you would be linguistically bankrupt.

The examples that follow show the differences between neutral diction and emotive diction.

Nouns

NEUTRAL	EMOTIVE
dissident, non-conformist	deviant, insurgent, rebel, revolutionary
enthusiast, visionary	dreamer, fanatic, zealot
farm worker/labourer	bumpkin, clodhopper, peasant, rustic, yokel
idiosyncrasy	affectation, eccentricity, fetish, oddity, peculiarity
industrialist, businessman	baron (as in *press baron*), magnate, mogul, supremo, tycoon
servant, subordinate	flunkey, lackey, underling
waste, debris, detritus	garbage, refuse, rubbish, trash

Adjectives

NEUTRAL	EMOTIVE
adventurous, enterprising	bold, daring, foolhardy, rash, reckless
evasive, elusive	furtive, shifty, sly, stealthy, surreptitious
private, confidential	clandestine, covert, secret, shrouded, veiled
undeveloped	backward, crude, primitive, raw
unusual, uncommon	bizarre, fantastic, mysterious, odd, peculiar, strange

Most of the adjectives above can be changed to adverbs ending in -ly, for example, *unusually, uncommonly, bizarrely, fantastically, mysteriously*. The adverbs then show the same contrast between neutral and emotive.

Verbs

NEUTRAL	EMOTIVE
complain	bewail, bleat, gripe, grouse, grumble, moan, whine, whinge
criticize, appraise, assess, evaluate, judge	attack, blast, lash, slam
debate, dispute	argue, bicker, clash, quarrel, squabble
fall, descend	crash, plummet, plunge, slump, tumble
reduce, contract, diminish, lessen	axe, butcher, chop, cut, slash
rise, ascend, climb, mount	rocket, soar, spiral
weep, lament	blubber, sob, wail, whimper

Several points emerge from these examples. In many contexts a range of neutral and emotive words is available and allows you to express precise shades of meaning and emphasis. The same person can be described as a *friend*, or as a *chum, colleague, comrade, confidant* or *crony*; the person remains the same, but the impression given to the reader differs with each word. The main differences are those between neutral and emotive words and, within a given range of emotive words, between favourable and unfavourable words. For example, of the emotive words listed above for the neutral adjectives *adventurous* and *enterprising*, the words *bold* and *daring* are favourable, and the words *foolhardy*, *rash* and *reckless* are unfavourable. Words used to express disfavour are sometimes said to be pejorative in function.

A neutral statement is by definition an impartial one. In most cases it is also a factual statement in which the key words – usually nouns, adjectives, verbs and adverbs – are used to denote or define, and in that sense to limit, the meaning of the statement. A neutral statement is denotative. In contrast, an emotive statement is a statement of opinion rather than fact. The key words are used for their connotations, that is, their associated meanings, and in that sense an emotive statement is connotative.

One of the most distinctive forms of emotive language is 'tabloidese', a use of language that is particular to tabloid newspapers. The aim of 'tabloidese' is to intensify the emotional impact of a word, sometimes at the expense of the word's precise meaning. Indeed, 'tabloidese' reduces a range of meanings to a single word; for example, the word *agony* covers a number of meanings that would normally be expressed by several words: *anguish, distress, grief, pain, sorrow*. In the same way, tabloid newspaper sub-editors use these single words to cover a range of meanings:

EMOTIVE WORD	RANGE OF MEANINGS
axe	abandon, cancel, dismiss, drop, omit, remove
blitz	attack, campaign, drive
blow	disappointment, disillusionment, rebuff, setback
boost	encourage(ment), improve(ment), incentive, increase
deal	arrange(ment), contract, exchange, negotiate, negotiation, transact(ion)
dump	abandon, dismiss, drop, omit, reject, throw out, throw away
fury	anger, dissent, opposition, rage
move	attempt, development, initiative, plan, scheme, venture
rap	admonish, caution, discipline, insult, reprimand, warn
set to	could, likely to, may, prepared, ready, will
storm	argument, conflict, controversy, debate, disagreement, discussion
top	distinguished, eminent, important, well-known

When the same words are used repeatedly to produce the same responses, often vague or confused responses, the words become clichés and the responses become conditioned reflexes.

Other emotive words favoured by the tabloid newspaper sub-editors are:

backs, blaze, blunder, bungle, ban, bar, bid, clampdown, clash, crackdown, curb, cut, dash (dash hopes, mercy dash), drama, feud, grab, looms, oust, outrage, probe, quit, quiz, rebel, riddle, rock, row, shake out, shake up, shock, slap, slam, snag, snub, soar, storm out, supremo, swoop, threat, vigil, zap.

These examples also show that a writer's main purpose in using emotive words is to give a ready-made interpretation that prevents the reader from reaching an independent conclusion. Some readers will be unaware that they are being manipulated in this way; others will see the writer's purpose and may then resist not only specific instances of emotive diction but the writer's entire statement; others still will see it as an amusing word game.

There is often an added amusement in tabloid headlines when the same words are used in different grammatical classes; for example, *shock* is used as an adjective in the headline, *Shock Death Sparks Probe*, but it could just as easily be used as a noun: *Death Probe Sparks Shock*. It is this confusion of word class that produces ambiguous and sometimes grotesque tabloid headlines such as these:

> HP firms up down-payments
> Reinforcements sent to massacre town
> UNO medics lick cholera outbreak
> Euro-climbdown over butter mountain
> Tories face split over arms
> Health heads foot trust bill

Finally, you should note that references to emotion are not necessarily examples of emotive diction. Statements such as *I am angry*, *She is in love* and *He is ambitious* are not emotive but neutral, factual, denotative statements. When the anger is expressed in these terms:

> I am angry with that greedy, lying trickster.

or love expressed like this:

> She is in love, the naïve, besotted fool.

or ambition like this:

> He is so ambitious he will cheat, betray or trample underfoot anyone who gets in his way.

then the key words – *greedy, lying trickster* and *naïve, besotted fool* and *betray or trample underfoot* – are clearly designed to arouse emotion.

Emotive Diction and Tone

Emotive words have a strong influence on the tone of your writing. The tone of a piece of prose, which is roughly comparable to tone of voice in speech, is a result of the combined effect of sentence structure, prose rhythm and, above all, of vocabulary.

Every piece of writing has a tone. You cannot escape tone by writing in a strictly neutral and impersonal way because those features, neutrality and impersonality, will create a tone. A prose style with a high frequency of concrete and monosyllabic words, along with a staccato rhythm produced by short sentences, could be effective in describing physical action or conveying psychological tension, but such a style could not be used to create a sense of tranquillity. A tranquil effect would require longer, more fluid sentences and a greater use of abstract and polysyllabic words.

Consider these two examples:

> Bask on silver sands in golden sunlight by day. Wine and dine beneath velvet skies until midnight.

> Lie on a compound of granulated silica, calcium carbonate and sodium chloride in temperatures of 25°C to 30°C from 0900 to 1800 hours. Eat and drink in the open air until 2400 hours.

In the first example, which is the kind of publicity copywriting found in holiday brochures, there are emotive connotations in the nouns *sunlight*, *skies* and *midnight*; in the adjectives *silver*, *golden* and *velvet*; and in the verbs *Bask*, *wine* and *dine*. The result is intended to be a warm, exotic appeal to the reader's self-indulgence. The second example expresses the same message as the first but in a register that is so absurdly inappropriate that the result is a parody of scientific language.

ECONOMY OF LANGUAGE

You should practise economy of language not only in your choice of specific words but in your syntax, that is, in your structuring of sentences and paragraphs. Long words and long sentences do not necessarily make a piece of writing more important or more authoritative; they may simply make it long-winded, pretentious or pompous. Economy will give a firmness, a suppleness, perhaps even a steely elegance to your prose style. You will then be able to write sentences that accommodate information more succinctly and that communicate the information to your reader more effectively.

One way in which journalists practise economy is by compressing a detailed description into the smallest number of words by using several adjectives to describe one noun, as in phrases like these:

Petite 27-year-old brunette mother-of-two Jane Marsh . . .

Prize-winning, best-selling Edinburgh-born author . . .

Ex-footballer and keep-fit fanatic Doug Kirk, now a fridge factory assembly-line supervisor . . .

That kind of economy is valid in tabloid newspapers, where it becomes another of the tabloids' daily word games. Our aim should be a less self-conscious style, a style that can transform the two long-winded sentences below:

A total of four firefighters, each of whom was wearing breathing apparatus, effected an entry to the warehouse, which was used for the storage of furniture, by means of a door at the side of the warehouse.

Margot Hunter, a soprano who has performed in a considerable number of operatic productions at an amateur level, has no wish to achieve professional status as an operatic soprano.

The information in these sentences would be accommodated more neatly and communicated more fluently if the sentences were rewritten:

Four firefighters wearing breathing apparatus entered the furniture warehouse by a side door.

Margot Hunter has sung soprano parts in many amateur opera productions but she has no wish to turn professional.

or

Opera soprano Margot Hunter has performed in many amateur productions but does not want to sing professionally.

Here are two longer passages.

Leonard Vedley's company, Metropolitan Assets plc, submitted an application for planning permission that would allow the company to demolish the old lifeboat station in Cradle Bay and, on the then vacant site, to construct a hotel with seventy-five units of bedroom accommodation and with car-parking provision for 100 vehicular units. A total in excess of 800 people, which constitutes the majority of the adult residents in the Cradle Bay area, lodged an objection to the application for planning permission on the grounds that the lifeboat station, although no longer being utilized for its original purpose, was nevertheless a structure of considerable social and historical interest. The residents went on to state that at this moment in time there was adequate provision of hotel accommodation in the area. Mr Matthew Ray, the Member of Parliament for the constituency that includes Cradle Bay, stated his willingness to give active consideration to the petition bearing the signatures of the greater proportion of the adult population in Cradle Bay.

Some specific points are worth noting before we look at the complete amended version of the passage above.

Phrases such as *submitted an application, lodged an objection* and *tendered his resignation* can normally be reduced to a one-word verb, *applied, appealed* or *resigned*. Phrases like *that would allow* or *which would permit* can often be reduced to *to allow* or *to permit*. The expressions, *seventy-five units of bedroom accommodation* and *100 vehicular units* – some people actually write like that – should be reduced to *seventy-five bedrooms* and *100 parking places*. *A total in excess of* should be written as *Over* or *More than*. The clause *which constitutes the majority* is an inflated way of writing *which is the majority*, and *utilized* is an inflation for *used*. When the residents *went on to state* they simply *added*; and when they wrote *at this moment in time* they meant *now, at present* or *currently*. *Adequate provision* normally means *enough or sufficient*. The long-winded reference to Matthew Ray's constituency can be reduced to *the local constituency*; *stated his willingness* should be reduced to *agreed*; and the pompous *bearing the signatures of the greater proportion of the adult population in Cradle Bay* should be *signed by most of the adult population in Cradle Bay*.

The amended version reads:

Leonard Vedley's company, Metropolitan Assets plc, applied for planning permission to demolish the old lifeboat station in Cradle Bay and in its place to build a seventy-five bedroom hotel with 100 parking spaces. Over 800 people, the majority of residents in the Cradle Bay area, objected on the grounds that, although the lifeboat station was no longer in use, it was a building of considerable social and historical interest. The residents added that at present there was enough hotel accommodation in the area. Mr Matthew Ray, the local Member of Parliament, agreed to consider the petition signed by most of the adult population in Cradle Bay.

Here is the second passage. If you apply the principles and techniques outlined above, you should be able to reduce the passage to a shorter and more effective statement.

A Rovers defender committed a foul on the United striker, who sustained an injury to his left shoulder and was taken to hospital for X-ray purposes. Subsequent to the fouling incident, there was an outbreak of fighting between the supporters of the rival teams. Police succeeded in putting an end to the fight but in doing so three officers suffered injuries of a minor nature; seven supporters were taken into police custody. In court on the morning immediately after the match, the first of the accused tendered a plea of guilty but pointed out that it was the first time he had committed any offence. The magistrates admonished the accused. The magistrates refused, however, to extend a lenient attitude towards the second accused, who had been convicted time and time again for criminal activities involving the use of violence. They decided to impose a custodial sentence of eighteen months' duration.

An amended version is this:

A Rovers defender fouled the United striker, who injured his left shoulder and was taken to hospital for X-ray. After the foul there was an outbreak of fighting by rival fans. Police stopped the fight, but three officers were slightly injured and seven supporters were arrested. In court the next morning, one of the accused pleaded guilty but said it was his first offence. The magistrates admonished him but they were not lenient with the second accused, who had many previous convictions for violent crime. They sentenced him to eighteen months in prison.

MISUSED AND MISUNDERSTOOD WORDS

It is easier to write bad or pretentious prose than to write simple or elegant prose. The attempt at simplicity or elegance is always worth making, however, because the reward is that you transmit your words, your thoughts, your ideas more effectively into the minds of your readers. The attempt is not always easy; the English lexicon is now so vast that no writer can know all the meanings of all the words. Some of the areas of confusion are discussed below.

A Common Root

Some root words or elements appear in several words and may even appear in two or more words in the same word class, making it difficult to distinguish the precise meanings of each word. For example, the Latin root *bene*, meaning well or good, appears in the nouns *benediction*, *benefaction*, *benefactor*, *benefice*, *beneficiary*, *benefit* and *benevolence*, all of which have the *bene* part of their meaning in common.

Other words with common roots and with parts of their meanings in common include:

administer, administrate	dependant, dependent
admission, admittance	electrify, electrocute
adversary, adversity	human, humane
adverse, averse	humanist, humanitarian
alternately, alternatively	imaginary, imaginative
ambiguous, ambivalent	judicial, judicious
amiable, amicable	luxuriant, luxurious
amoral, immoral	negligent, negligible
artist, artiste	personal, personnel
audience, audition	sociable, social
authoritarian, authoritative	stimulant, stimulus
biannual, biennial	technical, technological
captivate, capture	union, unity
centenarian, centennial	variation, variety
centurion, century	wonderful, wondrous
childish, childlike	xylograph, xylophone
coherence, cohesion	yoga, yogi
commitment, committal	zoology, zootomy
contemptible, contemptuous	

Homophones

English also has large numbers of homophones, that is, words with the same sound but with different spellings, like *rain*, *rein* and *reign*, and near-homophones like *flaunt* and *flout*.

The list that follows is merely a selection from the hundreds of homophones and near-homophones in the language.

allergy, allegory	gamble, gambol
bazaar, bizarre	genius, genus
boy, buoy	ghetto, grotto
broach, brooch	gorilla, guerrilla
cache, cash	gruelling, gruesome
calibre, calliper	hoard, horde
cartilage, cartridge	incognito, incommunicado
coarse, course	ingenious, ingenuous
chord, cord	lama, llama
choral, coral	lightening, lightning
cymbal, symbol	magnate, magnet
conscience, conscious	militate, mitigate
demist, demystify	moot, mute
dinghy, dingy	prodigy, protégé
disaffected, disinfected	right, rite, wright, write
eligible, illegible	stationary, stationery
executioner, executor	tycoon, typhoon
faint, feint	wrapped, rapped, rapt
flaunt, flout	you, yew, ewe

To confuse an executioner with an executor, a gorilla with a guerrilla or a lama with a llama could cause offence as well as amusement and would certainly undermine your authority as a writer.

Contrasting Pairs

Some words are paired because they are opposites or near-opposites, and the fact that they are constantly paired makes them inseparable. To recall one word seems to activate a conditioned reflex that triggers the other word so that, although we know the two words are different, we sometimes forget which word is which. *Concave* and *convex* can be distinguished because *concave* curves inwards like a *cave*. *Stalactites* and *stalagmites* can be distinguished by the mnemonic: *c* for *ceiling* and *g* for *ground*; stalactites grow downwards from the roof and stalagmites grow upwards from the ground. Can you distinguish these contrasting pairs?

artist, artiste

centrifugal, centripetal

critic, critique

emigrate, immigrate

fission, fusion

latitude, longitude

moral, morale

rational, rationale

review, revue

Inflation

Writers who choose their diction in order to impress their reader or to meet the formality of an occasion sometimes over-inflate their words and create the wrong meaning. For example, *advance* is inflated to *advancement*. Other inflations are these:

design, designate

differ, differentiate

escape, escapement

form, formulate

progress, progression

simple, simplistic

A similar tendency may prompt some people to use the word *refute*, which means to prove that something or someone is wrong, when the context requires *deny*, which means to reject. Disproving someone's case is a greater achievement than simply denying it, and so *refute* is wrongly used because it seems more emphatic or more important than *deny*. Similarly, the word *anticipate*, which means to take prior account of an event or even to forestall a possible future event, sometimes wrongly replaces the word *expect*, which means to wait for or to look forward to.

An opposite tendency seems to underlie the misuse of the word *decimate*, which means to reduce by one in ten but which is often used as if it meant to destroy. Perhaps the reason for this confusion is that *decimate* sounds like the first syllable of *destroy* followed by the last two syllables of *eliminate*

The negative prefix *dis-* in the word *disinterested* leads many people to think that *disinterested* means the same as *uninterested*, when it really means having no personal interest, that is, neutral.

Here is a passage that includes words that are sometimes confused.

> Scientists warn that we are *gambolling/gambling* with our natural *heritage/hermitage*. The problem, they say, is no longer a *moral/morale* question of *personal/personnel conscience/consciousness* but a question of the survival of the planet.
>
> Toxic *omissions/emissions* from *industrial/industrious sites/sights/cites* are causing *climatic/climactic* changes throughout the world. As a result, we are *loosing/losing* several *species/specious* every year because *their/there habits/habitats* are being destroyed.
>
> *Marine/maritime* pollution is damaging *coral/choral* reefs and *fowling/fouling* the world's *beeches/beaches*. Trees are *dying/dyeing* because of acid *rain/reign/rein* and *desert/dessert* areas are spreading. In Africa mountain *gorillas/guerrillas* are *prey/pray* to poachers; in South America *luxuriant/luxurious* tropical forests are being felled; in England the *barn/baron/barren* owl has become rare.
>
> *Astronomers/astrologers* claim that the *depletion/deletion* of the ozone *layer/lair* is causing damage on such a *cosmic/cosmopolitan* scale that the entire *echo-system/eco-system* could be *affected/effected*.

And here is the correct reading of the passage.

> Scientists warn that we are gambling [*Gambling* means taking risks or speculating; *gambolling* means leaping or frisking about.] with our natural heritage. [*Heritage* is what we inherit or what is handed down from a previous generation; a *hermitage* is where a hermit, a solitary person, lives.] The problem, they say, is no longer a moral question [A *moral* question is a question of right or wrong, good or evil; *morale* means confidence or self-confidence, and discipline.] of personal [*Personal* means individual or private; *personnel* means employees.] conscience [*Conscience* is one's awareness of the moral

quality of one's motives; *consciousness* is awareness, especially self-awareness, but with no moral implications.] but a question of the survival of the planet.

Toxic emissions [*Emissions* are substances that are emitted or given off by a plant or a process; *omissions* are things omitted or missed out.] from industrial sites [*Industrial sites* are places of industry, such as power stations or chemical plants; *industrious* means hard-working. *Sights* are what one sees; *cites* is the present tense of the verb *cite*, which means to quote or refer to.] are causing climatic [*Climatic* refers to the climate; *climactic* is the adjective from the noun *climax*.] changes throughout the world. As a result, we are losing [*Losing* means suffering a loss; *loosing* means setting loose or releasing.] several species [A biological *species* – the noun has the same form for singular and plural – is a class of animals or plants. The adjective *specious* can mean fair and pleasing, or outwardly pleasing but lacking substance or sincerity.] every year because their [*Their* is the possessive determiner meaning of or belonging to them; *there* is the adverb of place.] habitats [*Habitats* are the places where animals or plants normally live; *habits* are characteristic forms of behaviour.] are being destroyed.

Marine [*Marine* means of or belonging to the sea; *maritime* means commerce or navigation by sea. *Maritime* as a geographical term means bordering the sea, and in that sense the phrase *maritime pollution* is also acceptable here.] pollution is damaging coral [*Coral* is a small sea-creature, millions of whose skeletons form islands or reefs. *Choral* is an adjective referring to choirs and singing.] reefs and fouling [*Fouling* means making foul or dirty; *fowling* means hunting wild fowl, that is, birds.] the world's beaches. [*Beaches* spelled with *ea* are beside the *sea*; *beeches* spelled with *ee* are the trees.] Trees are dying [*Dying* is the ending of life; *dyeing* is a change of colour.] because of acid rain [*Rain* is the moisture that falls from the sky; *reign* is the rule of a monarch or chief; *rein* means to tie or check, as with a horse's reins.] and desert [A *desert* is a waterless wilderness; *dessert* is a pudding or sweet.] areas are spreading. In Africa mountain gorillas [*Gorillas* are the great apes; *guerrillas* are irregular troops engaged in small-scale war.] are prey [*Prey* is an animal hunted for food or as a trophy; the word has the same form as a verb and a noun. *Pray* means to ask humbly.] to poachers; in South America luxuriant [*Luxuriant* means abundant and normally applies to vegetation; *luxurious*, the adjective from luxury, means extravagant or excessive.] tropical forests are being felled; in England the barn [The *barn* owl is so called because it nests in barns, a *baron* is a lord; *barren* means sterile or unproductive.] owl has become rare.

Astronomers [*Astronomers* are scientists; *astrologers* are fortune-tellers.] claim that the depletion [*Depletion* means reduction or exhaustion; *deletion* means removal or erasure.] of the ozone layer [A *layer* is a level, in this case an atmospheric level or height; a *lair* is a resting place, especially an animal's.] is causing damage on such a cosmic [*Cosmic* means of the cosmos or universe; *cosmopolitan*, a noun and adjective, means at home in any part of the world, and thus a man or woman of the world.] scale that the entire eco-system [*Eco* is a contraction of *ecology*, the branch of biology that deals with animals and plants, their habitats and relationships; an *echo* is a reflected sound-wave.] could be affected. [*Affected* means influenced or changed; *effected* means brought about or produced.]

USING THE RIGHT WORD

Almost any passage of continuous prose in standard English will contain a mix of concrete and abstract nouns, just as it will contain a mix of monosyllabic nouns – that is, nouns of one syllable like the word *noun* itself – and polysyllabic nouns of two or more syllables, like the words *monosyllabic* and *polysyllabic*. Monosyllabic words often have qualities of immediacy and simplicity in contrast to the more formal quality of polysyllabic words:

MONOSYLLABIC	POLYSYLLABIC
work, job, trade	employment, occupation, profession, vocation
pay	remuneration
play	recreation
car	automobile
bus, coach	omnibus, charabanc
train	railway locomotive
school	educational institution
home	residence
shop	retail premises

Although concrete and monosyllabic nouns are likely to be more familiar and intelligible than abstract and polysyllabic nouns, a piece of writing with too high an incidence of concrete and monosyllabic nouns can lead to a self-conscious, mannered prose style and an oversimplification, or even a falsification, of the subject matter. Readers may feel that they are being 'talked down' to. When the concrete and monosyllabic quality extends from the nouns to other word classes, the result can be the strident prose of some tabloid news stories.

The language of journalism can be terse, supple and direct, but when a newspaper is written entirely in the style of the passage below – with a high proportion of concrete and monosyllabic nouns, short sentences and short paragraphs – then the style, and the newspaper, become monotonous.

Mountain cop saves seven . . . and then slams 'Sir'!

A police sergeant led a mountain mercy dash to the white hell of Ben Aird in the Scottish Highlands yesterday.

He saved six stranded schoolboys. And then slammed their schoolmaster!

Sergeant Eric McCall (42), leader of Glen Aird Mountain Rescue Unit, led an eight-man team up the killer peak.

Five climbers have died on Ben Aird this year. And four died last year.

The mountain cop found the seven – six schoolboys and their teacher – huddled in a hollow 2,000 feet up.

The seven are from King Alfred School, Manchester. On their way down the killer peak, they got lost in a blizzard.

Darkness fell. They were stranded – in sub-zero temperatures!

Glen Aird Youth Hostel warden, 57-year-old Archie Bell, raised the alarm.

Sergeant McCall and his team risked death in an all-night search.

The seven were found at first light. The rescue team led them to safety.

And then the mountain cop slammed teacher Harold Barton (38).

'Only a half-wit would take schoolboys up Ben Aird in these conditions,' said Eric. 'The man should be sacked!'

Two boys, Barry Appleton and Jason Wills, both 14, are suffering from exposure after their terrifying ordeal. The two are recovering in Newton Aird Hospital.

The passage above is modelled on the simplified form of standard English used in news stories in tabloid newspapers. A broadsheet newspaper reporting the same story would also use a simplified form of standard English, but with a more varied vocabulary, longer sentences and longer paragraphs than those in the tabloid press:

School party saved on Ben Aird

Two Manchester schoolboys are recovering in Newton Aird hospital, Inverness, after a night on a Scottish mountain in sub-zero temperatures.

The two, Barry Appleton and Jason Wills, were with four other boys and a teacher, Mr Harold Barton, from King Alfred School, Manchester. Descending Ben Aird, they lost their way in a blizzard, and when darkness fell they dug in for the night.

After an all-night search, Glen Aird Mountain Rescue Unit found the school party at first light and led them to safety.

Police Sergeant Eric McCall, leader of the rescue unit, said: 'Only experienced climbers should risk Ben Aird in these conditions.'

Mr Barton said: 'We are grateful to the Glen Aird Mountain Rescue Unit, although we were fully prepared with emergency food, extra clothing and survival equipment.'

A piece of writing with a high proportion of abstract nouns is likely to be distanced from the concrete familiar experience of everyday reality. Abstract nouns, apart from the words for emotions, are more likely than concrete nouns to be polysyllabic, and the combined effects of the abstract and polysyllabic qualities can give prose a ponderous or even a pretentious quality:

A singular consequence of anticyclonic meteorological conditions is chromatic and acoustic aberration of television transmission. Since these atmospheric phenomena are beyond human control, no amelioration of sound or vision can be effected by manipulating the controls of the television receiving apparatus.

AVOIDING AMBIGUITY

Even skilled and experienced writers occasionally make ambiguous statements:

Police were ordered to stop sleeping in shop doorways.

Her Royal Highness broke a bottle of champagne over her bows and then slid stern-first into the river.

In his farewell speech the retiring Member of Parliament for Newton Aird offered his best wishes to colleagues he had fought with for over thirty years.

Unintended absurdities like these may give amusement to the reader but they undermine the authority and credibility of the writer. Persistent absurdity also undermines the authority of the organization in which the writer works: the newspaper as well as the journalist, the local government department as well as the administrator, the education centre as well as the student.

Ambiguities and other errors can be eliminated by proof-reading a text, but effective proof-reading requires a level of language skills that few people possess. What students need is an explanation of how ambiguities arise and practical advice on how they can be avoided. This section, then, is concerned with the mechanics of English prose, not the creative ambiguities of literary criticism.

There are two general causes of ambiguity in written English. The first is that sense impressions or data in the writer's mind are not fully processed into the particular kind of thought required by written standard English. Only a tiny part of our thinking involves the use of words, and when it does it is often internal communication, confined to our own minds and not expressed in speech or writing. When we communicate with or within ourselves in this way, we do not need to specify the various subjects of our thoughts because we know, or think we know, exactly what we mean. The knowledge that forms the content of the internal communication may be complex and intricate, but knowledge at that stage in the mental process takes the form of sense impressions rather than logical, fully conscious thought or formally structured sentences.

The content of our internal communication is sometimes so obvious to us that we make the unquestioning, unthinking assumption that the content must be equally obvious to other people. But readers have no access to the ideas in our minds except through what we write; and the external expression of the ideas in written standard English requires us to recode the ideas into thought and language. The act of writing, then, involves a degree of intellectual detachment as we disengage ourselves from the purely internal form of communication so that we can consciously formulate the communication into thought and writing.

In that sense, we are our own translators, and by the merest extension of this role as translator we can practise another form of detachment so that we become the first readers of our own writing. If we assume the role of impartial readers we may be able to detect and eliminate ambiguities and other errors in our writing. The attitude of impartiality is vital. We cannot, of course, be truly objective observers since we are the subject of the observation, but we must at least adopt an attitude of critical neutrality if our reading is to be effective. We learn nothing about our writing, or about ourselves as writers, if we read our own work in a spirit of self-regarding infatuation or petulant defensiveness. Instead, we should try to imagine that we are outside observers approaching the work in a spirit of attentive curiosity, that is, with a mind that is alert as well as open. Only then will we begin to see what other readers see in our work.

The second general cause of ambiguity in written English is the nature of the English language itself. The English lexicon of over 500,000 words and variants; the large number of words with two or more meanings, that is, polysemous words like *bat*, *light*, *stock* and *tail*; the limitless number of syntactic permutations – all these factors make the English language an inexhaustible resource, but the same factors can make speech and writing a source of confusion and obscurity. Spoken English, especially informal speech, is tolerant of these ambiguities because the speaker can apologize, explain, rephrase or repeat the statement until the listener understands the meaning. Written English, on the other hand, is highly intolerant of ambiguity because the writer cannot be present to explain the ambiguity.

These two general causes of ambiguity take several different forms, all of which can be identified and eliminated. Some of the examples that follow have been adapted from the work of students and other inexperienced writers. The purpose is not to expose the writers but to expose the faults and to offer practical advice on how to eliminate the faults.

The Half-formed Thought

A common form of ambiguity shows a combination of the two general causes outlined above, that is, ideas that have not been fully formulated into thought, and half-formed thought that is not fully expressed in standard English.

In this first example the writer is discussing a novel:

> The actual time setting, which is some time around the turn of the nineteenth century, is relevant at times although not that important, because the book could be set in a different time.

The writer uses the word *time* at four points in the sentence but is either unaware that the word is being used in three different ways, or is aware of the differences but is unable to express them. The phrase, *The actual time setting*, means the historical period in which the novel is set; *some time around the turn of the 19th century* means at the end of the 19th century; *relevant at times* means relevant at some stages or in some chapters of the novel; and *a different time* means a different historical period. All this can be deduced by a patient and sympathetic reader, but the writer should not assume that all readers have these qualities. Instead, the sentence could have been written as:

> The historical period, which is the end of the nineteenth century, is relevant in some chapters but is not too important because the book could be set in a different period.

> or

> The historical period is the end of the nineteenth century, and although this is relevant in some chapters it is not vital because the novel could be set in a different period.

A sympathetic reader could probably deduce the meaning of this second example:

> A recruitment interview is a dialogue between two or more but it is not equal because one should control it while the other should do most of the talking.

The writer has some understanding of the balance of responsibilities in an interview, but the sentence is ambiguous because the responsibilities are not attributed to specific persons or formulated into precise thought and language. A clearer statement is:

> A recruitment interview is a dialogue between the interviewer and the subject, or interviewee, but it is not an equal dialogue. The interviewer should control the dialogue but the interviewee should do most of the talking.

or, even more explicitly:

> Although a recruitment interview is a dialogue between the interviewer and the candidate, it is not a conversation between equals. The interviewer should control the dialogue in such a way that the candidate does most of the talking.

You can avoid this common form of ambiguity by reminding yourself again that readers have no access to your thoughts except through what you write, and that you must therefore identify persons, places, objects and events as clearly as possible.

The Anonymous Pronoun

A particular variation of the first form of ambiguity is the form in which the writer unthinkingly assumes that the reader knows who or what is being discussed, even when the persons or things are not identified.

If a writer refers to two or more women in one sentence and then uses the pronoun *she* in the next sentence, the reader may have difficulty in knowing who *she* is. The same ambiguity arises if a reference to two or more men is followed by the pronoun *he*, if two or more groups of people are followed by *they*, and if two or more items are followed by *it*.

The writer of the first example below was a woman student discussing a novel written by a woman and featuring a woman as the central character. The student writer probably knew what the unidentified pronouns *it*, *her* and *she* meant, but the reader can only guess.

> I think it helps the reader to identify with her character. Perhaps the reader has the same thoughts and feelings as she follows her throughout the book.

The first *her*, in *her character*, could be the character created by the author or the characteristics, that is, the temperament and behaviour, of that character. The *she* in *as she follows* could be the reader of the novel or the author, both of whom were women. The second *her*, in *follows her*, is probably the central character but could be the author.

Something similar happens in this example:

> The Party has made a conscious decision to promote the policy in the city, and it is partly because of this that it is showing signs of growth.

The *it* that is showing signs of growth could be the political party, the policy or the city.

A reader could perhaps deduce what *it* was, and who *her* and *she* were in the previous example, by rereading the passages in which the ambiguous pronouns appear, but the reader may not have the time or the will. The examiner may have thirty other essays to read that night; the director of the local government department may have six more reports to read in a morning before attending a meeting in the afternoon; an employer may have fifty more letters of application and *curricula vitae* for one vacant post.

None of us can achieve absolute clarity, but it is in our own best interests to try to make our meaning intelligible.

Omissions

Wrong Numbers

News reports sometimes give statistical and arithmetical information in a simplified, slightly colloquial form that is widely accepted and understood but which, if interpreted literally by the reader, can still expose the writer to mild ridicule.

> A car left in a city car park is stolen twice a day.

> For the third Saturday in a row a child was lost in the shopping centre.

> Police report that five houses in the Cradle Bay district are broken into every weekend throughout the year.

The common cause of these ambiguities is that the incidence or frequency of the events in the statistics has been oversimplified; many cars, for example, become one car, which is stolen twice a day. The information could be expressed more fully and the words *on average* can sometimes be added:

> On average there are two incidents of car theft from city car parks every day.

> Police report that on average there are five cases of house-breaking in the Cradle Bay district every weekend throughout the year.

The second of the three examples above needs radical restructuring:

> A child was lost in the city shopping centre on Saturday, the third such incident in successive weeks.

Missing Links

Statements are sometimes ambiguous because the writers omit vital pieces of information. The omissions are more likely to occur when the writer is working under pressure, but even on these occasions the ambiguity is still the result of the writer's unthinking assumption that the reader will somehow know what the writer intends. In this first example the assumption is clear:

> Three homeless men shared the bed and breakfast.

Most readers will see at a glance that the term, *bed and breakfast*, is being used colloquially and that the word *accommodation* has been omitted from the end of the sentence, but some readers will also see the absurdity of the crowded bed and the single, shared breakfast. The ambiguity is avoided by identifying the circumstance correctly.

In this second example:

> Churchill's wartime speeches in Parliament were widely read in Britain and overseas.

most readers will realize that the speeches were reported in newspapers and that the public read these reports, but once again some readers of the sentence will notice the gap in the logic and thus will be more aware, at least momentarily, of the ambiguity than the intended meaning. This form of ambiguity is avoided by bridging the gap and identifying each stage in the sequence of events:

> Churchill's wartime speeches in Parliament were reported in the press and then widely read in Britain and overseas.

Two of the examples used in the introduction to this section show that the omissions can sometimes be absurd or even defamatory. The missing words are shown in square brackets:

> Police were ordered to stop [people from] sleeping in shop doorways.

> Her Royal Highness broke a bottle of champagne over [the ship's] bows and then [the ship] slid stern-first into the river.

The two sentences are structured in such a way that they bring together incongruous images or ideas; we separate the incongruities simply by adding the missing information.

Syntax

Juxtaposition

A similar form of absurdity can arise when the sentence includes all the necessary information but in a syntax, that is, a word order, that creates preposterous juxtaposition. Examples that have appeared in print include:

> The two thieves escaped in a stolen car which was driven by a third member of the gang fitted with false number plates.

> Ian Botham was feeding the elephants with his children before he set off on the next stage of the long march for charity.

> MI5 will take over the responsibility of hunting down terrorists from Scotland Yard's Special Branch.

In each case the absurdity can be avoided by restructuring the sentence:

> The two thieves escaped in a stolen car which was fitted with false number plates and driven by a third member of the gang.

> Ian Botham and his children were feeding the elephants before Mr Botham set off on the next stage of his long march for charity.

> MI5 will take over from Scotland Yard's Special Branch the responsibility for hunting down terrorists.

The way to avoid this form of ambiguity is to structure your sentences so that related items of information are as close together as possible, and dissimilar or contradictory items are kept apart.

Participial Phrases

Ambiguities can arise from the faulty syntax of sentences beginning with participial phrases. When a sentence opens with a participial phrase, the phrase must be followed immediately by a related noun, pronoun or noun phrase. For example:

> Driving along Princes Street, he saw the Castle silhouetted against the skyline.

The word *driving* is the present participle of the verb *drive*, and the words *Driving along Princes Street* form a participial phrase. The first word after the phrase is the pronoun *he*, which is directly related to the verb *driving* since it was he who was driving. Similarly, in the sentence:

> Beaten in the final of the 800 metres, Franky Dexter limped off the track.

The word *beaten* is the past participle of the verb *beat*, and the words *Beaten in the final of the 800 metres* form a participial phrase. *Franky Dexter*, the proper noun immediately after the participial phrase, is directly related to the verb *beaten*.

When the noun, pronoun or noun phrase is not directly related to the participial phrase, the result can be ambiguous and absurd. In these sentences:

> Flying across the Scottish mountains, a herd of red deer scattered in panic.

> Rowing across the Highland loch, an osprey caught a trout.

the noun phrase *a herd of red deer* and the noun *an osprey* are not directly related to the participial phrases, and so there is the momentary absurdity of deer that can fly and a bird that can row a boat. In both sentences the ambiguity is removed when a form of words including an appropriate noun, pronoun or noun phrase is added immediately after the participial phrases:

> Flying across the Scottish mountains, the helicopter pilot noticed a herd of red deer scatter in panic.

> Rowing across the Highland loch, the old poacher saw an osprey catch a trout.

The same rule applies to participial phrases beginning with the past participle:

> Educated in Canada, her books have been translated into seven languages.

> Killed in a road accident the previous month, the President awarded the decoration posthumously to the infantryman.

Here again there are absurdities: an educated book rather than an educated author, and a dead President coming back to life. The two sentences can be rewritten as:

> Educated in Canada, the author has had her books translated into seven languages.

> Killed in a road accident the previous month, the infantryman was awarded the decoration posthumously by the President.

The two faulty sentences that open with past participles benefit from a more radical editing:

> The author was educated in Canada, and her books have been translated into seven languages.

> The President awarded the decoration posthumously because the infantryman had been killed in a road accident the previous month.

Only

The misplaced word *only* is another source of ambiguity. The meaning of the sentence below changes according to the position of *only*:

> Sam borrowed a tape recorder from Derek.

When *only* is added to the beginning of the sentence:

> Only Sam borrowed a tape recorder from Derek.

the meaning is that Sam and no one else borrowed the tape recorder. If *only* is placed between *Sam* and *borrowed*, the implication is that Sam borrowed the machine as distinct from stealing it or damaging it. When *only* is placed between *borrowed* and *a tape recorder*, the implication is that Sam borrowed the tape recorder and nothing else. When *only* is placed at the end of the sentence after *Derek* the implication is that Sam borrowed from Derek and from no one else. If *only* appears between *recorder* and *from*, the sentence will be ambiguous; it could mean that Sam borrowed a tape recorder and nothing else or that Sam borrowed from Derek and no one else.

Multiple Meanings

Many simple, or apparently simple, English words have two or more meanings, either because the words are homonyms or because they are polysemous.

A homonym – the word means the same name or the same word – is a single form for two or more words with different meanings and different origins. For example, a shoemaker's *last*, a model of the human foot, is derived from the Old English word *last*, a footprint. *Last* in the sense of latest is from a different Old English word *laetest*. Last meaning endure or continue is from a third Old English word *laestan*. Three different words, each with a different meaning, have converged into the single form *last*.

A polysemous word – the noun is *polysemy* – is a word with two or more meanings, all of which have evolved from the same source. For example, the word *snake*, from the Old English word *snaca*, as well as denoting a reptile, is also a personal insult, a verb meaning to twist and turn literally or metaphorically, part of the compound words *snake-bird*, *snake-fish*, *snake-weed*, an exclamation in *Snakes alive!* and a colloquial term for an engineer's measuring tape.

Examples of words with multiple meanings are:

> air, bar, bat, bay, bit, cast, chap, die, dog, hack, vice, wake, ward, well, will, wind, yarn, yield.

Some of the polysemous words above, and many other words, have the same form both as noun and verb:

> bait, catch, engineer, guard, haunt, ring, trace, vault, veto, vote, water, zero, zigzag.

Other words have the same form both as adjective and noun:

academic, adult, delinquent, equal, evil, good, haemophiliac, introspective, neurotic, stoic, valuable.

Even the apparently simple expression, *put up*, has several different applications, especially if we include idiomatic and colloquial usages as well as standard English:

Mr Brown put up the *Vacancies* sign.

He put up an American couple for the night.

A child was put up to a prank by her brothers.

Mr Brown would not put up with rowdy guests.

Annoyed by one guest's behaviour, he shouted, 'Put up or shut up!'

Last year Mr Brown had to put up his prices.

This year he put up a plan to the local tourist association.

It is surprising, then, that polysemous words are seldom the cause of ambiguity in students' writing. Journalism, on the other hand, offers many examples. The use of the word *over* as a shorter form of *in connection with* leads to:

Police are holding two men over the fire in Edward Street.

An assistant finance officer has been suspended over the missing files.

Similarly, journalists' application of the word *case* to a variety of incidents and occasions leads to ambiguities such as:

Customs officials have been slammed in the smuggled arms case.

A company director is being held in a Moroccan drugs case.

Police are searching for an antiques dealer in a missing manuscript case.

The same kind of ambiguity appears in the example at the beginning of this section, where the words, *fought with* can be read as *fought against* or *fought alongside*:

In his farewell speech the retiring MP offered his best wishes to colleagues whom he had fought alongside for over thirty years.

The double grammatical function – noun and verb, or adjective and noun – of many words results in an endless succession of ambiguous newspaper headlines, some of which are so silly that they may be deliberate puns devised by newspaper sub-editors:

Health minister attacks dentists' body

Doctors back nurses' body

Labour left in pay bed fury

Children hit as teachers strike

Fish talks after skippers clash

Since all the ambiguities in this section arise from the meanings and grammatical functions of words, the only way to avoid the ambiguities – or, in your more frivolous moments, to create them – is to extend your vocabulary and improve your knowledge of grammar. The easiest way to achieve both these aims, and to improve your spelling at the same time, is to use a dictionary.

Officialese

Legal documents have to be written in a legalistic prose style, but the two examples below are in a form of language that is too often used in documents written for general readers. The extracts use a prose style that is known colloquially as officialese because it so obviously strives to be official, or even officious; the style is also known as gobbledegook, the nonsensical gobbling of a turkey.

The first example is adapted from a local government report.

> Both parties are agreed that the cause of the dispute is the rejection by the employees of the cleansing unit of a proposal by the District Council to pay them overtime money based on the amounts paid before the national strike action by the National and Local Government Officers Association, which has disrupted the District Council's normal pay process.

The parties may be agreed but it is difficult for the reader to understand exactly what they have agreed. Complex information like this can often be made more intelligible, without changing its meaning, if it is written in a simpler form. The example above can be simplified by breaking the information into shorter units of communication, that is, shorter sentences, and by changing the order of the information to provide a chronological sequence. Most of the original wording is retained in this revised version.

> The national strike action by the National and Local Government Officers Association (NALGO) disrupted the District Council's normal pay process. The District Council offered to pay employees of the cleansing unit overtime money based on the amounts paid before

the national strike action by NALGO. The employees rejected this proposal. Both parties, the District Council and NALGO, agree that the rejection of the pay proposal is the cause of the dispute.

The second example of unnecessarily ambiguous officialese is adapted from a company's staff handbook:

> The minimum holiday entitlement, irrespective of the employee's length of service, will be twenty days, not including statutory bank holidays, except when an employee terminates his employment before retiral age, or is dismissed from employment following agreed disciplinary procedures. When employment is terminated in either of these ways the employee's holiday entitlement for that year will be five days for each three months or part thereof of employment.

Similar changes can be made to the syntax of this second example, and the wording too can be changed. Since the minimum holiday entitlement is absolute, there is no need for the phrase, *irrespective of the employee's length of service*; and since statutory bank holidays are in addition to the twenty days, it is misleading to use the negative wording, *not including*. A simpler version of the second example is:

> The minimum holiday entitlement for all employees will be twenty days. In addition to the twenty days, all employees will receive the statutory bank holidays. Exceptions to this are, firstly, when an employee terminates his employment before retiral age, or, secondly, when an employee is dismissed from employment following agreed disciplinary procedures. When employment is terminated in either of these ways the employee's holiday entitlement for that year will be five days for each three months, or part of three months, of employment.

Miscellaneous

There remains a wide range of ambiguities that are difficult to classify, and thus difficult to avoid, because they are implicit in the English language. Groupings of words that are grammatically and syntactically correct can lead to statements that read like versions of the old music hall exchange:

> 'I didn't come here to be insulted.'
>
> 'No? Then where do you normally go to be insulted?'

Unintended variations on that exchange are:

Andrew left his friend to pay the bill.

Who paid the bill, Andrew or his friend?

Jeremy heard his sister from inside the house.

or

From inside the house Jeremy heard his sister.

Who was inside the house? Jeremy, or his sister, or both?

Mr Pendleton was not invited to the party because he was the *Clarion* editor.

Does that mean that Mr Pendleton's position as editor prevented him from being invited to the party, or that he was invited to the party but for reasons other than his editorship?

When you are writing under pressure it is particularly difficult to avoid these ambiguities. The more alert you are in your use of language, and the more you cultivate the role of reader as well as writer, then the greater your chance of detecting these double meanings. If you are in doubt, in this context or in others, then you should structure your sentences as explicitly as possible.

6 Writing Sentences

SIMPLE SENTENCES

The most easily identified unit of English language is the single word, and we have seen how words can be identified more precisely and used more effectively. But when language is used in the continuous prose of essays, reports, short stories or news stories, the significant units of language are the sentence and the paragraph.

A standard English sentence is the biggest unit of language that can be analysed grammatically, and the smallest unit that can be analysed for prose style. The two sets of factors, grammar and style, are interdependent. Good prose style requires a basis of sound grammar, and for that reason this chapter on sentence structure will take account of grammar and style. Before the main discussion begins, it may be helpful to look briefly at the mental activities involved in the writing of sentences.

All language, speech or writing, is a process of encoding. Electro-chemical energy in the left half, or hemisphere, of the brain is transformed into sense impressions; the impressions are refined into thought, that is, ideas, images and emotions; thought in turn is re-coded, or 'translated', into language, which is then structured and edited into written standard English.

If you are reading an account of these mental activities for the first time, the process may seem complex, but the fact that you are reading this paragraph proves that you are capable of all stages in the process. The final stage, encoding your thought in written standard English, differs from the others. Earlier stages are the result of innate, natural activities in the brain, whereas written standard English is the external expression of these activities by means of the alphabet, a medium that is not natural but invented.

Written standard English is more rule-bound than speech or one's inner thoughts before they are articulated as speech. The rules cover spelling, semantics, grammar, punctuation and syntax, that is, the structuring of sentences and paragraphs. The noun syntax and the adjective syntactic derive from a Greek word meaning arrange. These rules form a code or set of codes that must be applied to 'inner' language if the words in your brain are to be understood by readers. Anyone who is capable of the earlier stages of mental activity that lead to 'inner' language, and anyone who is reading these words, is certainly capable of learning and using the code.

When the code is known, the English language becomes an infinitely flexible, inexhaustible resource. The code enables you, the user, to be understood by, and thus to enter the thoughts of, all other readers who know the code. And the nature of the resource, over 500,000 words and variants which can appear in innumerable syntactic permutations, enables you to write wholly original sentences, combinations of words that have never been written before.

The Sentence Defined

A sentence is a group of words that must normally include a finite verb and must normally form a complete unit of communication. (The word *normally* is used in the definition above because there can be exceptions, that is, sentences which do not include finite verbs or which do not form complete units of communication.) Almost every passage of prose that extends to more than two or three paragraphs will have a mix of three types of sentence: the simple sentence, the compound sentence and the complex sentence. A fourth type, the compound-complex sentence, may also be present. All four types will be discussed in detail later in this chapter; this section focuses mainly on simple sentences.

A standard English sentence must normally include a finite verb, that is, a verb with a subject. The subject of a verb, and thus the subject of the sentence in which that verb appears, is the factor or agent responsible for the action or activity indicated by the verb:

SUBJECT	VERB	OBJECT
A thunderstorm	ruined	the barbecue.
Andrew and Hannah	entered	the yellow marquee.
We	followed	them.

These examples show that the subject of the verb is normally

a noun: *thunderstorm*

or a noun phrase: *Andrew and Hannah*

or a pronoun: *we*.

Verbs of command, that is, verbs in the imperative mood, break this pattern by implying the subject, *you*:

[You] Stop! [You] Listen! [You] Calm down.

A group of words without a finite verb is not normally acceptable as a standard English sentence. All verbs except the modal auxiliary verbs have non-finite forms. As we saw in the section on verbs, these forms are the infinitive:

to ruin, to enter, to follow

the present participle, which always ends in *-ing*:

ruining, entering, following

and the past participle, which is the form the verb takes after the auxiliary verb *have* or *had*:

ruined, entered, followed.

A group of words without a verb, either finite or non-finite, can communicate information to the reader but the group of words will be grammatically incomplete. Without the action or direction expressed by the verb the group of words is also likely to be stylistically incomplete. For these reasons standard English does not accept the following statements as sentences:

A new warning by the police to city motorists.

A second fatal accident this month on the city by-pass.

A one-year driving ban and a £1,000 fine for the careless driver.

If we add a finite verb to each sentence, and if we avoid the monotony of opening each sentence with a form of words such as *There is*, *There was* or *There will be*, we can produce sentences that are acceptable grammatically and stylistically:

Police *have issued* a new warning to city motorists.

For the second time this month a fatal accident *has occurred* on the city by-pass.

A one-year driving ban and a £1,000 fine *have been imposed* on the careless driver.

Each of the following statements has a verb, but because the verbs are in non-finite forms the statements are not acceptable as standard English:

Mr Leonard Vedley *to seek* planning permission for a Cradle Bay marina development.

A marina development *proposed* for Cradle Bay.

Mr Vedley *promising* 150 new jobs at the proposed Cradle Bay Marina.

The first verb, *to seek*, is the infinitive form; the second, *proposed*, is the past participle; the third, *promising*, is the present participle. We can change these non-finite forms into finite by adding auxiliary verbs:

Mr Leonard Vedley *is to seek* planning permission for a Cradle Bay marina development.

A marina development *has been proposed* for Cradle Bay.

Mr Vedley *is promising* 150 new jobs at the proposed Cradle Bay Marina.

With the addition of finite verbs, these statements meet the criteria of grammar and style and are thus acceptable as sentences.

Objects of Sentences

Three examples that were used above to illustrate the relationship between the subject and the verb in a sentence also illustrate the relationship between the transitive verb and the object:

SUBJECT	VERB	OBJECT
A thunderstorm	ruined	the barbecue.
Andrew and Hannah	entered	the yellow marquee.
We	followed	them.

The object of a transitive verb shows the result that follows from the action of the verb. An object, just like a subject, must normally include:

a noun: *barbecue*

or a noun phrase: *the yellow marquee*

or a pronoun: *them*.

All of these objects – *the barbecue, the yellow marquee*, and *them* – follow directly from the verbs. When the object follows the verb in this way it is known as the direct object. The object can be extended so as to add more information to a sentence, and these extensions are known as indirect objects because they normally follow indirectly rather than directly from the verb. The three sentences below are broken down into their component parts of subject, verb, direct object and indirect object.

SUBJECT	VERB	DIRECT OBJECT	INDIRECT OBJECT
The police	have issued	a new warnning	to city motorists.
A local businessman	will seek	planning permission	for a Cradle Bay development.
Mr Leonard Vedley	is promising	150 new jobs	at the Cradle Bay Marina development.

When the verb is transitive then it must, by definition, be followed by a direct object in order to make the sentence grammatically and stylistically complete, as these examples show:

City councillors took

The Chamber of Commerce will donate

Students at Central University need

With the addition of an object, each statement becomes a complete unit of communication:

City councillors took a difficult decision.

The Chamber of Commerce will donate £2,500 to local charities.

Students at Central University need a bigger library.

Together, the verb, the object and the indirect object are sometimes known as the predicate of the sentence, predicate in this context meaning the statement expressed by the subject. A sentence structure can be shown simply as subject and predicate:

SUBJECT	PREDICATE
The police	have issued a new warning to city motorists.
A local businessman	will seek planning permission for a Cradle Bay development.

Each of the sentences considered so far has only one finite verb, and such sentences are known grammatically as simple sentences. A simple sentence, then, can be expressed as:

> subject + verb + object + indirect object
>
> **or**
>
> subject + predicate.

Reduced to these formulae, sentences can be structurally as well as grammatically simple, and to avoid the risk of monotony most passages of continuous prose vary the types of sentence from simple to compound, complex and compound-complex. Even so, a great deal of variety can be achieved within the simple sentence by using various links and extensions.

Links and Extensions

One way of extending a simple sentence so that it conveys more information and adds variety to your prose style is to use the conjunction *and*, the adverb *also* and the linking phrases *as well as*, *along with*, *in addition to* and *on top of*:

> Vitesse Bordeaux *and* Cracow Solidarnoz met in the cup final.
>
> Charles Auriol, Chairman of Vitesse Bordeaux, is *also* chairman of three other companies in the Bordeaux area.
>
> Women *as well as* men sang in the streets of Bordeaux after Vitesse's cup win.
>
> The victory champagne, *in addition to* the brandy at half-time, affected the Vitesse Bordeaux Chairman.
>
> Their cup-winning bonus, *on top of* other cash awards *and along with* their annual salaries, made Vitesse Bordeaux the highest paid team in France.

Other words and phrases that can be used in the same way are: *besides*, *and besides* and *over and above*.

Noun Phrases

Another technique that is easy to use is to extend single words, notably nouns, adjectives, prepositions and adverbs, into phrases. A phrase is normally a group of two or more words without a finite verb. A noun phrase is a phrase in which the head word, or main word, is a noun.

Several noun phrases appear in the sentences immediately above:

> Chairman of Vitesse Bordeaux, chairman of three other companies, the victory champagne, the Vitesse Bordeaux chairman, Their cup-winning bonus, the highest paid team in France.

The head word in each of these phrases is a noun – *chairman* in three of the phrases, *champagne*, *bonus* and *team* – and by extending the nouns into noun phrases we add more information to the sentences and more variety to the sentence structures.

Adjective Phrases

Some of the noun phrases above contain adjectives:

> *other* companies, *victory* champagne, *cup-winning* bonus

but in each case it is clear that the noun is the head word and that the adjective is describing the noun. In other phrases, however, it is equally clear that the adjective is the head word, and such phrases are adjective phrases:

> Matthew Ray, the new Member of Parliament, is *much too ambitious*.

> The editor of the *Daily Clarion* is *hard-working, fair-minded and more objective than the former editor*.

> Kiln Acres, the site of the old brickworks, is *completely derelict*. The area is *the bleakest in the region*. The cost of reclamation, however, would be *far too high*.

Preposition Phrases

The earlier section on prepositions (see pages 74–7) showed the important role of this class of function words and showed too that a preposition appears as the head word in a preposition phrase:

> The Australian XV showed effort and artistry *in a high-scoring match*.

> Experienced archaeologists will excavate an Iron Age site *near the city centre*.

This third sentence ends with two preposition phrases, *for new orders* and *at home and abroad*:

> Electronic engineering factories are competing *for new orders at home and abroad*.

Further variation on the structure of the simple sentence can be achieved by placing the preposition phrase at the beginning of the sentence:

On the third Saturday in December city shoppers went on a Christmas spending spree.

After a heated debate the council accepted the planning proposal for the marina development.

Adverbial Phrases

The addition of an adverbial phrase allows you to extend the meaning of the verb of a simple sentence:

The editor publishes *without fear or favour*.

Slowly and painstakingly the archaeologists excavated the Iron Age site. *Only once before* had they dug near the city centre. Now they worked *with great enthusiasm*.

As a matter of urgency, electronic engineering factories are competing for new orders.

These examples show how, with the addition of a phrase, you can extend the meaning and the structure of a simple sentence. By changing the position of the phrase in the sentence, you vary not only the structure but also the prose rhythm and the internal emphasis, thus focusing your reader's attention on the part of the sentence you wish to highlight.

Links, Extensions and Prose Style

As a general rule, it is normally safer to use the simplest, least demonstrative linking device. If you strive for more elaborate links your prose style may begin to seem strained and contrived. You may also fall into the trap known ironically as 'elegant' variation, that is, a determination to avoid repeating a key word or phrase, even when the result of the avoidance is more obvious and more stilted than the repetition.

For example, a newspaper reporter writing about a photographer colleague who had won an award referred to the man first as *a prize-winning photographer*, a factual statement in standard English; then as *the ace lensman*, which is an instant journalistic cliché; as *the super snapper*, which is catchy, alliterative and colloquial but not standard English; and finally as *the prince of the pics*, a phrase chosen for its alliteration rather than its meaning. The news item would have been more effective if the reporter had avoided variation and instead had repeated the word *photographer*, the photographer's name and the personal pronoun *he*. As you can see from that example, the term 'elegant' variation is ironic because the variation is inelegant.

Wider questions of prose style arise from the use of descriptive links and extensions. If you rely entirely on phrases to extend simple sentences, a likely result is that your sentences will have a greater volume of information than the single verbs can properly support. The sentences may still be grammatically correct but they will be stylistically wrong if they draw the reader's attention away from your intended meaning and into your prose style. In this example:

> The fair-minded, hard-working city councillors, the elected representatives of the people, finally took a difficult decision on the marina development after a long and sometimes heated debate.

The single finite verb *took* is almost overwhelmed in the sentence. When a piece of writing has too great a volume of description, the prose style can become so florid and effusive that even a non-specialist reader will sense that there is something too highly embellished or self-conscious about the writing. The reader may suspect that your vivid description is merely windy rhetoric.

If you write simple sentences in a less descriptive style there could be another dilemma. A piece of continuous prose of two or more paragraphs written entirely in simple sentences could soon become boring for the reader. An unvarying formula of subject + verb + object could lead not only to repetition in the structure of the sentences but also to a repetitive, faltering or unnecessarily staccato prose rhythm. The dilemma is resolved by using a mixture of simple and longer sentences, that is, sentences with two or more finite verbs and thus two or more clauses.

COMPOUND SENTENCES

In the section on conjunctions (pages 77–8), we saw that a conjunction can be used to introduce a clause, that is, a group of words that is normally longer than a phrase but shorter than a sentence and that contains a finite verb. One example used the conjunction *either . . . or* and the two finite verbs, *stay* and *drive*:

> *Either* you stay overnight at Parsemer/*or* you drive on to the city of Grantown.

A second example used the conjunction *but* and the finite verb *is* in both clauses:

> Aldridge Tower at Upper Sallow is derelict/*but* Thornham Hall in Lower Sallow is still inhabited.

Similarly, the commonest conjunction, *and*, can be used to link two clauses in the same sentence:

> Rock bands attract one kind of audience/*and* folk groups attract another.

Two or more conjunctions can be used to link three or more clauses in a sentence, but the structure of a sentence can seem repetitive if more than two conjunctions are used:

> Some members of the council opposed the marina scheme/*but* a majority supported it/*and* the planning application was approved.

Sentences with two or more clauses linked by conjunctions are known as compound sentences; the word compound in this context means a combination of two or more factors. Each clause in a compound sentence has the same grammatical function and is known as a main clause or principal clause. A main clause without the conjunction can normally be detached from the rest of the sentence and stand alone as a sentence in its own right. If we apply that rule to the clauses in the compound sentences above, we find that all but one of the clauses form a complete sentence. The exception, *a majority supported it*, would be acceptable as a standard English sentence if the pronoun *it* were replaced by the noun phrase, *the marina scheme*:

> A majority supported the marina scheme.

Because the purpose of a conjunction is to link two units of language, in this context two main clauses, you may confuse your reader if you break the link and form two sentences while retaining the conjunction. There is no grammatical objection to a sentence that begins with a conjunction, but repeated use of this kind of structure can soon produce a mannered, unnecessarily staccato prose style:

> A team from the Young Farmers Club entered the annual raft race. And came second. The young farmers could have won. But their combined weight almost sank their raft. They raised over £1,000 for charity. And met their target. But they hope to do better next year.

All the sentences in the passage above are grammatically simple and yet the prose style is fussily ostentatious. Journalists sometimes use this breathless style in an attempt to inject interest in their subject matter, but the attempt will fail if the reader becomes more aware of the style than the content. A simpler effect is achieved if the grammatically simple sentences in the passage above are changed into compound sentences:

> A team from the Young Farmers Club entered the annual raft race and came second. The young farmers could have won but their combined weight almost sank their raft. They raised over £1,000 for charity and met their target, but they hope to do better next year.

The second version of the passage consists of three compound sentences and is more fluent than the first version with its seven simple sentences. Even so, the repeated use of the same structural device in the second version becomes repetitive by the end of the passage. The resources of simple sentences and compound sentences may not be enough to sustain a reader's interest over a longer prose passage, but when we turn to the third type of sentence, the complex sentence, we find an almost limitless number of options.

COMPLEX SENTENCES

A complex sentence consists of one main clause and one or more subordinate, or sub-clauses. The adjective complex here means composed of two or more related parts. As we have seen, a main clause is one that, if isolated from the rest of the sentence, can normally form a complete unit of communication and stand as a sentence in its own right. A sub-clause, on the other hand, cannot normally form a complete unit of communication or a complete sentence but depends for part of its meaning on the main clause. The sub-clause, then, is subordinate to the main clause.

In this complex sentence:

> Positron's drummer is Trick Fraser, who began his career in the National Youth Orchestra.

the main clause is

> Positron's drummer is Trick Fraser.

When we apply the test for a main clause we find that *Positron's drummer is Trick Fraser* is a form of words that is grammatically and semantically complete and can stand as a sentence in its own right. The remainder of the sentence:

who began his career in the National Youth Orchestra

contains the finite verb *began* with the pronoun *who* as the subject of the verb. The form of words, *who began his career in the National Youth Orchestra*, meets the grammatical requirements of a sentence, but it is clear that the words do not meet the require-ments of meaning or style and do not form a complete unit of com-munication. Instead, *who began his career in the National Youth Orchestra* depends for its meaning on the main clause and is thus a sub-clause in the complex sentence.

Descriptive Sub-clauses and Human Nouns

The statement, *who began his career in the National Youth Orchestra*, is a typical example of a sub-clause that describes a proper noun in the main clause, in this example the noun *Trick Fraser*. When the sub-clause describes a human noun in the main clause, the sub-clause normally begins with the relative pronoun *who*, *whom* or *whose*. The noun to which the relative pronoun relates is known as the antecedent, which means going before.

You may find it useful to think of *who* as being equivalent to *he*, *she* or *they*; *whom* as being equivalent to *him*, *her* or *them*; and *whose* as equivalent to *his*, *hers* or *theirs*. A simple mnemonic, or memorizing device will help you to file this point in your long-term memory:

who = he, she, they

whom = him, her, them

whose = his, hers, theirs.

A simplification in the grammar of descriptive sub-clauses is that the word *whom* can often be omitted in standard English. For exam-ple, in the sentence:

Trick Fraser is a musician *whom I admire.*

the sub-clause, *whom I admire*, which is the equivalent of *I admire him*, refers to the noun *musician* in the main clause. In this and in similar sentences the word *whom* can be dropped and the sentence can be be written as:

Trick Fraser is a musician *I admire.*

The words *I admire* still form a descriptive sub-clause referring back to the antecedent noun *musician*.

Standard English still requires the phrases *to whom*, *for whom*, *from whom*, *with whom* and *about whom*:

> The musician *from whom I learned most* is Positron's keyboards player, Ward Nettles.

> Positron's drummer, *about whom the critics are divided*, began his career in the National Youth Orchestra.

The sub-clause *from whom I learned most* is the equivalent of *I learned most from him* and refers to the antecedent noun *musician* in the main clause. The sub-clause *about whom the critics are divided* is the equivalent of *the critics are divided about him* and refers to the noun *drummer* in the main clause.

An example of a descriptive sub-clause beginning with the relative pronoun *whose* is:

> Trick Fraser, *whose parents are amateur musicians*, is leaving the group next month.

The sub-clause *whose parents are amateur musicians* is the equivalent of *his parents are amateur musicians*, and here the sub-clause relates to the antecedent proper noun, *Trick Fraser*.

A descriptive sub-clause referring to a human noun must begin with the relative pronoun *who*, *whom* or *whose*. The relative pronouns *that* and *which* relate only to non-human nouns in the main clause. Standard English does not tolerate a structure such as:

> Several musicians *that were once members of the National Youth Orchestra* are now playing professionally.

Inclusive and Exclusive Descriptive Sub-clauses

The meanings of descriptive clauses are often determined by the punctuation of the sub-clause. If we take the example:

> The fast bowler *who took six wickets* was named the man of the match.

the implication is that the singular noun *bowler* in the main clause is one bowler among others:

> The fast bowler *who took six wickets* [as distinct from the other fast bowlers] was named the man of the match.

But when the sub-clause is marked off by commas:

> The fast bowler, *who took six wickets*, was named the man of the match.

it is clear that only one bowler is being considered. The commas restrict the noun to one bowler, thus reinforcing the singularity of the noun in the main clause by making the noun not only grammatically singular but also singular in the sense of excluding all others.

Here is a similar example:

> The busker *who played the clarinet* entertained the Saturday shoppers.

Without the commas, the sentence implies that there may have been buskers who did not play clarinets or did not entertain the shoppers. When the commas are added:

> The busker, *who played the clarinet*, entertained the Saturday shoppers.

it is clear that only one busker is being referred to. The commas restrict the noun to one person only and thus make him or her an exclusive busker.

When the noun in the main clause is singular, the rules are these:

> If the 'who' clause is punctuated by commas, the commas restrict the noun to one person only and exclude all others.

> If the 'who' clause has no commas, there is no restriction; the noun is not exclusive but is one of several people.

When the noun in the main clause is plural the effect is different. In the examples that follow, the sub-clauses are again set in italic type. The words *Daily Clarion* are also set in italics to show that these words are the title of a newspaper.

> *Daily Clarion* journalists *who work unsocial hours* get overtime payments.

And when we restructure the same example:

> Overtime payments are given to *Daily Clarion* journalists *who work unsocial hours.*

the descriptive sub-clause *who work unsocial hours* clearly refers to the plural noun *journalists*. But does it refer to all journalists on the *Clarion* or only some of them? The ambiguity is easily avoided. If you write:

> *Daily Clarion* journalists, *who work unsocial hours*, get overtune payments.

or if you write:

> Overtime payments are given to *Daily Clarion* journalists, *who work unsocial hours.*

the effect of the commas is to make the sub-clause refer to all the journalists on the *Clarion*. The sub-clause marked off in commas not only describes the antecedent noun *journalists* but is similar in function to a statement in apposition to *journalists*, that is, to all the journalists. Commas make the plural noun all-inclusive.

When there are no commas the 'who' sub-clause refers only to some of the journalists. Thus the 'who' sub-clause in

> *Daily Clarion* journalists *who work unsocial hours* get overtime payments.

clearly implies that some *Clarion* journalists do not work unsocial hours and so get no overtime payments:

> *Daily Clarion* journalists *who work unsocial hours* [as distinct from other journalists who do not] get overtime payments.

When the noun in the main clause is plural, the rules are these:

> When the 'who' clause is punctuated by commas, the noun is all-inclusive and refers to everyone.

> If the 'who' clause has no commas, not everyone is included; the 'who' clause refers only to some of the people.

The old grammatical terms for sub-clauses with the same structure, but different punctuation and meanings, were 'defining' and 'non-defining' clauses, but these terms are themselves ambiguous.

Descriptive Sub-clauses and Non-human Nouns

When the descriptive sub-clause describes a noun that is not a person but is an animal or an inanimate thing, the sub-clause normally begins with the relative pronoun *that* or *which*. The distinction between *that* and *which* is both important and useful, especially when differentiating between inclusive and non-inclusive sub-clauses. In this sentence, for example:

> The drugs hot line *that was set up in the Cradle Bay district last year* is appealing for funds.

the sub-clause *that was set up in the Cradle Bay district last year* implies that there may have been other drugs hot lines in other places. But when we use the relative pronoun *which*, and punctuate the sub-clause with commas, the effect is different:

> The drugs hot line, *which was set in the Cradle Bay district last year*, is appealing for funds.

Now it is clear that only one hot line is being considered.

The same distinction between *that* and *which* is made when the noun in the main clause is plural. For example:

> Cradle Bay hotels *that depend on the tourist trade* are doing little business this year.

clearly implies that there are other hotels in Cradle Bay that do not depend on the tourist trade. With the replacement of *that* by *which*, and with the addition of commas, the meaning of the sentence is changed:

> Cradle Bay hotels, *which depend on the tourist trade*, are doing little business this year.

Now the sentence means that all the hotels depend on the tourist trade. Similarly:

> Clubs and societies *that meet in Wellington Hall* will pay an increased hire charge next year.

clearly implies that some clubs and societies do not meet in Wellington Hall, whereas this sentence:

> Clubs and societies, *which meet in Wellington Hall*, will pay an increased hire charge next year.

means that all the clubs and societies meet in the hall and will have to pay the new charges.

When the sub-clause describes a place or a location in the main clause, the sub-clause normally begins with the words *where*, *in which* or *at which*:

> There is the old boat yard *where/in which the first Cradle Bay lifeboat was built.*

If the sub-clause describes a date or a time in the main clause, the sub-clause normally begins with the words *when* or *at which*:

> Sunday morning is the time *when/at which the city centre is quietest.*

And finally, if the sub-clause describes an event or an occasion, the sub-clause can begin with the words *where*, *when*, *at which* or *in which*:

> Dr Somerford went to the graduation ceremony *where/at which/in which her niece was awarded a BA degree.*

Descriptive sub-clauses in complex sentences offer a wide range of syntactic options. For example, the simple sentences:

> Geoff Rimmer won the junior motor cycle scramble last year. He is competing again this year.

can be written as the compound sentence:

> Geoff Rimmer won the junior motor cycle scramble last year and he is competing again this year.

or as the complex sentence:

> Geoff Rimmer, who won the junior motor cycle scramble last year, is competing again this year.

The simple sentences:

> Geoff's machine was built by his father. Geoff is only seventeen years old.

can be reversed and linked in the compound sentence:

> Geoff is only seventeen years old, and his machine was built by his father.

or the two simple sentences can be integrated into the fluent and economic complex sentence:

> Geoff, whose machine was built by his father, is only seventeen years old.

The simple sentences:

> Cradle Bay was once a busy fishing port. Cradle Bay is now the site of the new marina.

can be restructured as the compound sentence:

> Cradle Bay was once a busy fishing port but is now the site of the new marina.

The two simple sentences can be restructured in two ways as a complex sentence. First:

> Cradle Bay, which was once a busy fishing port, is now the site of the new marina.

The main clause is *Cradle Bay is now the site of the new marina*; the sub-clause is *which was once a busy fishing port*. Second, we can restructure the two simple sentences as this complex sentence:

> Cradle Bay, which is now the site of the new marina, was once a busy fishing port.

In the second sentence the main clause is *Cradle Bay was once a busy fishing port*; the sub-clause is *which is now the site of the new marina*.

Some simple sentences cannot be linked effectively into a compound sentence. For example, when we link these two simple sentences:

> Geoff Rimmer's father, Jack, owns a lobster boat. The boat was built twenty years ago.

the result is a compound sentence which is structurally and stylistically weak:

> Geoff Rimmer's father, Jack, owns a lobster boat, and it was built twenty years ago.

But the two simple sentences can be integrated effectively in this complex sentence:

> Geoff Rimmer's father, Jack, owns a lobster boat *that was built twenty years ago*.

The main clause is *Geoff Rimmer's father, Jack, owns a lobster boat*, and the sub-clause is *that was built twenty years ago*. An alternative complex sentence, less fluent than the one above but still acceptable, is:

> The lobster boat *that Geoff Rimmer's father, Jack, owns* was built twenty years ago.

A final example shows how the information in two simple sentences can be integrated in several different ways to give variety to the structures and rhythms of your sentences. The two simple sentences are:

> Jack Rimer has lived in Cradle Bay for sixty years. Cradle Bay was once a busy fishing port.

From these two simple sentences we can form several complex sentences, each with the same essential meaning but with a different rhythm and emphasis. The sub-clauses are shown in italic type.

> Jack Rimmer has lived for sixty years in Cradle Bay, *which was once a busy fishing port*.

> Jack Rimmer has lived in Cradle Bay, *which was once a busy fishing port*, for sixty years.

> For sixty years Jack Rimmer has lived in Cradle Bay, *which was once a busy fishing port*.

> Cradle Bay, *where Jack Rimmer has lived for sixty years*, was once a busy fishing port.

The information can be structured as a main clause and two sub-clauses:

> Cradle Bay, *which was once a busy fishing port*, is *where Jack Rimmer has lived for sixty years*.

These examples, and especially the set of five variations on the single theme, show how the descriptive sub-clause and the complex sentence allow you to vary the length, structure, emphasis and rhythm of your writing. The examples also show that through the complex sentence you can organize information in a more integrated, fluent and economic style, a style that makes it possible for you to transmit your thoughts more effectively into the mind of your reader.

In the examples above, all the sub-clauses beginning with the relative pronouns *who*, *whom*, *whose*, *which* and *that*, describe nouns in the main clauses, and so the sub-clauses can be classified as adjective clauses.

Embedded Clauses

In some of the sentences above, the 'who' sub-clauses are inserted, or embedded, in the middle of the main clause. In this example:

> *Daily Clarion* journalists *who work unsocial hours* get overtime payments.

the main clause is:

> *Daily Clarion* journalists get overtime payments

and the sub-clause is embedded in the main clause.

This technique of embedding or inserting a sub-clause within the main clause has two sets of advantages: it allows your sentence to carry more information in an economic way, and it allows you to vary your syntax. But there is a danger in multiple embedding. If the main clause contains an embedded sub-clause, and if the embedded sub-clause itself contains another embedded sub-clause, the technique of embedding could begin to be counter-productive. For example:

> Positron's drummer, about whom the critics – most of whom are not professional musicians and whose knowledge of music is some-

times limited – are divided, began his career in the National Youth Orchestra.

The main clause, *Positron's drummer began his career in the National Youth Orchestra*, is interrupted by the embedded sub-clause, *about whom the critics are divided*. The sub-clause in turn is interrupted by two more embedded sub-clauses, *most of whom are not professional musicians* and *whose knowledge of music is sometimes limited*.

The end result is a fragmented, convoluted sentence that carries too much information. The subject of the main clause, *Positron's drummer*, is so far removed from the predicate of the main clause, *began his career in the National Youth Orchestra*, that the meaning of the main clause is partly obscured. The prose style becomes self-conscious and opaque, concealing rather than revealing the meaning, and irritating rather than informing the reader.

Sub-clauses as Objects of Verbs

In the opening section on sentence structure and style we saw that the verb of a simple sentence is often followed by a noun or pronoun, which is the object of the verb. The simple sentence then has the pattern: subject + verb + object. An extended version of this pattern appears in complex sentences when the sub-clause is the object of the verb in the main clause. Because this kind of sub-clause functions like a noun, it can be classified as a noun clause.

Such sub-clauses often begin with the relative pronoun *that* or *what*:

> Jean-Paul Chambery, manager of Vitesse Bordeaux, thought *that his goalkeeper was excellent.*

The sub-clause, *that his goalkeeper was excellent*, is the object of the verb *thought* in the main clause, and tells us what was thought. Similarly:

> In the second half, Chambery saw *that Cracow Solidarnoz had lost their rhythm.*

The sub-clause, *that Cracow Solidarnoz had lost their rhythm*, is the object of the verb *saw* in the main clause.

The examples above show the sub-clause beginning with *that*. As a variation of the same structure you can open the sub-clause with *what*:

The Bordeaux team knew *what they had to do to win*.

The sub-clause, *what they had to do to win*, is the object of the verb *knew* in the main clause, and tells us what the team knew. Similarly:

Solidarnoz's manager did not understand *what had gone wrong with his plan*.

The section that follows will show how a third type of sub-clause opens up an even wider range of syntactic options.

Adverbial Clauses

When the sub-clause modifies, or affects the meaning of, the verb in the main clause, many more syntactic options become available. Because this kind of sub-clause modifies the verb in the way an adverb does, the sub-clause is sometimes known as an adverbial clause, and this section will consider the structure and function of the main types of adverbial clause.

Clauses of Opposition

There are many ways of structuring sentences so that the sub-clause indicates opposition or contrast to the action of the verb in the main clause. A sub-clause of opposition often begins as follows:

although, despite, in spite of; if, even if; provided that, so long as, as long as; in case, lest, unless; however, no matter, whether, whatever.

This variety of words and phrases not only offers you a range of options in structuring your opposition sub-clauses but also allows you to select the precise degree of opposition or contrast – the condition to be met or the concession to be made – that is required in each sentence. Too many writers ignore this range of options and choose instead the single, sometimes faulty, 'however' structure for every opposition clause.

We have already seen (pages 201–3) that the simplest way of indicating opposition or contrast is to write two main clauses joined by the conjunction *but*. Some teachers and journalists, reacting to the overuse of the 'but' clause and reacting unnecessarily to any use of *But* as the first word in a sentence, began to use 'however' clauses and structures in a confused way.

Here is an acceptable use of a 'however' clause:

> The reporters could not satisfy the *Clarion* editor *however hard they worked.*

The meaning of the word *however* in the sub-clause, *however hard they worked,* is *no matter how,* or *in whatever manner* or *by whatever means.* If the sequence of main clause and sub-clause is reversed the result is an equally acceptable sentence with the same meaning and the same use of the 'however' clause:

> *However hard they worked,* the reporters could not satisfy the *Clarion* editor.

Similarly, in the correctly structured sentence:

> Beppi's Bistro could not attract new customers *however hard the manager tried.*

or in the same sentence reversed:

> *However hard the manager tried,* Beppi's Bistro could not attract new customers.

the word *however* at the start of the sub-clause means *no matter how* in both forms of the sentence.

Here are typical examples of the other, sometimes confused, use of *however*:

> *However,* the editor was a fine journalist.

> *However,* the *Clarion* editor sometimes muttered a compliment.

> *However,* Beppi's Bistro still made a small profit.

> *However,* Beppi still had his regular customers.

This second use of *however* differs from the first use above. Now the word *however* means *nevertheless,* or *even so,* or *despite this,* or simply *but*; and it was the retreat from *but* that led to this use of *however.* Each sentence in the second group has only one verb and thus only one clause; the word *however* is working as a single word, an adverb, and not as a clause. *However* is sometimes used, not to indicate opposition, but as a vague intensifier like *Basically, Hopefully* or *Frankly,* at the beginning of a sentence. When a comma is inserted after the word *However,* the single-clause structure is clear, but the comma is often wrongly omitted.

'Does it matter?' students sometimes ask about this and other aspects of standard English. It matters for several reasons. First, when the comma is wrongly omitted there can be genuine confusion between the two different 'however' structures. For example:

> *However you feel*, sentence structure can clarify the meaning of what you write.

is not the same as:

> *However*, you feel sentence structure can clarify the meaning of what you write.

Although the word order is identical the 'however' structures, and their meanings, are different. The first, the sub-clause, *However you feel*, means *No matter what you feel* or *Irrespective of how you feel*. In the second structure the word *However* can be seen as an adverb meaning *nevertheless, despite this* or *even so*; but when the second structure is used loosely so that the opening word *However* acts as a link with the previous sentence, *However* is an adverbial conjunction with the same effect as *but*.

When two structures – in this case, the 'however' sub-clause and the single word *However* – become confused in this way, one of them tends to displace the other and a useful part of the language is lost. Another danger for the writer is that those readers who are aware of the difference between the two structures may have to break the continuity of their reading in order to work out the intended meaning. Even a momentary break diverts the reader away from your meaning and into the mechanics of your prose style; if the comma is wrongly omitted after the single word *However*, the break is longer still and the reader's sympathy may be lost.

Another important reason is that the variety, along with the rhythmic and structural energy that comes from variety, is abandoned for the same repetitive *However* structure. When this happens, even a non-professional reader begins to sense the writer's limitations. Repetition can be avoided and the single-clause structure can be made more effective by varying the opening words of the sentences:

> The reporters, however, respected the editor.

> The *Clarion* editor, however, sometimes muttered a compliment.

What matters here and elsewhere is that your capacity for subtle and complex thought, and your ability to communicate that thought to your reader, should not be restricted or undermined by your use of language.

Other Sub-clauses of Opposition

The 'however' sub-clause creates a clear sense of opposition, and the same strength of feeling is created by sub-clauses beginning with the adverbials:

even if, no matter, whether, whatever, despite, in spite of

as in this example:

Even if local residents object, the marina development will go ahead.

The 'even if' sub-clause is equally effective if it follows the main clause:

The marina development will go ahead *even if local residents object*.

A similar effect is created when the sub-clause, either before or after the main clause, begins with the adverbials:

No matter, whether, whatever, despite, in spite of

as in:

No matter what local residents say, . . .

Whether local residents object or not, . . .

Whatever local residents say, . . .

The terms *despite* and *in spite of* could be more succinctly effective if used in adverbial phrases – that is, groups of words without a finite verb – rather than as sub-clauses:

Despite local objections (adverbial phrase), the marina development will go ahead.

In spite of local objections (adverbial phrase), . . .

Sub-clauses beginning with the adverbials:

provided, provided that, so long as, as long as, in case, lest, unless

normally imply that some condition has to be met or some concession made before the action of the verb in the main clause can prevail. Thus:

Provided enough good climbers volunteer, a fells rescue unit will be formed.

A fells rescue unit will be formed *as long as enough good climbers volunteer*.

and:

Miriam Levy will not feel confident in the piano solo *unless she gets more rehearsal time*.

The National Youth Orchestra rehearsed Elgar's overture 'In the South' *in case they needed an encore.*

Provided that and *lest* are now slightly archaic in standard English; the alternatives, *provided* and *in case*, are normally used.

Two similar options are available in sub-clauses beginning with the words *although* and *if*:

Miriam Levy felt nervous *although she had rehearsed the solo thoroughly.*

If Miriam felt nervous it was not apparent in her polished performance.

The 'if' sub-clause tends to be overused, but repetition is easily avoided by using the range of options outlined above.

Finally, for the direct comparison of two or more persons or things, sub-clauses beginning with *as, as if* and *than* are effective:

The atmosphere in Beppi's is *as lively as it was.*

Beppi Serafini spoke about his Bistro *as if it were a gourmet restaurant.*

Beppi's prices are much higher *than they were last year.*

You can work variations on 'as' and 'than' clauses by using the phrases, *as much as, more than, less than.*

When we apply some of these techniques to two simple sentences, we can produce a variety of different structures, all of them conveying the same essential meaning. The two simple sentences:

Franky Dexter has been selected for the 800 metres. He missed most of last season because of injury.

allow the following variations, one of which is the obvious but useful device of reversing the order of the main clause and sub-clause:

Franky Dexter has been selected for the 800 metres *despite/in spite of missing most of last season because of injury.*

Despite/in spite of missing most of last season because of injury, Franky Dexter has been selected for the 800 metres.

Franky Dexter has been selected for the 800 metres *although he missed most of last season because of injury.*

Although he missed most of last season because of injury, Franky Dexter has been selected for the 800 metres.

217

The following two simple sentences:

> Franky could win the race. He will have to train hard.

can be rewritten as one compound sentence:

> Franky could win the race but he will have to train hard.

When the techniques of the complex sentence are applied, we find several variations, again including changing the positions of the main clause and sub-clause:

> Franky could win the race *if he trains hard.*

> *If he trains hard*, Franky could win the race.

> Franky could win the race *provided he trains hard.*

> *Provided he trains hard*, Franky could win the race.

Two more variations are available by embedding the sub-clause within the main clause:

> Franky, *provided he trains hard*, could win the race.

> Franky could, *if he trains hard*, win the race.

This compound sentence:

> The training might prove rigorous but Franky is determined to win.

can be restructured as several versions of a complex sentence:

> *Even if the training proves rigorous*, Franky is determined to win.

> Franky is determined to win *even if the training proves rigorous.*

> *No matter how rigorous the training proves*, Franky is determined to win.

> Franky is determined to win *no matter how rigorous the training proves.*

> *However rigorous the training proves*, Franky is determined to win.

> Franky is determined to win *however rigorous the training proves.*

Stronger Opposition Structures
Some expressions of opposition – *therefore*, which always implies a direct and logical consequence, *even so*, *otherwise*, the slightly archaic *nevertheless*, and of course *however* – have emphatic overtones that call for firmer punctuation and structuring than in most other opposition sub-clauses. Similar to these intensifiers of opposition are the intensifiers of agreement and confirmation, *indeed* and the slightly archaic *furthermore*.

Standard English does not accept constructions such as:

> The drugs hot line ran out of funds, *the service therefore had to be abandoned.*

> Only five experienced climbers volunteered, *even so a fells rescue unit was formed.*

or, to indicate agreement:

> Mike Carter is the youngest player in the Australian XV, *indeed he is the youngest first-class player in Australia.*

These three examples lack the completeness and unity of communication that are the stylistic requirements of sentence structure. Each example consists of two statements, and this must be shown in one of two ways. You can use a semicolon to divide one sentence into two constituent statements:

> The drugs hot line ran out of funds; *the service, therefore, had to be abandoned.*

> Only five experienced climbers volunteered; *even so, a fells rescue unit was formed.*

> Mike Carter is the youngest player in the Australian XV; *indeed, he is the youngest first-class player in Australia.*

In the three examples above, the effect of the semicolon is to produce compound sentences consisting of two main clauses. The commas before and after *therefore*, after *even so* and after *indeed* introduce momentary pauses that reinforce the emphatic nature of these main clauses.

Another option is to make the separation more explicit by writing two sentences:

> The drugs hot line ran out of funds. The service, therefore, had to be abandoned.

> Only five experienced climbers volunteered. Even so, a fells rescue unit was formed.

> Mike Carter is the youngest player in the Australian XV. Indeed, he is the youngest first-class player in Australia.

Here again the commas before and after *therefore*, and after *even so* and *indeed*, confirm the emphases in these sub-clauses.

A third tactic is to omit the words *therefore* and *even so* and to restructure the statements as integrated complex sentences consisting of a main clause and a sub-clause of reason (see below) or a sub-clause of concession. The end result is not quite the same because the emphatic quality of *therefore* and *even so* is lost:

> *Because the drugs hot line ran out of funds,* the service had to be abandoned.

> A fells rescue unit was formed *although only five experienced climbers volunteered.*

Clauses of Comparison, Manner and Method

When the element of contrast takes the form of comparison rather than of outright opposition, or when you wish to express the manner or method in which something was done, several options are available.

One option lies in the ready-made comparison that exists in the comparative forms of adjectives and adverbs. In the example below, the oblique line, /, shows the division of the clauses:

> Hill farmers in the Northwest claim/that costs are *much higher/than they were last year/*but that incomes are *lower/than they have been for many years.*

The comparative adjective *higher* describes the noun *costs*; the sub-clause of comparison, *than they were last year*, modifies the verb *are*. Similarly, the comparative adjective *lower* describes the noun *incomes*, and the sub-clause of comparison, *than they have been for many years*, modifies the second verb *are*.

Comparisons can also be drawn by using the forms *as . . . as*, *more . . . than*, and *less . . . than* as adverbial phrases. In the sentence below, the phrases *as hard as* and *less hopefully than* are adverbials.

> Most farmers are working as *hard/*as they can/but they face the future *less hopefully/*than they have ever done.

The adverb *hard* modifies the verb *are working*, and the sub-clause of comparison is *as they can*; the comparative adverb *less hopefully* modifies the verb *face*, and the sub-clause of comparison is *than they have ever done*.

The same form of words, *as . . . as*, can be used to introduce a sub-clause of manner or method, which modifies the verb in the main clause by telling us how something was done:

> Dr Craig broke the news about the drugs hot line *as gently as he could.*

Variations on *as . . . as* appear in the clauses of manner and method in the next two sentences:

> *Just as he had feared*, the venture collapsed through lack of funds.

> Dr Craig felt *as if he were personally responsible for the failure.*

Manner and method can often be expressed as effectively through a phrase as through a clause:

> Dr Craig broke the news *as gently as possible*.

> He felt *personally responsible* for the failure.

Clauses of Reason and Purpose

A standard way of explaining the reason or purpose of the action in a main clause is to structure a sub-clause beginning with the words *because, since* or *as,* which are normally interchangeable. An additional flexibility of this and most other complex sentences is that the positions of the main clause and the sub-clause can be reversed:

> Central University Students' Association's Green Week was poorly attended *because/since/as the event was not publicized.*

> *Because/since/as the event was not publicized,* Central University Students' Association's Green Week was poorly attended.

> *Because Central University Students' Association's Green Week was not publicized,* the event was poorly attended.

A sub-clause of reason beginning with the word *for* is now used less frequently than before, possibly because there are the other options suggested above and possibly because it is being displaced by the other use of *for* as a preposition: *a prize for the winner, time for tea.* But the structure can still be used effectively:

> At the end of the debate on capital punishment MPs did not vote along party lines, *for they saw the issue as one of personal conscience, not party dogma.*

Another, more explicit, way of indicating reason is to use the word *reason* itself:

> *The reason Matthew Ray voted against capital punishment* was his fear of making a fatal error.

In the sentence above, the main clause is *The reason was his fear of making a fatal error.* The sub-clause, *Matthew Ray voted against capital punishment,* could be classified as an adjective clause describing the noun *reason*, but the grammatical classification of the clause is less important than the writer's ability to use it effectively. The phrase *the reason why*, although repetitive, is accepted as correct idiom.

When we turn from clauses of reason to clauses of purpose, we find once again that the English language has evolved in inconsistent ways. Sub-clauses of purpose beginning with the words *that*, *so that* and *in order that* can still be written, but they sound archaic in current standard English. Structures like these:

> Train hard *that you may win.*

> Train hard *so that you may win.*

> Train hard *in order that you may win.*

are seldom written today. Instead, the first two structures are usually reduced to the infinitive form of the verb *to win*:

> Train hard *to win*

The third sub-clause above, *in order that you may win*, is normally reduced to *in order to win*. The reduced forms, *to win* and *in order to win*, can still be classified as clauses.

Clauses of Cause and Effect

Sub-clauses of cause and effect can be based on the expressions *so . . . that* and *such . . . that*:

> The Green Week was *so badly attended that* the stall-holders outnumbered the visitors.

> The event was *such an embarrassment that* the Vice-President of the Students' Association resigned.

Grammatically, the words *so* and *such* are in the main clause, and *that* is in the sub-clause, but it is easier to think of the words, *so badly attended that* and *such an embarrassment that*, as indivisible phrases.

Clauses of Time and Place

In sentences expressing time, it is the difference or similarity in time between the main clause and the sub-clause that determines the particular structure to be used. Sub-clauses indicating simultaneous or contemporaneous action normally begin with the adverbials:

> when, whenever, while, as, as soon as, just as, even as

as these examples show:

> *When she is sick of the city* Barbara returns to the Isle of Skye.
>
> *Whenever she sets foot on the island* Barbara feels free.
>
> She walked down to the shore *while the village was still asleep*.
>
> Rain began to fall *as Barbara walked along the shingle*.

The phrases *as soon as*, *just as* and *even as* normally indicate a sharper sense of immediacy or even a suddenness:

> *As soon as/Just as/Even as she reached the bay* the oystercatchers flew off.

Differences in time between the main clause and the sub-clause are expressed by the words *before*, *after*, *till*, *until* and *since*:

> Upstart Genes played for an hour *before Positron came on stage*.
>
> Positron's road crew went to work *after the audience left*.
>
> The crew kept going *till/until every item was in the van*.
>
> Fran Prasana has been singing with Upstart Genes *since she left art college six years ago*.

Finally, sub-clauses of place normally begin with the words *where*, *wherever*, *anywhere* and *everywhere*. *Where* is a simple indication of place:

> Upstart Genes' tour ended *where it had begun*, in Hamburg.

Wherever, on the other hand, means at or to any place, or no matter where, and is almost synonymous with the word *anywhere*, which means in any place:

> In their first year as a band Upstart Genes played *wherever/anywhere they could*.

An example of a sub-clause beginning with *everywhere* is:

> Now Upstart Genes attract big audiences *everywhere they play*.

The word *nowhere* is probably more effective as a phrase than as a clause:

> The harsh grandeur of the Isle of Skye is like *nowhere else in the world*.
>
> On some parts of the island signs of human habitation are *nowhere to be seen*.

The following examples confirm that when simple sentences are transformed into complex sentences containing adverbial sub-clauses, the results can be varied, fluent, economic and persuasive. These two simple sentences:

> At the age of sixteen Felicity Ward wrote news items for her local newspaper. She was still at school at that time.

can be rewritten as:

> At the age of sixteen Felicity Ward wrote news items for her local newspaper while she was still at school.

> At the age of sixteen, while she was still at school, Felicity Ward wrote news items for her local newspaper.

> Felicity Ward wrote items for her local newspaper when she was sixteen and still at school.

> Felicity Ward wrote news items for her local newspaper when she was a sixteen-year-old schoolgirl.

> When she was aged sixteen and still at school, Felicity Ward wrote news items for her local newspaper.

> Felicity Ward, when she was sixteen and still at school, wrote items for her local newspaper.

These two simple sentences:

> At the age of nineteen, Felicity went to Central University. There she began to edit the University magazine *Zymogen*.

can be written as a compound sentence:

> At the age of nineteen, Felicity went to Central University, and there she began to edit the University magazine *Zymogen*.

or as the complex sentence with two sub-clauses, one of time and one of place:

> When she was nineteen, Felicity went to Central University, where she edited the University magazine *Zymogen*.

When the two simple sentences are integrated into one complex sentence with a main clause and two sub-clauses, the information is not only accommodated more compactly but is also delivered more fluently to the reader.

The following three simple sentences:

> Felicity edited *Zymogen* for three years. She then graduated. She joined the *Daily Clarion* as a reporter.

can be restructured in these complex sentences:

Felicity edited *Zymogen* for three years until she graduated, after which she joined the *Daily Clarion* as a reporter.

For three years Felicity edited *Zymogen* until, after graduating, she joined the *Daily Clarion* as a reporter.

When Felicity graduated after editing *Zymogen* for three years, she joined the *Daily Clarion* as a reporter.

COMPOUND-COMPLEX SENTENCES

The three simple sentences:

Felicity Ward edited *Zymogen* for three years. She then graduated. She joined the *Daily Clarion* as a reporter.

lend themselves to a dual technique, that of the compound sentence and the complex sentence integrated in one and the same sentence. The resulting sentence consists of two main clauses and one sub-clause and is known as a compound-complex sentence:

(a) Felicity Ward edited *Zymogen* for three years until she graduated, and then she joined the *Daily Clarion* as a reporter.

(b) After Felicity Ward had edited *Zymogen* for three years, she graduated and joined the *Daily Clarion* as a reporter.

(c) When Felicity Ward had edited *Zymogen* for three years, she graduated and joined the *Daily Clarion* as a reporter.

(d) Felicity Ward graduated after she had edited *Zymogen* for three years, and then she joined the *Daily Clarion* as a reporter.

In sentence (a) the adverbial conjunction *until* introduces the sub-clause of time, *until she graduated*; the simple conjunction *and* introduces the main clause *and then she joined the Daily Clarion as a reporter*, which is grammatically equal in status to the main clause that opens the sentence, *Felicity Ward edited Zymogen for almost thee years*. In sentence (b) the adverbial conjunction *After* introduces the sub-clause of time *After Felicity Ward had edited Zymogen for almost three years*; the simple conjunction *and* introduces the second main clause *and joined . . . as a reporter*, which compounds with the other main clause, *she graduated*, to form the compound part of the compound-complex sentence. Sentence (c) opens with a sub-clause of time, continues with the main clause, *she graduated*, and ends with the second, or compound, main clause *and joined . . . as a reporter*. Sentence (d) opens with the main clause, *Felicity Ward graduated*, continues with the sub-clause of time, *after she had edited Zymogen for three years,* and ends with the second main clause, *and then she joined the Daily Clarion as a reporter*.

Compound-complex sentences can have more than two main clauses and more than one sub-clause:

> When Fran Prasana, who was studying art at Central College, told her family that she was joining Upstart Genes as the lead singer, her father was alarmed and her mother was bewildered but her young sister was delighted.

In the sentence above, there are three main clauses:

> her father was alarmed

> and her mother was bewildered

> but her young sister was delighted

and three sub-clauses:

> When Fran Prasana told her family

an adverbial sub-clause of time modifying the repeated verb *was*;

> who was studying art at Central College

an adjective sub-clause which describes the proper noun, *Fran Prasana*;

> that she was joining Upstart Genes as the lead singer

a noun sub-clause as object of the verb *told*.
  Here is a a second example:

> Upstart Genes rehearsed whenever they had time, played gigs anywhere they could and travelled hundreds of miles a week, but they did not achieve the success they longed for until Fran Prasana, whose voice is ideal for the band, joined them.

In this second sentence there are four main clauses:

> Upstart Genes rehearsed

> [Upstart Genes] played gigs

> and [Upstart Genes] travelled hundreds of miles a week

> but they did not achieve the success

and four sub-clauses:

> whenever they had time

which is clearly an adverbial sub-clause of time modifying the verb *rehearsed*;

> anywhere they could

an adverbial sub-clause of place modifying the verb *played*;

> [that] they longed for

an adjective sub-clause describing the noun *success*;

> until Fran Prasana joined them

an adverbial sub-clause of time modifying the verb *did not achieve*;

> whose voice is ideal for the band

an adjective sub-clause describing the proper noun, *Fran Prasana*.

Together, complex sentences and compound-complex sentences present you with an almost inexhaustible fund of syntactic options that allow you to write with fluency, economy, variety and, because you will write combinations of words that have never been written before, with originality. The chapters that follow will show how these qualities can be sustained over longer passages of writing.

7 Constructing Paragraphs

A sentence was defined as a complete unit of communication; a paragraph can be defined as a number of sentences forming a complete sequence of communication.

Standard English allows almost unlimited freedom in the lengths and structures of paragraphs, from the one-sentence paragraph found in journalism to the paragraph of many sentences and hundreds of words found in textbooks and in many non-fiction works. The sequence can be as simple as a factual description of items with something in common, for example, the posters, postcards and pictures in your room, or as subtle as a series of ideas in a train of thought, or an analysis of the elements in a person's character, or the logical stages in a formal debate or academic argument.

By assembling a number of related observations in this way you create a thematic as well as a syntactic cohesion; that is, in arranging your sentences into a paragraph you are also arranging your ideas into a unified intellectual structure. Even a simple paragraph can help you to clarify and organize your thoughts and to communicate these thoughts more clearly to your reader.

Paragraphing is also used to structure dialogue when there are two or more speakers, a function that is explained on page 106.

Paragraphs, like most aspects of written standard English, were devised by printers. When early printers saw that a new topic was being introduced or a new speaker was about to be quoted, they marked that point in the text with a symbol like the letter P or like the letter P reversed. Then, to make these changes of topic clearer still, printers began to set each new topic in a new line, indented from the left-hand margin. The custom became standard practice and so another convention was added to written English.

Because a paragraph normally consists of a sequence or series of related observations rather than a single observation, a paragraph will normally have two or more sentences. Paragraphs consisting of a single sentence are acceptable in standard English; indeed, the one-sentence paragraph can be an effective way of making a short definitive or emphatic statement.

PARAGRAPHING THE FACTS

Here is an example of a simple paragraph in which a number of related facts are assembled in a sequence:

> The front page of modern broadsheet, or 'quality', newspapers normally carries five or six news stories. A prominent headline above the leading story is designed to catch the reader's eye, and this appeal is strengthened by the use of news photographs, sometimes in full colour. Colour is also used in front-page advertisements, including house advertisements in which the newspaper promotes selected articles in that day's issue.

The three sentences form a sequence of observations on a single topic, modern broadsheet newspapers. The first sentence is grammatically simple, the second is compound and the third is complex. The first sentence introduces the topic and also offers the first of several factual statements; the two sentences that follow offer additional information on the same topic. Although the end result is certainly a paragraph, it reads like a loosely assembled catalogue of items. If we cast the topic into sharper relief, the effect would be to identify the topic, and also focus the reader's attention, more precisely.

We can achieve this precision by including a topic sentence, that is, a sentence that clearly identifies the topic, or subject, of the paragraph. The topic sentence is sometimes known as a key sentence because it serves as the metaphorical key that unlocks the meaning of the paragraph. The simplest method is to place the topic sentence at the beginning of the paragraph, and if the topic sentence were as direct as this:

> Newspaper design is constantly changing.

the subject would be unmistakable. A more revealing topic sentence is:

> A newspaper achieves its effects through page design as well as editorial content.

The precise focus gained by an introductory topic sentence can be reinforced by a deliberately structured closing sentence, or exit line, which brings the paragraph to a controlled conclusion rather than an abrupt or faltering halt. The conclusion of a paragraph, and more importantly the conclusion of an essay, report or dissertation, is not simply an ending but an interpretation, a reasoned opinion that you reach at the end of the sequence. An effective closing sentence for the demonstration paragraph above is one that assimilates and refocuses the information in the preceding sentences of the paragraph:

> The effect of these devices is to make the modern broadsheet newspaper a visual as well as a written medium of communication.

With the addition of the introductory topic sentence and the closing sentence, the paragraph is more sharply defined; it is also a more firmly structured and self-contained statement with an introduction, a development and a conclusion. Thus:

> A newspaper achieves its effects through page design as well as editorial content. The front page of modern broadsheet, or 'quality', newspapers normally carries five or six news stories. A prominent headline above the leading story is designed to catch the reader's eye, and this appeal is strengthened by the use of news photographs, sometimes in full colour. Colour is also used in front-page advertisements, including house advertisements in which the newspaper promotes selected articles in that day's issue. The effect of these devices is to make the modern broadsheet newspaper a visual as well as a written medium of communication.

But what if we had to develop the subject of newspaper design rather than bring it to an end? If the paragraph on broadsheet newspaper design is followed by a paragraph on tabloid newspaper design then the finality of the closing sentence, *The effect of ... medium of communication*, is out of place. Instead, we need a sentence that functions both as an introduction to the new topic and as a link or bridge that creates continuity from one paragraph to the next.

You can do this by stating the new topic and the link explicitly in the first sentence of the second paragraph:

> Tabloid, or 'popular', newspapers are even more dependent on page design.

The word *Tabloid* introduces the new topic, the words *page design* establish the link, and the words *even more dependent* suggest that the subject is about to be extended by means of a contrast or comparison.

Another option is to write a longer, slightly more ambitious sentence that not only introduces the new topic and makes the link between the paragraphs but also integrates the topics:

> Page design is even bolder in tabloid newspapers, where there are bigger headlines, more photographs and a greater use of colour.

By extending the link in this way the sentence creates the continuity that leads your reader effortlessly from one paragraph to the next. The second paragraph, like the first, could then be developed in a factual way:

> Some editors attach so much importance to visual effects that they allow the designer rather than the chief sub-editor to plan the front page. The focal point is always a photograph, and wherever possible the photograph is a close-up in full colour.

The closing sentence of the first paragraph referred only to broadsheet newspapers, but the sentence can easily be adapted by adding a reference to tabloid newspapers and by changing *medium*, the singular form of the noun, to *media*, the plural:

> The effect of these devices is to make modern newspapers, both broadsheet and tabloid, visual as well as written media of communication.

When we summarize the tactics used in this demonstration passage we find that the whole sequence is introduced by a topic sentence:

> A newspaper achieves its effects through page design as well as editorial content.

The remainder of the first paragraph confirms and illustrates the topic sentence by giving details of the front page design of broadsheet newspapers.

Continuity from the first paragraph to the second is achieved by a linking or bridging sentence, which also serves as the topic sentence for the second paragraph:

> Page design is even bolder in tabloid newspapers, where there are bigger headlines, more photographs and a greater use of colour.

The second paragraph develops the subject of the new topic sentence, the front page design of tabloid newspapers, and thus creates a contrast with the first paragraph.

At the end of the second paragraph the closing sentence summarizes and integrates the sequence in a firm conclusion:

> The effect of these devices is to make modern newspapers, both broadsheet and tabloid, visual as well as written media of communication.

The end result of the process is this:

> A newspaper achieves its effects through page design as well as editorial content. The front page of modern broadsheet, or 'quality', newspapers normally carries five or six news stories. A prominent headline above the leading story is designed to catch the reader's eye, and this appeal is strengthened by the use of news photographs, sometimes in full colour. Colour is also used in front-page advertisements, including house advertisements in which the newspaper promotes selected articles in that day's issue.
>
> Page design is even bolder in tabloid newspapers, where there are bigger headlines, more photographs and a greater use of colour. Some editors attach so much importance to visual effects that they allow the designer rather than the chief sub-editor to plan the front page. The focal point is always a photograph, and wherever possible the photograph is a close-up in full colour. The effect of these devices is to make modern newspapers, both broadsheet and tabloid, visual as well as written media of communication.

Apart from the elements of summary and interpretation in the closing sentence, the entire demonstration passage consists of factual observations. When the subject of a sequence is more philosophical, or your treatment of the subject more speculative, you should normally apply different principles of organization.

PARAGRAPHING IDEAS

If we treat the same subject in a different way, evaluating newspapers, news and readership rather than giving a factual account of the contents of the front page, we should use different structuring tactics. In the second demonstration passage the information is first presented in a historical sequence but as a series of fragmentary notes, which is the way many essays and paragraphs begin.

> *Daily Mail* launched 1896; by 1900 mass circulation of 1 million copies a day at half-penny a copy. Cost low because long print run gave low unit cost, and income from advertising; cost made it affordable; daily publication – new issue every morning – made it disposable; newspapers as commodities to be used and discarded. Since newspaper was disposable, so news too was disposable. Then news as a commodity, read and then discarded; news agencies selling news – e.g., Press Association and Reuters. Now newspaper adver-

tising managers sell space to advertisers by promising thousands or millions readers. If readership bought and sold, then readers too are a commodity.

The notes begin with a factual statement about the *Daily Mail* and end with the rather dramatic statement that newspaper readers are themselves a commodity. If the notes were to be used for a news story in the press, the reporter would apply the legitimate journalistic principle of changing the chronological order and beginning with the final outcome to create topicality and immediacy in the introductory sentence, colloquially known as the 'intro'. Our present purpose is better served by accepting the existing order of the material because the notes can be written as a logical train of thought that develops like a crescendo until it reaches the forceful conclusion.

Although the notes begin with a reference to the *Daily Mail*, that reference alone cannot form the topic sentence because the real subject of the sequence is not the *Mail* but mass-circulation newspapers and their readers. With that in mind, the notes could be edited into this paragraph:

Britain's first mass-circulation newspaper was the *Daily Mail*, which was launched in 1896. Only four years later, in 1900, the *Daily Mail* had a circulation of one million copies a day. Part of the *Daily Mail's* popular appeal was its cheapness, one half-penny, at a time when other newspapers cost up to ten pence. The low cover price was possible because the long print-run led to low unit costs; that is, the expense of news-gathering, writing, editing, typesetting and printing was spread over one million copies compared to the 50,000 or 100,000 copies of other newspapers. Another factor influencing the cover price was that some of the *Daily Mail's* income came from advertising revenue, which meant that part of the production cost was borne by advertisers. Mass-circulation newspapers became easily affordable and, since a new edition appeared every morning, they came to be seen as disposable, things to be used and then discarded. As newspapers came to be treated as commodities, so too did their contents. Organizations that existed to buy and sell news – the Press Association, the national news agency established in 1868, and Reuters, the international news agency established in 1851 – increased their activities to meet the growing demands of newspapers and their readers. Newspaper proprietors, unlike most of their editors, saw their publications as commercial operations rather than as information services, and sold space in the pages of their newspapers to advertisers. Advertising agencies were formed to buy and sell space just as the news agencies bought and sold news, and so the spaces, along with the advertisements that filled them, came to be seen as commodities. Today, most newspapers have advertisement managers, who sell space to advertisers and advertising agencies by promising so many thousands or millions of readers. The promise is made in letters, or 'mailshots', to advertising agents and in newspapers' self-promoting house advertisements, the assumption being that whoever reads the newspapers also reads the advertisements. Now that readerships are being bought and sold in this way, readers too have become commodities in the world of mass-circulation newspapers.

Since the introductory sentence prompts the train of thought that flows through the remainder of the paragraph, the sentence can be seen as a topic sentence, but it is not the only one. The paragraph is designed as a crescendo, a gradual accumulation of meaning that ends with the claim in the closing sentence. The final words, *the world of mass-circulation newspapers*, summarize the argument and also echo the opening words of the first sentence. But the closing sentence attempts more than this; it is the realization of the entire sequence, and for that reason the closing rather than the introductory sentence should be seen as the topic sentence.

When the closing sentence is designed to serve this double purpose, the paragraph should be structured in an even more strictly progressive way, so that it moves inexorably towards the finishing stroke, the 'punch line'. The demonstration passage does this by creating a continuous train of thought fashioned from linked, sometimes overlapping, ideas and through the increasing emphasis on the words *read*, *reader* and *readership*.

At the beginning of this chapter we saw that standard English allows great flexibility in the lengths and structures of paragraphs. A measure of this flexibility is the fact that the demonstration passage above could be divided into two or even three paragraphs. A second paragraph could begin at *As newspapers came to be treated as commodities*, and a third paragraph could begin at *Today, most newspapers have advertisement managers*. On occasions like these, when the subject matter gives no firm indication of paragraph length and you have to use some other criterion, the best practice is to structure your paragraphs to meet the needs and abilities of your reader. Put simply: judge the number of words and ideas that your reader can take without a paragraph break.

PARAGRAPHING PEOPLE

From time to time you will be required to discuss people's lives, their characters or careers. The people may be historical figures or characters from novels and plays; they may be characters you create in your own short stories; the character may even be yourself, or that version of your self you present in your *curriculum vitae* or CV. For these reasons the third demonstration passage is biographical.

The information is given in standard English sentences but in a deliberately repetitive style and in a random sequence. The length of the passage, approximately 220 words, may call for more than one paragraph and for some editing in the form of simple additions or deletions.

> His second book, *In at the Kill: Blood Sports in Britain*, once again caught the public imagination. His powerful descriptions and starkly revealing photographs of blood sports persuaded many landowners to ban hunting on their land. His third book, *Plight of the Otter*, was described by *Living Land* magazine as 'A mysterious, disturbing work that invites comparison with Gavin Maxwell's *Ring of Bright Water* and Henry Williamson's *Tarka the Otter*'. His new book, *The Vanishing Countryside*, will be published in June. Michael Ashton, 38, was born in York and educated at Central University, where he gained a degree in botany. His new book will be as controversial as his first three. His first book, *A Poisoned Heritage: Britain's Rivers and Waterways*, identified those industries and local authorities that were polluting our rivers and forced many of the offenders to change their practices. Michael Ashton's new book, *The Vanishing Countryside*, shows how thousands of acres of British countryside – woodland, wetland and moorland – have been destroyed in the last ten years. Michael Ashton taught botany in a secondary school for six years and then became a full-time writer. His new book identifies the government departments, local authorities and private developers who are responsible for the destruction. His new book is likely to be as controversial as his earlier work.

Despite the random order of the information and the repetitive prose style, the subject of the passage is clear: Michael Ashton, a campaigning author on environmental causes, is about to publish his fourth book.

The first task, then, is to find a logical sequence for the material. A single reading of the passage is enough to see the chronological order in the phrases, *His first book*, *His second book* and *His third book*, and since these phrases indicate the stages in the writer's career we could organize the entire passage as a time sequence, beginning with the sentence:

> Michael Ashton, 38, was born in York and educated at Central University, where he gained a degree in botany.

We could continue with the next stage in his career, editing the material to avoid clumsy repetition:

> He taught botany in a secondary school for six years before becoming a full-time writer.

and we could end with the three sentences that refer to the latest stage in his career, once again editing the material to give fluency and variety to the sentence structures:

> Michael Ashton's new book, *The Vanishing Countryside*, not only shows how thousands of acres of British countryside – woodland, wetland and moorland – have been destroyed in the last ten years, but also identifies the government departments, local authorities and private developers who are responsible for the destruction. *The Vanishing Countryside* will be as controversial as his first three books.

An attraction of this kind of sequence is its simplicity; the paragraph follows a strict biographical order from past to present. A particular attraction here is that although this passage does not have the crescendo effect of the second passage, it nevertheless moves systematically towards a conclusion. But the danger in this method is that the end result may seem too plodding an account.

Biographical material sometimes benefits from placing some of the most recent information at the beginning of the passage in order to create immediacy and topicality. An added benefit of this kind of structuring is that you identify the character in terms of his achievement, his current reputation and his present circumstances rather than the remote and sometimes irrelevant circumstances of his birth and early life.

The demonstration passage lends itself ideally to this kind of treatment; and since the subject is not simply Michael Ashton but the campaigning or controversial nature of his books, this approach allows us to place a topic sentence at the beginning and the end of the sequence. The complete sequence would then read like this:

> A new book by Michael Ashton, the writer who campaigns on environmental issues, will be published in June. *The Vanishing Countryside* will not only show show how thousands of acres of British countryside – woodland, wetland and moorland – have been destroyed in the last ten years but will also identify the government departments, local authorities and private developers who are responsible for the destruction.
>
> Readers of Mr Ashton's three previous books now expect such dramatic disclosures. In his first book, *A Poisoned Heritage: Britain's Rivers and Waterways*, the author identified those industries and local authorities that were polluting our rivers, and forced many of the offenders to change their practices. He caught the public imagination again in *In at the Kill*, when his powerful descriptions and starkly revealing photographs of blood sports persuaded many landowners to ban hunting on their land. *Plight of the Otter*, his third book, was described by *Living Land* magazine as 'A mysterious, disturbing work that invites comparison with Gavin Maxwell's *Ring of Bright Water* and Henry Williamson's *Tarka the Otter*'.
>
> Mr Ashton, 38, was born in York and educated at Central University, where he gained a degree in botany. He taught botany in a secondary school for six years before becoming a full-time writer. *The Vanishing Countryside* is likely to be as controversial as his earlier work.

Information on the forthcoming book is structured into a cohesive unit that forms the first paragraph; details of the three previous books also form a cohesive unit; biographical material forms most of the third unit. The remainder of the third unit, the promise of controversy and the deliberate echo of the first sentence in the passage, is an effective closing sentence. The end result is a sequence in which the flow of information and the pattern of interest generated by the flow are entirely different from the pattern in the demonstration passage on newspaper readership. Now the structure is similar to a biographical news release or news story: the most topical information is in the first two paragraphs, the impetus of which sustains the short third paragraph.

One of the minor demands of this and other biographical

sequences is to avoid repeating the same form of the person's name: *Michael Ashton*, or the same term of address: *the author* or simply *him*, without falling into the pitfall of 'elegant' variation. In the passage above, the person is identified in paragraph one with the words *Michael Ashton, the writer who campaigns on environmental issues*; in paragraph two, the longest of the three paragraphs, as *Mr Ashton, the author* and *he*; in paragraph three as *Mr Ashton* and *He*. That is all the variety that is needed to establish and maintain the person's identity.

INFORMATION STRUCTURING

The underlying requirement in paragraphing is not so much a test of your writing skills as an exercise in classifying the information you have gathered. Most writers have little difficulty with broad classifications and find that the exercise in classification becomes clearer still when they compile written lists, noting the items of information under appropriate topic or sub-topic headings.

Some writers have difficulty, however, in organizing information within a paragraph and in organizing the sequence of paragraphs in the final written work. The difference between the internal structure of a single paragraph and the overall structure of an essay is one of scale; the two are versions of the same problem, and the problem can be solved by applying the appropriate method of organization to both tasks. The two main methods are to arrange your material as a time sequence, that is, chronologically, or as a subject sequence, that is, thematically.

Chronological Structuring

When you are dealing with information that can be dated and thus classified by the month or year or century, a chronological sequence from past to present, from the most remote to the most recent, is the simplest way of arranging your material. Subjects that can be structured in this way range from historical studies to biography and autobiography, and from sports reports to theatre reviews, all of which can be seen as linear progressions through time. The subject of travel can also be treated in this way because every journey is both a geographical and a chronological sequence.

If you feel that the past-to-present structure is too rigid, you can vary the pattern, as we did in the demonstration passage on the author Michael Ashton, by beginning in the present before giving an account of the past. The opening sequence would be followed by the historical or chronological account, which would normally bring the reader up to date and back to the present. The complete sequence, whether a paragraph or a longer work, would then be a firm, symmetrical structure.

With a little more planning you can introduce even more variety by making comparisons of past and present, cutting carefully from one to the other in such a way that each is more clearly defined by the contrast. In an essay or report this alternating structure should be at intervals of three or more paragraphs because too frequent cutting could confuse your reader.

Variations of this technique can be effective not only with subjects that have an obvious chronological basis but with almost any subject that has a past: popular culture, policing the cities, the American novel, children's comics, a football club or a county cricket club. By structuring your material in such a way that the conditions and values of the past seem to interact with those of the present, you can inject into your writing the energy and creative tension that come from contrast and comparison. The pitfall to be avoided is that of giving so much attention to the past that every subject becomes a historical study.

Essays, reports and dissertations often make multiple demands because their overall themes include two or more related but distinctly different topics, each of which has its own history. Examples of this are a project on the theme of British military aircraft in the Second World War, or a local survey of two or more businesses or employers, or an account of the performance of the British economy under three successive governments.

In cases such as these the only way to make the exercise manageable, especially at the planning stage, is to divide the overall subject into its component subjects, each of which could include several topics. For example, the project on British military aircraft could have three main sections: fighter, bomber and reconnaissance aircraft, each of which could be treated historically. The section on bombers could be further sub-divided into four topics: the Wellington, Stirling, Halifax and Lancaster. Each topic, in turn, could be discussed in one or more paragraphs.

You could then structure the final project report in separate historical sections, but you would almost certainly find that you wished to make references that cut across the rigid compartments.

In the section on bomber aircraft, for example, you would wish to make occasional references to the main British fighter aircraft of the Second World War, the Spitfire and the Hurricane. Similarly, in the sub-section on the Wellington bomber, you would probably have to make cross-references to, or comparisons with, the other bombers. In effect, the chronological framework would be carrying an added thematic dimension, and the result could be a more flexible and fully detailed report than the chronological approach alone would allow.

Thematic Structuring

When your subject cannot be structured in terms of time or geography, you must use a thematic structure; that is, you must organize your material in the way that best illustrates your theme. This is how you would normally approach abstract or semi-abstract subjects: religion, philosophy, morality, education, human values and human character. Since the last of these, human character, is a constant theme in the discussion of plays, novels and even some poems, we could take as our example an essay on some of the central characters in the novels of Graham Greene.

At the planning stage it would again be helpful to subdivide the overall theme into component parts, and in order to make the subject manageable you could compile lists of characters and characteristics. You could even draft separate sections according to the publication dates of the novels: Henry Scobie in *The Heart of the Matter*, Alden Pyle in *The Quiet American*, Jim Wormold in *Our Man in Havana*, and Charley Fortnum and Eduardo Plarr in *The Honorary Consul*. But once you had compiled your notes you would find that a strictly separate treatment of the characters would result in four or five brief statements rather than the single cohesive statement required in an essay. To achieve cohesion, you must integrate your separate sets of notes by making comparisons and cross-references from one character to another. Some standard biographical information would be useful in establishing the characters' identities, but in an essay on Greene's characters it would be more important to show how the characters think and act, how they treat their families and their friends, how they respond to physical danger, or solitude, or despair, or temptation. These characteristics would form the real subjects of the essay.

Within the general thematic approach there are three main

methods of structuring your material. You can use the balanced structure of the first demonstration passage in the previous section, where all the information on broadsheet and tabloid newspaper design was of equal importance. That passage depended for its final shape on the introductory and closing sentences. Apart from those two sentences, and the broad division into broadsheet and tabloid newspapers, the order of information could be changed without affecting the meaning or the impact of that sequence.

A second method is to arrange your material in ascending order of importance, sentence by sentence and paragraph by paragraph, as in the second demonstration passage, which works systematically to the conclusion that newspaper readers are a commodity.

The third method, which is really a variation of the second, is to arrange your material in descending order of importance, as we did in the demonstration passage on the writer, Michael Ashton.

The thematic approach, then, requires you to make two main decisions. You must decide which of the three structuring methods is the most appropriate: a balanced presentation of the information, a presentation in ascending order of importance, or in descending order. The second decision is really a set of decisions, because once you have chosen one of the three methods outlined above, you must decide on the order of the sentences in the paragraphs, and the order of the paragraphs in the essay. Only you can make these decisions, but there are some firm guidelines that can help you to make them.

Guidelines for Thematic Structuring

If the items of information within a single paragraph are of equal or similar importance, and if each paragraph in the total work is of similar importance, you have little choice but to use a balanced structure. The sequence would then be a measured progression, which would take its final shape from your introductory and closing sentences.

If the items of information differ in their importance or their level of difficulty, you should structure the items in an ascending or descending order of importance. The importance of an item of information can often be assessed by using human values as your criteria. Information has an obvious importance if it refers to matters of human life or death, physical safety or suffering, or if it refers to human qualities such as love or hatred, tolerance or bigotry, education or ignorance. The information may have a genuinely global or cosmic importance if it refers to the condition of the planet earth and the surrounding atmosphere. Sometimes the importance of the information is a matter of size or scale: a footballer's transfer fee, the crime rate, a long spell of exceptionally hot or cold weather; and sometimes it is a matter of uniqueness, strangeness or mere novelty: the first heart transplant, an unexpected result in a parliamentary by-election or a new fashion in clothes.

One way of assessing the level of difficulty of the material in your paragraph or essay is to assess your audience. The smaller and more specialist your audience, the greater is the likelihood that it will understand what you write. If your reader is a subject teacher or an examiner, you can normally assume that he or she will understand the intellectual content of your writing. If you are writing for a large, non-specialist readership, you should normally explain your subject in fuller, clearer or simpler terms. But you should remember that your readership, whether one person or one million, may be as intelligent as, or even more intelligent than, you are. If you try to patronize or outwit your audience you may antagonize them, and lose them.

The final decision is whether an ascending or descending order of information is the more appropriate. An ascending order, from the least to the most important information, should be used if you are constructing an academic argument or if you are presenting a case that requires explanation and examples. Your individual paragraphs should proceed in graduated stages so that the accumulation of evidence or examples gives increasing force to your argument until, when you reach your conclusion, your readers are convinced by your case.

A descending order, from the most important information to the least, should be used when you wish to catch the attention or the imagination of your reader as quickly as possible. The descending order is effective when some of your information has qualities of immediacy or news value. As we saw in the previous section, this kind of structuring is used in news reporting, where the interest generated in the opening sentences or paragraphs can sustain the rest of the story. The descending order is also the most appropriate one for communicating information that has varying degrees of urgency, such as warnings, instructions or advice. Priority would, of course, be given to the most urgent items of information.

STRUCTURAL VARIATIONS

Diversity is a source of energy and interest. You can sustain the energy of your prose and the interest of your reader if you vary the structures of your sentences and paragraphs. The technical skill that allows you to create variety in your writing, or at least to avoid repetition, could also be a source of personal satisfaction. Repetition of key words, including the opening words of sentences, and repetition of the structures and lengths of sentences will bore the reader. The reader may also see the lack of variety as a symptom of the writer's lack of skill, and when that happens the writer loses authority and credibility. As the Introduction to this book warned: If the reader cannot trust the writer's use of language, how can the reader trust the writer's message?

Variety is difficult to sustain when you are writing to a deadline or under examination conditions, but a planned, prepared piece of writing should have a first paragraph with more structural variety than this:

> The *Northern Chronicle* is a weekly newspaper and is published every Thursday. A member of the Northern News Group, it was established in 1899. It sells for 35 pence and has an average circulation just in excess of 35,000. Its circulation area is Normouth and the surrounding villages. It contains between 20 and 26 pages, and includes the occasional supplement, such as the 'Home and Garden' section which came with the 16th April issue.

The paragraph offers a great deal of varied information, but the variety is partly obscured by the repetition of the opening word, *It*, *Its* and *It*, in the third, fourth and fifth sentences, and by the similarities in the structure of these sentences. The effect of that structural repetition is to create the illusion of semantic repetition; that is, the different items of information sound alike. There is repetition too in *a weekly newspaper and is published every Thursday* in the first sentence, since *every Thursday* is weekly; and there is an unnecessary echo of *circulation* in sentence four. With some restructuring, the paragraph could be written as:

> The *Northern Chronicle*, a member of the Northern News Group, was established in 1899. Published every Thursday at 35 pence, the *Chronicle* has an average circulation of just over 35,000 in Normouth and the surrounding villages. Editions range from 20 to 26 pages and include occasional supplements such as the 'Home and Garden' section in the 16th April issue.

Simply by varying some of the opening words of the sentences in a paragraph and, on the larger scale, by varying some of the opening words of the paragraphs in an essay, you can maintain variety in your prose style. If you also vary the lengths and structures of the sentences, your prose style will generate an energy that will attract and sustain the reader's interest.

NARRATIVE TACTICS

This chapter on paragraphs, along with the earlier chapter on sentences, shows that the linear nature of writing – line by line, sentence by sentence, and paragraph by paragraph – gives every piece of continuous prose a narrative structure. The chapters also show that you can control the structure in various ways to make your writing more effective. What is less obvious is that prose also includes narrative viewpoints and narrative speeds, and that by controlling these factors you can create another range of effects.

Narrative Viewpoint

Narrative viewpoint includes the complex question of the author's role and presence in his or her own work, but our concern is with simpler aspects of the subject: the fact that the writer's viewpoint normally determines the reader's viewpoint, and that the writer can control the angle of vision.

The claim is best illustrated by the visual medium of television. When television records a confrontation between rioters and police, the camera is normally behind the police lines, and so the viewpoint of the audience watching the news bulletin is similar to the viewpoint of the camera and the police. The physical viewpoint then becomes the audience's emotional and intellectual viewpoint; the audience would have to make a conscious effort in order to imagine how the event would seem from the other side. Similarly, when television records a sporting event the viewpoint is normally that of a spectator. But when a camera is mounted on a Formula 1 racing car, or a miniature camera is fixed to a ski boot or placed in the off stump of a cricket wicket, the viewpoint is transformed to the more dramatic one of the participant.

Something similar happens in writing. You can write from the viewpoint of the spectator or of the participant or, if the need arises, you can alternate from one to the other. If your writing is reasonably competent most readers will accept your viewpoint; that is, they will see the subject in your terms. Even an examiner, who normally reads in a spirit of critical detachment, will accept your viewpoint if your style and content are accurate.

A writer of prose non-fiction, unlike a novelist or dramatist, is seldom required to make fundamental changes of viewpoint, but if the need arises in your writing you should make the change explicitly. In a report that takes account of the views of two or more persons or groups – management and workers in industry, manufacturers and consumers in the market place, staff and students in schools or universities – you should use a clear form of words to indicate the change from one set of views to the other:

> Those were the views on pay and conditions expressed by the directors of Normouth Engineering Ltd. The employees expressed different views.
>
> or
>
> When the employees of Normouth Engineering Ltd were consulted, they expressed views that differed from those of the directors.
>
> A survey of 150 customers found that what they meant by the term 'Value for Money' was in sharp contrast to what the manufacturers meant.
>
> Interviews with over 100 students at Central University clearly established that students' expectations of higher education were not the same as the expectations of the academic staff.

These major changes in direction are sometimes easier to control than minor changes, because the smaller the shift in direction, the less obvious the narrative tactic should be. And when the task is not to change direction but simply to maintain the normal narrative progress of descriptive or historical accounts, of reports or summaries, the tactics should be imperceptible to the general reader.

This summary on the subject of the Highland Clearances proceeds by a series of awkward lurches:

> It began in the middle of the eighteenth century. The clan system was breaking down in the Highlands and Islands at this time. This was due to the fact that the clans were defeated at the Battle of Culloden in 1746. After the battle some clan chiefs were executed, some were imprisoned, some went into exile like their leader Charles Edward Stuart. Also at this time some of the landowners wanted the land for sheep farming but the land was occupied by clansmen.

The passage shows that the writer has some understanding of the period, but the passage would be more convincing if it were written in a more coherent prose style; the structural coherence would then make the history more coherent and thus more intelligible to the reader. The paragraph could be restructured as:

> The long process known as the Highland Clearances began in the middle of the eighteenth century. After the defeat of the clans at the Battle of Culloden in 1746, the clan system was breaking down. Some clan chiefs had been executed, some were imprisoned, and others had gone into exile like their leader, Charles Edward Stuart. In the same period, land occupied by clansmen was wanted by some landowners for sheep farming.

The second version begins with a clear topic sentence and avoids the vagueness of *It*. Any sentence, and especially the first sentence in a sequence, that opens with the word *It* will seem vague or ambiguous to some readers; and any sequence that begins with the words, *It began* or *It all began*, will sound hackneyed. Other hackneyed and uneconomic phrases in the first version of this passage are *This was due to the fact that* and *Also at this time*. *This was due to the fact that* can normally be replaced by the single word *because* or *since*; alternatively, as the second version shows, the information introduced by these words can be linked with other information. In addition to these changes, the second version integrates the information more fully, and in restructuring the information the second version varies the lengths and structures of the sentences. The end result is a more fluent and cohesive sequence, and these syntactic qualities give fluency and cohesion to the information so that the message is delivered more effectively to the reader.

Narrative Speed

Narrative pace or tempo is the last tactic to be considered in this chapter. A reader's sense of the narrative pace of any piece of continuous prose should, ideally, be determined by the nature of the subject matter. A subject that is inherently exciting will create the impression of speed in the reader's mind, whatever the reader's actual reading speed may be. Conversely, a subject that is inherently leisurely will create a sense of ease. The ideal solution is seldom attainable, and so we must use other tactics to control the tempo of our prose.

The simplest tactic is to be explicit. If you want to create the impression of speed, use the noun *speed* and its synonyms:

> fleetness, haste, hurry, quickness, rapidity, swiftness, velocity.

You can also use the adjectives and adverbs:

> fleet, hasty/hastily, hurried/hurriedly, quick/quickly, rapid/ rapidly, rushed, swift/swiftly,

and the associated verbs:

> accelerate, dart, dash, fly, hurry, hurtle, race, rush, scurry, shoot.

This tactic can be used not only to control the tempo of your prose but also to create other effects: anger, bewilderment, confidence, fear, greed, panic. The word implants the idea in the reader's mind.

A danger in this method is that the sentences may become so overloaded with signals that readers feel they are being told what to think. Some readers will resent the writer's attempt to manipulate them; these readers and others will be more aware of your technique than of the meaning you wish to convey.

An equally effective but less obvious tactic is to control the tempo of your prose by creating syntactic structures and prose rhythms.

> Barbara walked slowly along the shore. Shingle scrunched beneath her feet. She enjoyed the sound. The sea was calm. Mist drifted over the water. She heard the faint sounds of a boat. The boat was hidden by mist. She heard a slow creaking of oars. She heard a gentle rippling sound. She heard voices. The voices were muffled by the mist.

Despite the words, *slowly*, *calm*, *drifted*, *faint*, *slow*, *gentle* and *muffled*, the paragraph fails to communicate ease or tranquillity because the flow of information is repeatedly interrupted by the full stops at the ends of the short, crudely structured sentences. By integrating the eleven short sentences into a smaller number of longer sentences we can change from staccato into a smoother, or legato, rhythm, and from a broken, agitated prose style to a more fluid and continuous style:

> Barbara walked slowly along the shore, enjoying the sound of the shingle that scrunched beneath her feet. Mist drifted over the calm sea. She heard the faint sounds of a boat that was hidden by mist: a slow creaking of oars, a gentle rippling sound and muffled voices.

The eleven sentences of the original have been reduced to three, and with slight structural editing the first two sentences of the new version could be written as one:

> Mist drifted over the calm sea as Barbara walked slowly along the shore, enjoying the sound of the shingle that scrunched beneath her feet.

Most readers are not consciously aware of the rhythmic effects of syntax in continuous prose; rhythm is something they associate only with music or poetry. Readers are, however, intuitively aware of the influence prose rhythm exerts in controlling the flow of information and creating the right tone and atmosphere. These are powerful effects, and when you achieve these effects without exposing your structural tactics – that is, when you achieve these effects imperceptibly – your readers will be more, rather than less, impressed by what you write. Specialist readers will also be impressed because technical skill, in prose writing as in poetry or music or sport, brings an added satisfaction to the audience as well as to the practitioner.

8 Planning and Writing Essays

An essay written for school, college or university on a topic drawn from any one of a number of subjects – economics, history or poetry – is an academic essay, and an academic essay is an exercise in scholarship. Convention requires you to observe certain methods of writing, which in turn lead to distinct kinds of structure.

The academic essay begins by introducing the topic and its context, for example, mass-consumer advertising in Britain today. At this early stage your viewpoint should normally be one of intellectual curiosity as an expression of an open and alert mind, but in the course of the essay the viewpoint may change as you introduce evidence in the form of examples or case studies. In examining the evidence you will reach a series of reasoned interpretations, which will lead to the viewpoint that forms the conclusion of the essay.

If some of the evidence is contradictory you can use the differences to develop a case study into a comparative study. If the evidence is inconclusive you should say so, but you are still allowed to conclude the essay with a distinct final viewpoint.

In contrast, the free essay, one that invites a personal train of thought rather than a specific academic argument, is not so much a form of scholarship as an exercise in linguistic inventiveness, especially when the topics are unseen until you enter the examination room where the essay has to be completed in one or two hours. The freedom of the free essay is the negative freedom of being relieved, at least partly, of the burden of proof and of the need to offer evidence for all your claims. It is also the positive freedom, freedom of expression in the intellectual content of the essay, that is, your ideas; in your use of language and style in expressing these ideas; and in the shape and structure that accommodate the ideas. Indeed, language, style and structure are important features in their own right in the free essay, whereas in the academic essay these features are vehicles for the intellectual argument.

Examples of this freedom and linguistic inventiveness appear in the leader columns, that is, the statements of editorial opinion that are designed to 'lead' public opinion, in the broadsheet press. Newspaper leaders are essays; third leaders – by convention they are lighthearted or mischievous or satirical in theme and treatment – can be good examples of the idiosyncratic English essay.

These definitions of the academic and the free essay are deliberately brief because what young writers need is not another general discussion but practical, procedural advice on how to get started, how to sustain or develop a topic and how to reach a conclusion.

WRITER'S BLOCK

Newspaper leader writers are professional essayists, but even they can experience the chaotic fluttering of half-formed ideas or the sullen stupefaction that prevents them from getting started. The leader writers know what the topic is. They know the viewpoint they will assume. They know the style and tone they will adopt. But they cannot formulate the opening sentence. The problem is widespread but largely unexplained. In its acute form, a form that can last for days or weeks and affects novelists and poets rather than journalists, it is sometimes called *writer's block*. The blockage has two main causes.

One is the writer's uncertainty of the role he or she will play in the new piece of writing. All writers play a role in their own work. Few writers ask themselves the explicit question: What is my role in the piece I am about to write? But most writers realize, perhaps at an intuitive rather than a fully conscious level, that they must come to terms with their sense of self, or with an edited version of self, if their words are to ring true.

Before you dismiss the idea as far-fetched or pretentious, consider the way you edit your experience for a *curriculum vitae* to present the most appropriate or the most favourable version of your self. Or consider the self-consciousness, the awkward sense of self, you sometimes feel when having your photograph taken, and then the slightly different sense of self you feel when you see the version of you in the print of the photograph. Or at an everyday level, consider the person you are when you relax with your close friends compared to the person you are when you are with parents or grandparents or with strangers.

Actors have a highly developed sense of self and role, and they still use the word *persona* and the concept of persona, as do playwrights in the term *dramatis personae*. The word originally meant a mask; the actor who wore the mask – of a saint or a devil or a king – took on the characteristics, the identity, of the saint or the devil or the king. Writers too wear masks: the cynical journalist becomes the impassioned moralist when he writes his newspaper's first leader; the middle-aged mother becomes a chillingly macabre story-teller in her crime novels; the retired teacher, seemingly a suburban nonentity, writes visionary poetry to critical acclaim. The persona allows the writer to liberate or to develop part of his or her identity that is not expressed in everyday life.

And you? You will already have assumed a persona for your essays, or your short stories and poems. If you have not, or if you are unsure of your persona and role, you can experiment in early drafts of your essays until you find a mask that fits, one that allows you to write as well as you can, and one that you can sustain.

The other cause of the block is this. Before we can write a sentence we must formulate that sentence in our brains. As we have seen, the neurons, or nerve cells, and the connections, or synapses, encode the brain's electrochemical energy into language and then into standard English. If we wish to write something new, not original in a profoundly creative sense but simply different from anything we have written before, we must first make new connections of neurons and synapses. One of the functions of the brain is to do just this, and in that sense the brain is constantly redesigning itself throughout its working life. But the time the brain takes to make a new connection is variable and unpredictable, from a split second to years.

If you have difficulty in making the mental connections needed to start an essay, especially under examination conditions, you must compromise by using the existing connections, and thus the existing language, in your brain. The result may be an opening sentence that is less original and less striking than you would have wished, but you will at least have started on a train of thought.

Two forms of compromise should, however, be avoided: the dictionary definition of the topic:

> The *Shorter Oxford English Dictionary* defines an advertisement as 'a public announcement'.

and a quotation on the topic:

> Samuel Johnson in his series of essays, *The Idler*, wrote, 'Promise, large promise, is the soul of an advertisement.'

You should avoid these methods of opening your essay because they are such hackneyed gambits that it almost impossible, even with a penetrating observation like Johnson's, to breathe new life into the technique. Avoid them, too, because your reader may see these introductory techniques as signs of desperation or shallow opportunism; that is, signs that you could think of nothing better, or that you did not even take the time to think. How then does one begin? Curiously enough, a slight adaptation can transform these overused introductions into something more acceptable.

GETTING STARTED

Instead of opening your essay with the flat dictionary definition you can write this:

> The *Shorter Oxford English Dictionary* leaves many questions unanswered when it defines an advertisement as 'a public announcement'.

You can then develop the essay by discussing some of the questions raised by advertising, and by offering some of the answers. A similar adaptation is this:

> No dictionary definition, not even the *Shorter Oxford's* definition of an advertisement as 'a public announcement', can capture the complexity of modern mass-consumer advertising.

Here again the introduction implies the development that will follow, in this case, a discussion of the complexity of modern advertising. A variation like this:

> No dictionary definition can capture the ingenuity and diversity of modern mass-consumer advertising. The *Shorter Oxford's* definition of an advertisement as 'a public announcement' gives no indication of the fact that advertising is the main form of popular culture in the Western world.

clearly implies that the topic will be developed in a positive, perhaps an enthusiastic, way and might even reach the conclusion that modern advertising is not just a form of popular culture but of popular art.

Similar sets of variations can be worked on quotations. The Johnson quotation, for example, can be adapted like this:

> When Samuel Johnson wrote, 'Promise, large promise, is the soul of an advertisement', he probably had in mind coffee houses, inns,

theatres and publishers, the main advertisers in the eighteenth century. He could not have imagined the multicolour fantasies of power
and pleasure promised by modern advertising.

You would then develop the essay by analysing some of the multicolour fantasies. Another variation is this:

'Promise, large promise, is the soul of an advertisement', wrote
Samuel Johnson in the middle of the eighteenth century. Today, the
promise is even greater, but it has less chance of being fulfilled than
the promise in a syndicated horoscope.

The subsequent discussion could expose the false promises of current 'lifestyle' advertising. A similar development could follow from
an introduction like this:

When Dr Johnson wrote, 'Promise, large promise, is the soul of an
advertisement', in the middle of the eighteenth century he was clearly
being ironic. Advertisements have no soul.

One more example shows how the technique can be applied
to other subjects. Arthur Miller, the American playwright, was
quoted in *The Observer* as saying, 'A good newspaper, I suppose,
is a nation talking to itself.' That last sentence would make a rather
flat opening to an essay, but the sentence and the quotation can be
re-cast like this:

The American playwright Arthur Miller was probably thinking of
affairs of state, of politics and human rights, economics and the arts
when he said that a good newspaper is a nation talking to itself. But
when a nation talks to itself the dialogue includes gossip, rumour,
scandal and fantasy.

An introductory paragraph like the one immediately above would
allow you to discuss tabloid as well as broadsheet newspapers and
would allow you to compare and contrast the two.

A safe and effective tactic is to open with a factual statement that
allows you to develop the essay in any one of a number of ways:

Mass-consumer advertising has infiltrated many areas of modern
life.

The mass media of newspapers, magazines, independent radio and
television depend on advertising for their survival.

One last way of getting started carries a risk, but you may think
the risk worth taking if it leads to an arresting or an original
introduction. The method is to begin with a key sentence in the

form of a distinctive, or even a provocative, statement that immediately indicates your viewpoint and sets the tone of the work that follows. This kind of introduction would also be an immediate indication of the persona you were adopting in the essay. Here are some examples:

> Newspaper readers as well as newspapers have become commodities in the battle for advertising and circulation.

That sentence was the conclusion in a demonstration passage in the chapter on paragraphs, but the sentence could be equally effective as the introduction, which could then be followed by a wide-ranging discussion of broadsheet and tabloid newspapers, of their relative contents in terms of advertising as well as editorial matter, of their different news values, of newspaper readerships and circulation figures. This second example is adapted from an earlier introductory statement above:

> Mass-consumer advertising is now the main form of popular culture in the Western world.

Here is an arresting introduction on a different topic:

> Slang transforms the human predicament into the human comedy.

The risk we take in introductions like these is that the form of words that we believe to be witty or original may strike our reader as immature or melodramatic. Another risk is that your introduction commits you to certain lines of development, and the more narrowly angled your introduction is, the more limited you are in developing your themes. An advantage that we gain is that, even if the introduction is less witty or original than we had hoped, it nevertheless throws the topic into sharp relief and focuses the reader's attention more precisely.

This kind of introduction resembles the 'intro' and the 'angle' of the journalist, and the techniques of journalism are worth considering here. Journalists, especially news reporters and to a lesser extent feature writers, are warned never to open a story with an abstraction, a generalization, a set of numbers or statistics because these 'intros' are too impersonal to catch the reader's attention. Instead, the reporter is trained to look for the human angle in a story and to use the human angle as the 'intro'. At worst, the search for the human angle leads to gross breaches of privacy; at best, the technique is an act of recognition that adds humanity to what would otherwise be a lifeless piece of writing.

The journalist would not write an 'intro' like this:

> Homelessness in the Grantown area has risen by 27 per cent in the last year.

Instead, he or she would open the feature article or the news-feature like this:

> Grace Garland and her two small children – three-year-old Martin and four-year-old Ben – live in one small room of a Grantown hotel where they share a bathroom with two other families. The Garlands, and over 6,000 other people in Grantown, are homeless.

The young journalist might write this:

> A growing number of disabled people in Grantown are gaining a new sense of purpose and a new self-confidence through the work of the Grantown Disabled Support Group.

But the editor would prefer this:

> Mike Giles raised over £3,000 for charity last year when he completed a half-marathon and two five-mile fun runs – in a wheelchair.
>
> Mike (37), of 29 Almond Street, Grantown, has found a new sense of purpose and self-confidence since he joined the Grantown Disabled Support Group last year.

Feature articles and essays are two different literary forms, each with its own conventions; even so, the essayist can learn lessons of immediacy and humanity from good journalism.

DEVELOPING THE ESSAY

The best way to sustain and develop a topic over the 500 words or 1,000 words of the essay is to gather the evidence – facts, examples, quotations or case studies – and then to organize the material into a recognizable structure. The chapter on paragraphing offered practical, procedural advice on how information can be edited and expressed as a continuous, structured narrative sequence; and in showing how dictionary definitions and quotations can be adapted for use as introductory sentences or paragraphs, the section, Getting Started, has shown how the topics of advertising and newspaper readerships could be sustained and developed throughout an essay. There are other ways of sustaining and developing a topic.

One radical method is to choose a topic to which you are

opposed – a single European currency or European state, the end of amateurism in sport, payment for university education, the building of more motorways – because hostility can result in forceful writing, especially when the hostility is controlled and well informed. You may also find that in exploring your opposition, either at the research stage or in the act of writing, you are forced to clarify your views on the topic.

You should also note appropriate opportunities for comparative studies, because when you compare and contrast two things you find that one plus one equals more than two. That is, when two sub-topics are brought together for comparison, the act of bringing them together and comparing them produces a third sub-topic. The comparison is normally a study of two things, two sets of ideas, two policies, but the essayist can create a comparison by changing his or her narrative standpoint. The subject remains the same, but you look at it from a different angle. The dangers of this technique are that two contrasting views, one for and one against, could cancel each other out, and a rapidly alternating viewpoint could produce a form of pantomime prose: 'Oh, yes, I did!' 'Oh, no, you didn't!'

One way of creating a contrast is to ask questions in your essay:

> What would be the effect on the news industries if all mass-consumer advertising were to cease?
>
> Who can believe the promises in mass-consumer advertisements?
>
> Does slang satisfy some social or personal need that cannot be met by standard English?
>
> Does the division between broadsheet and tabloid newspapers mark a division in our society?

Only a few such questions can be asked in an essay of up to 1,000 words; too many questions will make the device mannered and obtrusive. The questions should not be rhetorical but must be answered, because a missing answer will create a gap in the dialogue that the reader may be unwilling to bridge.

Questions can be used as major turning points in your essay. Each new stage in your train of thought should be linked to the previous stage or should emerge as if naturally from the previous stage so that the complete essay forms a continuous, unbroken sequence. A question can be used to introduce a new stage in your essay, not just a new sub-topic but a new viewpoint. In an essay on slang, for example, you could discuss areas of life in which slang is used, with examples of slang from these areas, and then you could change direction, change your narrative viewpoint, by asking the question above:

> Does slang satisfy some social or personal need that cannot be met by standard English?

Similarly, you could discuss the differences between the contents of broadsheet and tabloid newspapers and then ask the question:

> Does the division between broadsheet and tabloid newspapers mark a division in our society?

The question can form the opening sentence, perhaps the key sentence, of a new paragraph; the question can be equally effective as the last sentence in a paragraph, to be followed by your answer in the next paragraph.

A range of other devices can be used to mark a new stage in your train of thought. A time-switch from one period to another can be introduced by a form of words like this:

> Mass-consumer advertising was transformed by the introduction of colour television and newspaper colour supplements in the 1960s.

> Newsprint was rationed during the Second World War, but by the mid-1950s newspapers began to publish more pages.

The time-switch can be made by even simpler devices:

> As we enter the twenty-first century we may find ...

> A common practice in the nineteenth century was ...

> A century later, we find that ...

> Between 1980 and 1990 there was little change ...

> Since 1990, there has been rapid change ...

The same kind of device can be used to mark a change of location:

> In France, too, the problem of ...

> Conditions in the north of England, however, ...

> When he returned to the United States he found ...

And a range of other devices allows you to change direction in almost any essay:

> Turning to foreign policy, the President said, ...

> On the problem of violent crime, the Prime Minister warned that ...

In his poems as in his novels, Thomas Hardy explores the themes of . . .

Another Scottish poet, Hugh MacDiarmid, was a contemporary of Edwin Muir's, but MacDiarmid's vision of Scotland is . . .

There are irreconcilable differences between the news values in the broadsheet press and those in the tabloids. . .

Compared to the *Daily Telegraph*, the *Daily Mirror* is . . .

The Conclusion

The conclusion should be a logical outcome of the argument and evidence that form the bulk of the essay. And since any reasoned interpretation of the evidence is acceptable, the conclusion can be the outcome of your interpretation. Two essayists, for example, the leader writers of the *Daily Telegraph* and *The Guardian*, can use the same evidence to reach entirely different conclusions. But if you spend 750 words contending that modern mass-consumer advertising is a social evil, you cannot use the last fifty words of the essay to conclude that advertising is harmless. If you spend the bulk of your essay arguing that the broadsheet press, or the press in general, is a safeguard against tyranny, you cannot end with a claim that the press is a capitalist conspiracy designed to maintain one political party in power.

Two other forms of conclusion should be avoided. One is the old slogan:

Someone should do something about it.

and variations on the slogan:

The local council should take positive action to end this abuse.

The government should intervene now before it is too late.

These could be acceptable conclusions to essays on aspects of local or central government, but they should not be used as easy, multi-purpose options.

The second kind of conclusion can infuriate the reader. It is the conclusion that introduces a new development or a new train of thought that is more promising or perceptive than all that has gone before, a striking new departure that has the effect of undermining the bulk of the essay. This, the conclusion that is a new beginning, is the obverse of the writer's block, or perhaps an indirect consequence of the block. It takes time to think our way into a topic, time to create the new connections in the brain without which we cannot write anything original, or perhaps anything at all, and time to orientate ourselves in the new mental landscape. And when we finally orientate ourselves, we find that the examination time has expired.

These principles of structure – introduction, development and conclusion – are applied in the three demonstration essays that follow. In each case the introduction determines, at least partly, the narrative viewpoint.

The first demonstration essay opens with the introduction in support of mass-consumer advertising, and so the paragraphs that follow the introduction give a sympathetic treatment to the topic.

Advertising: a Case for the Defence

No dictionary definition can capture the ingenuity and diversity of modern mass-consumer advertising. The *Shorter Oxford*'s definition of an advertisement as 'a public announcement' gives no indication of the fact that advertising is the main form of popular culture in the Western World.

Britain began to adopt American techniques of mass-consumer advertising in the 1950s, but it was not until the late 1960s, after the introduction of colour television and newspaper colour supplements, that British advertising became a major form of popular culture.

Today, with the exception of the BBC, most of the mass media – television, radio, newspapers and magazines – depend on advertising for their survival in their present forms. Independent radio and television are dependent on advertising for over 95 per cent of their income, the remainder coming from publications and sales of programmes; broadsheet newspapers and most magazines are 75 per cent dependent.

Advertising is not confined to the news media; it is our most widely shared cultural experience. Advertisements appear on billboards and shop fronts, in railway, underground and bus stations, on buses and taxis. They appear in sports grounds and, in the form of sponsorship, they sustain football, rugby, cricket, athletics, golf, snooker, darts and bowls. So completely have we accepted advertisements we even wear them on shirts and sweaters, shoes and boots, baseball caps, umbrellas and hand-luggage. But it is in the colour magazines and on television that modern advertising is most vivid, inventive and witty.

In a finely printed colour magazine the subject of the advertisement – the perfumed woman, the powerful car, the succulent food – assumes an almost luminous form. The art director and photographer use their knowledge of composition, colour, texture, lighting and camera angles to produce intensely realized, sometimes idealized, images. It is not the fault of the advertisers if their pictures are more alluring or more revealing than the editorial photographs in the same publication. Nor is it the fault of the advertising copywriters if their texts are wittier, happier or more literate than those of the journalists.

Television has the added elements of sound and movement that allow the advertiser to transform the still lives of magazine advertising into the entertaining dramas of television advertising. Indeed, television advertising is a recognized form of entertainment that has attracted eminent film directors while they have been 'resting' between films. Alan Parker (*Midnight Express*) directed the amusing Cinzano and Birds Eye advertisements; Ridley Scott (*Blade Runner* and *Alien*) directed the nostalgic Hovis advertisements; Ken Russell (the televised *Lady Chatterley's Lover* as well as feature films) directed the acrobatic, melodramatic Black Magic advertisements. Other cinema directors who have made television advertisements include Lindsay Anderson, Jack Gold, Joseph Losey, Karel Reisz and John Schlesinger.

These directors have created cinema in miniature: there are identifiable central characters, often with casts of supporting characters or even crowds of extras; there are story-lines that have a clear development and resolution; the locations and the background music heighten the emotion just as they do in the cinema, but without the violence. If television advertising is something of an insiders' game in which directors and advertising agencies try to impress each other, then the viewer benefits through the humour, the inventiveness, the sheer creativity of some of the work.

Television and colour magazines confirm that mass-consumer advertising is not only the main form of popular culture in the Western world; it is a highly popular form of minor art.

Moralists still argue that mass-consumer advertising is a corrupting influence, but without this income, newspapers and magazines would be smaller and more expensive, and most independent radio and television companies would cease to exist. Sport, too, would be affected: if sponsors withdrew their support there would be fewer clubs, fewer events, fewer sportsmen and women. The loss, not only of entertainment but of information, education and employment, would be a greater social evil than the alleged evil of mass-consumer advertising.

But is anyone really corrupted by advertising? Is it not the case that the vast majority of people now regard advertising in the same way as they regard horoscopes, or football pools, or television soap operas? We may read the horoscope and momentarily fantasize that we are going to be rich and famous again, or that yet another beautiful woman or handsome man is going to fall in love with us, but we know the horoscope is merely a silly and harmless entertainment, just as we know that most television soap operas are fantasies, and that we have as much chance of winning a fortune on the football pools as we have of hang-gliding across the Atlantic.

Mass-consumer advertising comes into the same category, except that advertisements are always good news and always have happy endings.

The second essay on advertising opens with one of the hostile introductions and then presents a moral and political case against advertising.

Advertising: the Face Behind the Mask

When Samuel Johnson wrote, 'Promise, large promise, is the soul of an advertisement', he probably had in mind coffee houses, inns, theatres and publishers, the main advertisers in the eighteenth century. He could not have imagined the multicolour fantasies of power and pleasure promised by modern advertising.

What mass-consumer advertisements promise is not the reality of power and pleasure but a fantasy, and the aim of the fantasy is not to inform or enable the television viewers or the readers of colour magazines but to manipulate them by arousing their fear, their greed and their hope.

Advertisements for soaps, perfumes, cosmetics and toiletries play on the personal fears of women. Some advertisements imply that women are inferior as wives and mothers and that they are betraying their husbands and children if they, the women, do not get the weekly wash sparkling clean with the advertised brand of washing powder. Similarly, women who do not use the advertised brands of soap or toothpaste are implicitly accused of being unclean and therefore socially unacceptable. And women who do not use a certain perfume or shampoo or deodorant will be unacceptable as sexual partners. The advertisements promise an end to these fears if women buy, and go on buying, the advertised products.

The promise of a better life is also implicit in food and drink advertisements, which are designed to arouse the appetite and to promise instant gratification. Advertisers and the psychologists who advise them say that the central element in this area of advertising is *appetitiveness*, but this is simply another word for *greed*.

In what is sometimes euphemistically called *lifestyle advertising*, the promise of gratification is symbolic rather than physical, but the promise is no less real or powerful for offering to relieve emotional rather than physical hunger. Some car advertisements are clearly designed to arouse, and symbolically to fulfil, a masculine wish for power. Television advertisements show the driver exerting power over the environment, over the police, over business rivals and, almost inevitably in this genre of advertising, over women.

A common factor in most of these forms of advertising – perfumes, clothes, cars, holidays, food and drink – is that the fantasy promise of self-improvement masks the underlying appeal to self-indulgence. By arousing our fears, our greed and our fantasies of power, the advertiser is manipulating not only our spending habits but our way of life and our vision of life, because the advertiser encourages us to see all things as commodities which are available at a price. And the price is greater than the advertisers and their powerful clients would have us believe.

The advertising agencies' wealthiest clients are multi-national corporations: oil companies, drug companies, motor manufacturers and others. Some of these organizations have annual incomes that are greater than the national incomes of the countries in which they operate. The organizations exert enormous influence. They may persuade a government to produce crops for export while the people of the country go hungry. They may force down the price of raw materials so that the supplier country is trapped in debt. They may use their influence to hold down the price of labour and thus the people's standard of living.

International capitalism, often described as the free market, is primarily concerned with the control of commodities, raw materials and labour costs, and with the manipulation of interest rates, currency exchange rates and investment capital – all with the aim of increasing productivity and profit. The free market is not interested in people except in their roles as producers or, more importantly, as consumers, of the market's goods and services.

To emphasize consumption when we live in a world of limited resources that are unevenly divided among the world's population and that in some cases, for example, oil and natural gas, should be carefully conserved rather than rapidly consumed – to emphasize this is irresponsibility on a global scale.

Mass-consumer advertising is the human face on these inhuman forces. Advertisements address us in a language of caring familiarity about our physical appearance, our attraction to members of the opposite sex, the state of our health. They speak knowingly, too, of our emotional states, our fears and hopes and dreams; they even suggest how these dreams might be realized.

But when we look behind the mask we see that the free market is not interested in our personal freedom. As consumers we are encouraged to experience only the fantasy, the illusion, of power and pleasure; the realities of power and pleasure rest partly with the advertising agencies but mainly with the organizations that are the agencies' clients.

The third demonstration essay explores a different topic, slang.

A Pickled Wally – Slang and Society

Slang transforms the human predicament into the human comedy. It punctures pomposity and pretentiousness, reduces our ideals to bawdy jokes, and even turns tragedy into farce.

Slang is an alternative to standard English and expresses an alternative, unofficial, attitude to life, a way of thinking as well as a way of speaking. The differences between the two forms of language are most obvious when they deal with serious issues or intimate circumstances: money, wealth and poverty; food, drink and drunkenness; crime, police, prison and prison officers; the human body and bodily functions; emotional or extreme states of mind; and death.

Someone who is mentally ill, or more commonly someone you describe as mad because you strongly disagree with him, is *barmy, loony, loopy, nuts*; is a *bampot* or a *nutter*; is *off his nut, off his rocker* or *off his trolley*. He might also have been called *bonkers* until tabloid newspapers redesignated that word as slang for sexual intercourse. Someone who dies *snuffs it* or *has bought it*, or in an earlier age might have been said to have *kicked the bucket* or *popped his clogs*. Someone in prison is in the *nick*, the *clink* or the *slammer*. Features of the human anatomy – *bum* for buttocks, *bonce, noddle* or *nut* for head – are renamed. So too as are bodily functions, for example *crapping* for defecating and *piddling*, *riddling* or *widdling* for urinating.

One human condition alone, drunkenness, has generated dozens of slang words and phrases, a few of which are: *bevvied*, *blotto*, *canned*, *groggy*, *legless*, *lit-up*, *pickled*, *pissed*, *plastered*, *sloshed*, *smashed*, *stoned*, *tiddly*, *tight*.

The examples above confirm that slang punctures pomposity, but the examples also show that some slang expressions are so intent on denying not only the formalities but also the grim realities of life, so intent on shutting out the pain, that sometimes the result is itself black and brutal comedy. A standard English statement like *The fool was so drunk he was arrested* becomes the harsh humour of *The wally was so pissed he got nicked*. But the main effect of slang is to make the condition or the problem it describes sound less ominous, less threatening, almost friendly at times. *A hairy shunt in an old banger*, for example, sounds less serious than a *hair-raising crash in an old car*.

Slang also makes the occasion or the condition seem more vulgar in both senses of the word: of the common people, and unrefined or coarse. As a result, slang in its vulgar, unofficial way is as far removed from standard English as euphemism is in its over-refined or sanitized way. The standard English words *poor*, *moneyless* or *indigent*, become the slang *skint*, *broke*, *strapped* or *in stook*, and the euphemism *financially embarrassed*.

The two registers, slang and euphemism, are also ways of avoiding taboos, that is, forbidden words or forbidden topics. Although there are now few if any absolute taboos in Western society, there are still words that are thought to be too obscene, or too indelicate, for use in public or in polite company. A key word is the standard English *lavatory*. *Lavatory* itself – the word originally meant a washing place – was once a euphemism, but is now seen as being too blunt and has been replaced by the more widely used *toilet*; *loo* remains a colloquial term, hovering on the edge of polite usage but not acceptable in formal standard English. The many euphemisms for lavatory include *the men's room, the ladies' room, the Gents', the Ladies'*, and the phrases *to wash your hands, to go upstairs, to freshen up*. Slang avoids all delicacy in words like *bog*, *crapper* and *lavvy*, a diminutive of *lavatory*. Euphemism avoids the taboo by skirting delicately around the edge of the subject; slang takes a more direct stance and uses words that defy or mock the taboo.

Does slang, then, meet some social need? It meets the need to discuss taboo subjects, as we saw in the paragraph above, but it meets another, more important need. Many slang terms – *nosh*, *gob*, *lolly*, *pong* – are widely understood, but distinct social groups or sub-cultures have their own slang vocabulary. The slang of the comprehensive school differs from that of the boarding school, and the slang of both differs from that of men in prison; the slang of jazz musicians differs from that of journalists.

Journalists' slang include the terms *bleed*, to print a photograph to the edge of a page; *blow-up*, to enlarge a photograph; *crop*, to reduce the size of a photograph; *kill*, to abandon an article; *pix*, pictures or photographs; *puff*, favourable publicity; *splash*, the main news story on the front page.

Slang registers like these are so distinctive that they function like codes, uniting the members of the sub-culture or speech community and excluding others. To that extent, slang still meets the need for secrecy, or at least for solidarity, implied in the French loan word *argot*, which is now a synonym for *slang*. The word originally meant the language of thieves and rogues, and although *argot* has outgrown that meaning it remains a useful reminder of the separate, sometimes subversive, nature of slang.

Because the various registers of slang develop in isolation from each other and from written standard English, they are highly volatile forms of language. The 1950s' terms, *spiv*, *ned* and *teddy boy*, now seem absurdly archaic, and so too do the 1960s' expressions, *fab*, *groovy*, *hip* and *cool*. Slang also varies from one age group to another, and even from one social class to another.

Clearly, slang meets several needs. It reduces the pompous to the comic and the intimidating to the familiar. It confirms the identity of a professional or social group, and at the same time it excludes those who do not know the language. It is an affirmation of life, a vulgar and defiant humour in the face of adversity. And in meeting these needs, slang reminds us yet again of the flexibility, the diversity and the vitality of the English language.

9 Writing Letters and Reports

LETTERS

Simply to defend our rights as ordinary citizens we sometimes have to write formal letters of complaint: to the Inland Revenue, to the local council, to a Member of Parliament, to the manager of a shop or other business, to a newspaper for publication on the readers' letters page. The more effectively our letter is written and presented, the more likely it is to be taken seriously.

Some mechanical rules have to be observed. You must, for example, 'top and tail' your letter in a standard way. Across the top of the page, or offset to the right side at the top of the page, you must write your address; immediately underneath your address, or offset to the left side of the page, you must write the date. The inclusion of your telephone number is optional.

Beneath your address and the date, and on the left side of the page, you should write the name, the official position and the address of the person to whom you are writing. If you are unsure of the person's name and position, you could telephone the organization in which the person works and tell the switchboard operator that you are about to write to the organization and that you would like to know the name and position of the appropriate person. If you still cannot identify a person by name or position, use the job title you think most appropriate in the context: Managing Director, Publicity Officer, Director of Planning. Always target your letter as precisely as possible; otherwise, in a large organization your letter could be passed from one department to another over a period of weeks until someone accepted responsibility.

Letters addressed to named individuals must, as a matter of courtesy and consistency, use the person's name as a greeting: *Dear Ms Drummond* or *Dear Dr Marsh*. Letters addressed to a job title, especially when you are unsure if the holder of the job is male or female, must normally open with the slightly absurd greeting *Dear Sir or Madam*. In some cases you can use the job title itself as the greeting: *Dear Editor, Dear Councillor, Dear Chairman*.

Simple rules apply to the 'tail' of the letter. If your greeting uses the person's name or job title – *Dear Ms Drummond* or *Dear Editor* – then you must close with the words *Yours sincerely* (with a capital *Y* in *Yours* but a small letter *s* in *sincerely*) and your name. If your greeting uses the form *Dear Sir*, *Dear Madam* or *Dear Sir or Madam*, you must close with the words *Yours faithfully* and your name. When you write as a spokesperson for an organization and not as a private individual, at the end of your letter you must identify yourself by this additional role as well as your name; for example, *Ms Jane Thomson, Press Secretary, Grantown Camera Club* or *Dr Victor Arne, Chairman, Cradle Bay Civic Society*.

The content of the letter will depend on the nature of the message you wish to transmit, but some guidelines apply to a large number of occasions. State your precise purpose in your opening sentence, and use subsequent sentences and paragraphs to add essential detail:

> I write to confirm the reservation I made by telephone today. The reservation is for a single room, with dinner, bed and breakfast, from the evening of 20 September to the morning of 25 September, 19--.

> As Secretary of Grantown Camera Club, I write to thank you and your Company for generously sponsoring our annual exhibition.

> I write to complain about the excessive delay by Grantown Council Planning Department in dealing with my application for planning permission.

In a letter that makes an enquiry, a suggestion or a complaint, try to make it as easy as possible for the recipient of the letter to meet your request. For example, in the third case above, the complaint to the Director of Planning, the writer could state:

> My planning application is entirely straightforward and could be dealt with as a purely routine item of business. Even if your department wished to put my application to the Planning Committee, this could have been done at one of the Committee's monthly meetings.

Throughout your letter you should use words and syntax in a way that is most likely to create the kind of tone that will lead to the result you want. The language should be neutral rather than emotive. An aggressive, threatening or sarcastic tone may be less effective than a positive, formally correct tone, especially if your letter is passed to a third party for arbitration, as we shall see in the next set of guidelines.

Towards the end of your letter, briefly restate your main purpose. In the letter of complaint to the director of planning, the restatement could take this form:

> I suggest that one of these two procedures, routine approval or submission to the Planning Committee, be followed now.

Since a letter of complaint is likely to be more difficult, and more important, than most other formal letters, further guidelines are worth noting:

> Do not engage in specialist dialogue with an expert unless you yourself are an expert in the same field,

> Do not threaten legal action unless you have the time, the nervous energy and the money to sustain a case,

> Do not threaten action that is illegal,

> Do state the possibility of reference to an appropriate third party who may act as arbitrator. There are established, inexpensive grievance procedures such as: appeals to a Parliamentary Commissioner, or Ombudsman; to a formal complaints commission such as the Press or Broadcasting Complaints Commission; to your local councillor; your Member of Parliament; your Member of the European Parliament.

We can now apply these guidelines to a simulated case study. Assume that a private individual believes that the planning department of the local council is guilty of excessive delay in dealing with her application. She writes this letter of complaint to the director of the department:

25 St Michael's Lane
Cradle Bay
Grantown GR1 1BC

23 May 19--

Telephone: Grantown
(1234) 56789

The Director of Planning
Planning Department
Grantown Council
High Street
Grantown

Dear Sir

I write to complain about the excessive delay by Grantown Council Planning Department in dealing with my application for planning permission.

On 11 February 19-- I sent a completed application form for outline planning permission for the construction of a one-storey extension to the rear of my house at 25 St Michael's Lane, Cradle Bay, Grantown. The application was acknowledged by your department in a standard letter dated 20 February 19--, but I have received no further response since that date.

I have made five telephone calls and two personal visits to your department in an attempt to discover how my application is being processed. On each occasion members of your department were unable, or unwilling, to tell me what decision had been reached or what progress had been made in processing my application. This lack of response is wholly unsatisfactory.

My planning application is entirely straightforward and could be dealt with as a purely routine item of business. Even if your department wished to put my application to the Planning Committee, this could have been done at one of the Committee's monthly meetings. I suggest that one of these two procedures, routine approval or submission to the Planning Committee, be followed now.

I shall copy this letter to my local Councillor, Mrs Alice Desai, and to my Member of Parliament, Mr Matthew Ray.

Yours faithfully

Ms Dika Riesl

People in business also write letters of complaint, to local or national government departments, and sometimes to fellow-businessmen in the same business community. In this second simulated case study we should assume that Mr Jack Hartford, the transport manager of a timber supplies firm, Grantown Timbers Ltd, finds that there has been a fall in the standard of work by Malley Auto Servicing, the garage that services the vehicles of Grantown Timbers Ltd. The decline in standards is so serious that a formal, written complaint is necessary; a complication is that Mr Hartford and the garage owner, George Malley, know each other socially as well as professionally. Mr Hartford telephones Mr Malley to discuss the problem informally; he then confirms the main points of the telephone conversation in this formal letter. Since the letter is from one business to another, the 'topping and tailing' is different from that in the previous letter. Here, the sender's address includes a telephone number and a fax number; the signature at the end includes the sender's business role as well as his name. The tone of the letter is formal but the final paragraph strikes a positive and conciliatory note.

Grantown Timbers Ltd
Grantown Industrial Estate, Grantown GG1 2PQ

Telephone: 9876 543210   Fax: 9876 543 2100

10 November 19--

Mr George Malley
Proprietor
Malley Auto Servicing
London Road
Grantown GG2 5SP

Dear George
I write to confirm the main points of the telephone conversation we had today, 10 November.

There has been a serious decline in the quality of service provided to Grantown Timbers Ltd by Malley Auto Servicing in recent months.

On several occasions between August and 1 November this year your mechanics failed to correct serious faults in our vehicles. The faults included:

electrical circuits on a Mercedes 20 tonne truck
steering on a Volvo X97 tractor unit
steering and brakes on a Ford Escort van
roll bar on a Trex 50 all-terrain vehicle

and several other less serious faults on five Grantown Timbers vehicles.

In addition, your invoices for July and August this year include accounts for work that was not done by you. These errors, notably for new exhaust systems for two Mercedes trucks and complete sets of tyres for three of our Land Rovers, were drawn to the attention of your Accounts Department at the time. Despite this, your Accounts Department has re-submitted these invoices to Grantown Timbers Ltd.

On a less serious point, my drivers report that their vehicles are being returned in a dirty condition, with oil stains on seat covers and interior panels.

This quality of service is wholly unsatisfactory and cannot be allowed to continue. Unless there is an immediate improvement I shall be forced to close our account with you.

I understand that you have been experiencing serious problems with two employees and that you are in the process of appointing a new floor manager and a cashier. I hope these problems will soon be resolved so that our two firms can resume the excellent working relationship we had until this year.

With good wishes.

Yours sincerely

Jack Hartford
Transport Manager

REPORTS

A report is an account of an investigation and a statement of the conclusions that emerge from the investigation. The report may be the result an internal investigation by an organization into aspects of its own operation, or it may be the result of an investigation by an external, independent consultant. The structure and style of a report will normally be determined by the house style of the organization, but some features are common to all reports.

1. A report should be factual and objective, and for these reasons should be expressed in neutral diction and an impersonal prose style. A report should have a logical, sequential structure, as outlined in the points that follow.

2. First, the report must identify the circumstances that prompted the need for the investigation. This section can be headed **Background** or **Introduction**.

3. There should normally be a statement of the **Terms of Reference**, that is, the conditions, criteria or rules within which the investigation was conducted and the report was written.

4. The report should then state the **Procedure** adopted by the authors. Procedure can include an indication of the scope and scale of the investigation; a brief description of the methods of investigation: expert testimony, interviews, random surveys, questionnaires, site visits; and, optionally, a brief statement of the reasons why those investigative methods were used.

5. A vital section of the report is the **Findings**, a strictly factual statement of what the investigation discovered.

6. At that point the authors of the report could state their **Conclusion**, that is, their reasoned interpretation of the findings.

7. If the findings identify a problem, the authors should offer their **Recommendations** on how the problem can be solved. The conclusion and recommendations can be presented as two separate sections or as a single joint section headed **Conclusion and Recommendations**.

These guidelines are applied in the two simulated case studies that follow. The first is a report on Fasta Foods Ltd, a food-processing company that supplies the hotel and catering industry. Believing that something is seriously wrong with the company's operation, the management committee call for an urgent report by an independent firm of management consultants, Gascoigne, Whistler, Vaughan. The sequential structure of the report is emphasized by a simple double system of numbers and headings. The report below would be accompanied by a covering letter and an appendix, which would include statistics, costs and analyses.

The Recruitment, Retention and Promotion of Staff
of Fasta Foods Ltd

A report by Gascoigne, Whistler, Vaughan
Management Consultants

CONFIDENTIAL

Introduction
In the past two years Fasta Foods Ltd has had difficulty in recruiting
and retaining appropriate staff. The average annual turnover of staff
in the two-year period is 24 per cent, ranging from 8 per cent in the
Administration and Accounts Departments to 39 per cent in the Production and Delivery Departments. At a meeting of the Management
Committee of Fasta Foods on 5 September 19--, it was stated that
the problems of staff recruitment and retention were affecting the
profitability of the Company. The meeting agreed that Gascoigne,
Whistler, Vaughan, Management Consultants, be commissioned to
investigate the problem as a matter of urgency and to report back
to the Management Committee of Fasta Foods within one month.

What follows is the report by Gascoigne, Whistler, Vaughan.

1. Procedure
Gascoigne, Whistler, Vaughan interviewed all Heads of Departments
of Fasta Foods individually. Questionnaires were issued to all
employees to be completed anonymously, and this produced 157
replies, a response rate of 78 per cent. A copy of the questionnaire
and a summary of the main findings are enclosed with this report;
summaries of the interviews are also enclosed.

2. Findings
2.1 Recruitment
It was found that Fasta Foods has no consistent policy on the recruitment of staff. Some vacancies, particularly in the Accounts Department, are advertised in the local press; candidates are required to
apply in writing, the best candidates are invited for personal interview and the final selection is made on the basis of the written
application and the interview. Other employees, notably in the Production, Delivery and Plant Maintenance Departments, are recruited

through local Job Centres or by word-of-mouth and personal contact with existing employees. Staffing in the Production Department sometimes resembles a system of casual labour rather than full-time employment.

The lack of a clear and consistent policy on the recruitment of staff means that there is no corporate view of the kind of experience, qualifications, age profile or personality required of new recruits. Consequently, there is no corporate control over the standards of new recruits.

2.2 Wages and Salaries

Several complaints were received about wages and salaries. On investigation, however, it was found that the wages of employees on hourly rates compare favourably with those in other local industries. Monthly salary levels are slightly above the national average for the food and drink industry.

2.3 Training

Fasta Foods has no policy on in-service training. New recruits may be offered advice by their Heads of Department or supervisors, but this is done in a random, unstructured way. Fasta Foods does not take advantage of the experience and expertise of existing employees.

2.4 Promotion

Although Fasta Foods has no written policy on promotion, the practice is to promote existing staff, normally on the recommendation of the Head of Department.

It was found that several employees promoted from existing staff within the last five years had insufficient experience or ability to meet the demands and responsibilities of their new, higher level posts. This has led to recurring irregularities in stock control which have seriously affected production flow, and to recurring interruptions to delivery programmes which have damaged customer relations.

The quality of promoted staff, along with topic 2.5, Conditions, proved the most controversial. Ninety-eight of the 157 respondents to the questionnaire expressed some degree of dissatisfaction with or mistrust of their immediate superiors.

2.5 Conditions

Fasta Foods meets the minimum statutory requirements for health and safety at work, but Gascoigne, Whistler, Vaughan received eighty-four complaints from the hourly paid staff about conditions. Complaints referred to the lack of cleanliness in toilets, in the refectory and in the workplace generally. The segregated refectories, one for hourly paid workers and the other for salaried staff, was bitterly resented by many respondents. Complaints were also received about the lack of parking space and the lack of a nursery for the children of women employees.

3. Recommendations

3.1 Promotion

As a matter of urgency we recommend that Fasta Foods introduce a clear policy on promotion.

We recommend:

(a) that all promotions be centrally controlled by the Personnel Office

(b) that all candidates for promoted posts must complete an appropriate application form

(c) that short-listed candidates, three where possible, be interviewed

(d) that interviews be conducted by at least two senior members of Fasta Foods, one of whom should normally be the Personnel Manager or the Assistant Personnel Manager

(e) that existing staff should be promoted only on merit.

Staff who are promoted on these criteria will be more effective as managers, leaders and exemplars.

3.2 Conditions

We strongly recommend that the working environment of hourly paid employees be improved.

We recommend:

(a) that the Management Committee consider ending the segregation of the adjoining refectories, which already share the same kitchen and menus

(b) that new furnishings and fittings be provided for the hourly paid refectory

(c) that the hourly paid refectory, the toilets and the workplace generally be maintained at a higher standard of cleanliness

(d) that the Management Committee consider the establishment of a nursery for the children of employees. Estimated costs of nursery provision are shown in the Appendix to this report

(e) that an annual ballot be held for company parking spaces, other than parking spaces for promoted staff.

We believe that these changes will remove the main sources of conflict between management and employees, and between salaried staff and hourly paid employees. Fasta Foods would then be in a better position to retain good staff and also to reduce the absentee rate.

3.3 Wages and Salaries

We recommend that Fasta Foods' monthly newsletter publish the wage and salary scales of other employers in the area and other major companies in the food and drink industry. This will demonstrate that Fasta Foods' rates are above average.

3.4 Training

If Recommendations 3.1 (a) to (e) were introduced, there would be no need for extensive training. As a short-term measure, however, we recommend that some promoted staff be required to attend in-service training; the training could be given by experienced members of the existing staff. Training of two hours per week for a trial period of eight weeks could be introduced at one month's notice. An outline training programme is included in the Appendix.

We believe that the proposed changes would lead to more effective management, more harmonious management–employee relations, and a greater degree of job satisfaction for a majority of employees. These changes, in turn, should result in better recruitment and retention of staff and, as a consequence, improved efficiency, productivity and profitability for Fasta Foods.

Signed: Gardner Vaughan
for Gascoigne, Whistler, Vaughan

1 October 19--

The second simulated case study takes the form of an internal report. This second report is structured even more firmly than the report above: the sequence of items in *Findings* is repeated in the subsequent sections, *Conclusion* and *Recommendations*; *Recommendations* (b) and (c) are given as a joint section since the two topics are closely linked.

Carlton Crates and Containers Ltd

Mr Wilf Sutton
Managing Director

Report on Carlton Crates and Containers Gazette

Background
During the period from June to 1 November this year, formal complaints about inaccuracies in the Company's house journal, *Carlton Crates and Containers Gazette*, were made by the Chairman of the Company and by the Secretary of the Women's Hockey Section. Informal complaints about the content and quality of the magazine were also received during the same period.

1. Terms of Reference
The Managing Director, in his memorandum of 15 November 19--, instructed the Personnel Department to investigate complaints about the Company's monthly house magazine, *Carlton Crates and Containers Gazette*, and to make recommendations.

2. Procedure
Between 20 and 27 November, interviews were conducted with all Heads of Departments and with members of the committee of the Staff Association. Between 30 November and 15 December brief interviews were conducted with non-promoted staff in all departments, a total of thirty persons.

3. Findings

(a) Printing
On four occasions in the last six months the house magazine has been delivered late by the printer. For example, the September edition, which should have been delivered by 28 August, did not arrive until 13 September, by which time several events listed in the magazine had already taken place.

The finished product is of poor technical quality: design and layout are old-fashioned, photographs and other illustrations are badly reproduced, and the quality of printing is inconsistent.

(b) Contents

Recent issues of the magazine have contained many typographical errors, notably misplaced captions for photographs. In the July edition the picture caption for the dog show, 'Boxer Bitch is Champion', appeared beneath the picture of the Women's Hockey Section; the photograph of the Company Chairman and his wife was captioned 'Congratulations on the biggest catch of the season – a 10 lb trout'; the names of some of the visiting French trade delegation were printed in the adjoining article, 'This Month's Recipe'.

(c) Staffing

The magazine is edited by the Advertising Manager and his staff, none of whom have previous experience of editing. There is no clear system for the collection of news items from Company clubs and societies or from individual employees, nor is there an agreed system of distribution of the magazine throughout the Company.

4. Conclusions

(a) Printing

Complaints about the quality of the printing, and the delivery service by the printer, are fully justified.

(b) Contents

Editorial control, for example, proof-reading and layout, is inconsistent and occasionally erratic. This has caused distress to the Chairman and his wife, and to members of the Women's Hockey Section.

(c) Staffing

The Advertising Department has neither the expertise nor the time required to produce a better quality monthly magazine.

5. Recommendations

(a) Printing

The printing of the magazine should be put out to competitive tender on the basis of print quality as well as cost. Quality and delivery should be specified in any contract with a printer, and should be closely monitored.

(b) Contents and (c) Staffing

A part-time editor should be appointed, either from within the Company or by advertising the post; alternatively, the Company could commission a freelance editorial consultant. The editor should exercise close control over contents and production, and should monitor the service provided by the printer.

Each department should nominate a departmental reporter who would undertake information-gathering and news-gathering on a continuous basis. The Staff Association should be encouraged to use the magazine to publicize all Staff Association events. A free 'small ads' service should be offered to all employees.

Monthly distribution of the magazine could become the responsibility of the Mail Room.

Additionally, it is recommended that the title of the Company's house magazine be changed from *Carlton Crates and Containers Gazette* to the simpler title, *Carlton Gazette* or *Carlton News*.

PJ Minster
Assistant Personnel Officer

22 December 19--

INDEX